Alternatives to Valium

ABOUT THE AUTHOR

Alastair McKay grew up in North Berwick. He has written for *Uncut* magazine, the *Evening Standard*, *NME*, *The Scotsman*, *Scotland on Sunday*, *The Sunday Times*, *The Guardian*, *Black Book*, *Out*, *Blah Blah Blah* and *The Independent*. He lives in London with his partner, his spirited daughter and a lazy cat.

Alternatives to Valium

How Punk Rock Saved a Shy Boy's Life

Alastair McKay

First published in Great Britain in 2022 by Polygon,
an imprint of Birlinn Ltd

Birlinn Ltd
West Newington House
10 Newington Road
Edinburgh
EH9 1QS

www.polygonbooks.co.uk

1

ISBN 978 1 84697 581 3
eBook ISBN 978 1 78885 494 8

Typeset by 3B Type, Edinburgh

Contents

For Rosebud

Write your own bloody bibles!
—Colin Vearncombe

Sleeve Notes

A few years ago, I asked Tom Petty how his songs had been influenced by his life. As a rule, songwriters aren't keen on unpicking their work, and Petty was no exception. He didn't want to get into specifics. 'Life is so difficult,' he said. 'And easy. It's just a chain of spontaneous events.'

For Petty, the flashpoint of inspiration was a childhood visit to the set of the film *Follow That Dream*, where he noticed girls handing records over a fence for Elvis Presley to sign. In the heat of that Florida moment, Petty reckoned that if he had a record, he could get Elvis's autograph. Possibly – though he didn't say this – he also realised that if he played music, he could be the one getting all the attention. 'I traded my Wham-o slingshot for this box of records,' he said.

I never had a catapult, but I grew up at a time when acquiring records was a rite of passage. Not just any records. The correct records. This was a matter of identity and endless dispute. My formative years coincided with the punk explosion, a cultural spasm in which music was assumed to have profound and unpredictable power. There was a before, and there was an after.

This book inhabits both moments. It is a fanzine disguised as a memoir. It is inspired and informed by music, so it takes the form of an album, with two distinct sides. The first side is about childhood, and the struggle to find a voice. The second side is about interviews, and learning how to listen.

Revisiting those interview cassettes was both chastening and enlightening, and not just because they had to be rescued from redundant technology. Interviews are a dance of suspicion and performance. They are also a form of autobiography, an interrogation in which fame exists as a kind of trick-mirror. What is it that the interviewer hopes to find out? Why do you ask? And why is it that the worst thing in the world is the sound of your own voice?

SIDE ONE
Play It Loud

I

Mr Stenhouse, Philip Larkin, Going to Hell

M r Stenhouse was quite clear. The word 'fuck' was fine, as long as the context justified it.

We were fifteen years old, and my favourite teacher was giving us permission to swear.

He looked around the classroom. 'For instance,' he said, 'I'm about to retire, but often I get the urge . . .' He walked to the corridor, opened the door, and flicked a Harvey Smith. 'I often get the urge to go to the headmaster and say, "Fuck your pension!"'

He was paraphrasing Philip Larkin's 'Toads', in which the poet imagined throwing off the anura of work and living like the lispers, losers, loblolly-men and louts, who did as they pleased, without starving.

Looking back, I can see there was a bit of Larkin in Mr Stenhouse. Nothing loblolly, but he used to talk about standing outside Bus Stop – a fashion boutique in Edinburgh – in a way that reminded me of Larkin watching a disco through the condensation on a Scout hut window. He cultivated the idea that youth was a party to which he was not invited. Once, he asked us to define the concept of love. Being fifteen, and Scottish, we were not good at this. 'You know nothing about love,' he concluded, without cruelty.

Occasionally he would examine our barathea lapels for badges and ask us to explain the meaning of Thin Lizzy. Then, with an expression of intense bafflement, he would observe that some of the modern groups had taken to smashing their guitars. 'Now, why would they do that?' he'd demand. 'If they didn't want to play the guitar, surely they could have given it to someone who did.'

Mr Stenhouse had another routine, which makes sense now, but didn't then. 'Who can tell me the most beautiful city in Europe?' he would say. The answer was Edinburgh, though none of us could understand why. At fifteen my experience of Edinburgh was C&A, where they had Kubrick-style surveillance cameras on the ceiling and Rorschach blot carrier bags; Easter Road, where Hibernian toiled; and the multi-storey car park at Castle Terrace – the first place I ever saw the phrase 'no loitering'. What did it mean, to loiter?

But I was beginning to appreciate the city's natural geography. Specifically, this meant a circuit from Waverley, south to Hot Licks in Cockburn Street, up the close to Phoenix in the High Street, down to the Other Record Shop in St Mary's Street, and across town to the Ezy Ryder Record Exchange, which reeked of denim and was staffed by the rudest men in the world. Then it was back to Bruce's in Rose Street, and on to Hell in Thistle Street. I favoured Hell, because their carrier bag said 'I Got It in Hell'. But it was at the Other Record Shop that I bought my first punk record: 'Neat Neat Neat' by The Damned.

It's fair to say that North Berwick was not the epicentre of punk. I have a photograph taken by accident from the window of my teenage bedroom. It's the free shot, the blank you shoot when you wind the film into the camera, so it's blurry. It shows the new houses in what we used to call the Field, their windows blazing in a winter dusk. There are spindles of hedge, not yet knitted, and an apologetic tree. The road is blue.

This was our second North Berwick house. It was a new-build, detached, on the edge of town. I remember visiting the site before it was built. Our future home was string, pegged on damp earth, and we walked through the rooms, imagining. When we moved in, my brother set up his portable stereo on the living-room floor and played '5.15' by The Who, loud. We danced on bare boards. It was as if we were trying to paint the emptiness with noise.

North Berwick itself was a peaceful place, with occasional ruptures. Witches were burned on the seafront in 1590. Robert Louis Stevenson had a holiday home in the Quadrant, which inspired his novel *Catriona* in 1893. For a week in the early 1970s, the Law – the 600-foot volcanic frown on the south horizon – smouldered after being set alight by vandals. Later, the lookout post at the Law's summit, next to the whale's jawbone, was daubed with the letters MRS, short for Midnight Riot Squad. It was the MRS who assaulted my brother in the Lodge grounds, one Friday after Scouts. They wore *Clockwork Orange* boiler suits and politely asked my brother his age before kicking him in the balls. I was eleven, and small, so I was allowed to pass.

Mostly, life was safe. North Berwick had been a seaside resort, but the advent of foreign travel was turning it into a retirement village. It had become a beautiful place to die.

❋

5

On 7 June 1977 I rode my mail-order self-assembly racing bike to the Harbour Pavilion. The Piv was a sad building next to the swimming pool. It had once hosted seaside variety shows; now the main hall was dark. The corridors were filled with puggies and table football. On that day, the day of the Queen's Silver Jubilee, I scored three cherries on a one-armed bandit. As the machine spewed its jackpot, the manager of the Piv ejected me from the premises. Winning was not permitted.

The streets were quiet and the sun was out as I cycled from the harbour to the High Street, to stare at the Melody Centre. The record shop was run by Mr Stewart, a patient soul who, seven months earlier, had refused to sell me a Bonnie Tyler record on the grounds that it wasn't the sort of thing I liked. Perhaps he understood that the escapist promise of 'Lost In France' was more to do with being lost in the tidal pull of Bonnie Tyler's hair than the romantic geography of the song.

Mr Stewart wasn't keen on punk, but he knew what sold, so he arranged the picture sleeves of the punk singles around the bottom of his shop window. I got 'Sick Of You' by The Users in there, on the basis of its cover. That was good. I also got a 45 by The Depressions, which was bad. The Depressions were managed by Chas Chandler, who had been in The Animals and managed Slade. Their gimmick was peroxide hair. But the song was no good. 'God Save The Queen' by the Sex Pistols was in the middle of the window, but the Jamie Reid sleeve was reversed, so the image of the Queen with a safety pin through her nose was hidden from public view. It was quite satisfying, this half-censorship.

That same June, I bought a copy of *Sniffin' Glue* from Bruce's in Edinburgh. *Sniffin' Glue* was the punk fanzine. It was half-literate, urgent and passionate. In that issue there was an editorial by Danny Baker, whose career would later stretch from being the *NME*'s disco correspondent and hanging out with a bewildered Michael Jackson to selling Daz and delivering quick-fire repartee as the host of the STV game show *Win, Lose or Draw*. 'Have you noticed how amused the other press is to find out punks like other types of music?' Danny Baker wrote. 'Look sunshine, we don't need mum, dad or Sniffin' Glue to let us know what to dance to, BUT the new wave is more than music to you and me, it's our megaphone for Youth. Positive Youth. Spelt P-U-N-K and put over as rock 'n' roll.'

Not long after that I made my own fanzine, *Blow Your Nose on This*. It was a montage of crap, Xeroxed by a friend's mother during her lunch hour at the golf club factory. On page two of issue two I reprinted the *East Lothian Courier*'s review of the Sex Pistols' LP. 'So what if all the tracks sound more or less the same?' the review moaned. 'It's still the ideal Christmas gift for the punk rocker in your life.' Next to that I had pasted the famous image, taken from *Sideburns* fanzine, of three guitar chords, A, E and G, alongside the legend 'This is a chord. This is another. This is a third. Now form a band.'

I became the singer of The Instant Whips. I couldn't sing, so I wore a hat. While the Scottish country dance group The Rowan Trio had a cigarette break at the Seniors' Dance, I retched through 'Ging Gang Goolie', 'I'm A Believer' and 'The Worm Song'. It was a high-concept show. A cardboard pig was suspended above the stage and at the end of our cover of The Goodies' version of 'Wild Thing', I kicked a Chad Valley drum kit into the crowd, causing a small wound on the breast of a popular fourth-year girl. The girl's boyfriend was the captain of the rugby team. He was not impressed.

If that performance was a cry for help, the next was a letter to Social Services. The show took place in the function room of the Nether Abbey, a hotel favoured by rugby players, the owner of which was reputed to be Rod Stewart's cousin. Musically, we were marginally more competent, and the repertoire had expanded to include the Ramones' 'Rockaway Beach'. We had assumed punk names. I was Captain Pugwash, the guitarist was James Bondage, and the half-Danish drummer was Björn Hope. Band practices took place at Björn Hope's house, using a biscuit tin for a drum kit, unless Björn's mum was baking pastries. Once, when we were halfway through a wretched cover version of Alternative TV's hymn to erectile dysfunction, 'Love Lies Limp', the drum kit was requisitioned by Björn's mum. She needed the tin for a batch of scones.

I had written a song for that Nether Abbey show. I must have liked it, because I had the lyrics run off on the school's Fordigraph machine and handed out at the door. The purple ink smelled like victory.

The song was called 'Smoke Signals'. This was the chorus: 'You narrow-minded sycophant/I'd rather be a rubber plant/ Than be like you.'

If there were easier ways to make friends, I hadn't discovered them.

2

The Happy Smile Club

As a journalist, I have an emergency question for interviews that are going badly. The question is marginally more subtle than applying jump leads to a stopped heart, and is only required in dire circumstances, when a conversation has been predictable or unenlightening. 'What,' I will blurt out, 'is your first memory?'

Psychologists might dispute the relevance of such a question. Many first memories aren't memories at all. Young children's brains aren't wired for posterity. The stuff that lodges there is often a collage of family anecdote, fiction and cultivated regret. With celebrities, the possibility of invention, or corruption of the image, is magnified by repetition, but it's a process that is universal. Your first memory is the thing you remember when you are asked about your first memory. Whether it happened like that isn't the point.

I have two first memories, and no real way of working out which came first. Both are completely true. Both are entirely consistent with the way I think about myself.

Here is one of my first memories.

I am running along a cinder path. The path, if we are to add some retrospective context, skirted my parents' house in Seaton Sluice, Northumberland. I am chasing my childhood friend, Kimberley. I stumble and fall onto my face, smashing my nose. The bone is too soft to break but it bends slightly, leaving my profile with a boxer's kink and giving me a lifetime of nosebleeds.

Here is another of my first memories. This takes place in that same house in Seaton Sluice. I have reconstructed the outside of the building from family photographs, but the inside is a haze of soft sunlight. My mother is ironing clothes. My brother, Colin, is not there. As a memory, this is a non-event but I have processed it over the years. It's not about the ironing. It's about being alone with my mother because my brother has started school. Am I lonely or secure with my mum? The memory comes with no emotion attached. It is just a scene. So maybe both. Security and loneliness can co-exist.

Another memory. A trivial one, which also manages to be a lifelong trauma. There is physical evidence for this one.

By now I am at school. No longer in Seaton Sluice, the McKay family has moved home to Scotland because my dad has a job at the new power station in Cockenzie. My brother, two years older than me, records the move in a school jotter. Alongside a drawing of some mountains, a car, a giant sun and a stripe of blue sky draped along the top of the picture, he writes: 'Yesterday afternoon my mammy and brother Alastair went to Allan's, Whitley Bay to get a multi-directional, one-hundred-shot water pistol. Of course, this was all happening when I was at school. It has a thing on the top near the end of the hole where the water comes out of. Like all water pistols it has a long range. This is a picture of the pistol. Firing.' In the drawing, the pistol is chimney-red with a yellow trigger. A thin jet shoots across the page.

There is more. In between further reminiscences about *Thunderbirds*, toy guns and Jesus rising from the dead and turning sadness into joy, Colin records the family's weekend search for a new home. 'We even looked in Musselburgh,' he writes. 'My daddy let me in a furnished Show house. We only saw 1 house for sale but we did not go in it.' The teacher has added a red tick next to this paragraph.

My brother continues. 'On Saturday we went to Woolworths in Whitley Bay to get a Thunderbird 1 with variable wing movement. I am now saving up for a Thunderbird three. They are 6s, 11d. Peter Holmes is saving for Thunderbird 5. They are 32 shillings and 11d.'

In later life Colin will become a lawyer, skilled at controlling conversations with a series of elongated ums and errs. There will be digressions and hesitations but he will always bring the conversation home.

Under the heading 'Our customers' he writes: 'We have had lots of people looking for a house. My daddy has had one customer. My mammy had the rest. We have not sold the house. We have not found a house with a school near it. We have pictures of bungalows and we all like the same one. On Sunday I went to the Spanish City with my mammy, daddy and brother Alastair. It was great fun there. My daddy had a try at darts and won a toy atomic submarine.'

Where is this story going? It is going with the McKay family to another seaside town, North Berwick. After an exhaustive search that includes a block of flats near a roundabout outside Musselburgh and a quiet road in Gullane, we settle in Lady Jane Gardens, a new street, not yet finished, in North Berwick. Quite a few of the neighbours also work at the power station, all living in identical houses. Lady Jane was – is – a terrace of shell pebbledash homes with painted wooden facades and coal bunkers by the front doors. The houses are not quite semi-detached. Ours costs £4,000, almost enough to break the family's finances. But the street is neighbourly, verging on communitarian. The mums hold coffee mornings, which my brother and I eavesdrop on while sheltering under the living-room table, muttering 'Up periscope!' as we appear between the leaves of the extendable dining table, scattering millionaire's shortbread and melting moments between the fronds of the deep shag.

The talk at those coffee mornings is often explicit. In 1966, the Swinging Sixties are on the cusp of making an appearance in North Berwick. They will stay on this cusp for a long time. A hint of self-expression is being added to the industrialised housewifery. As well as catalogue parties – sealable containers from Betterware, novelty soap on a rope from Avon – there is yoga, the pill, SodaStreams.

Money is tighter than people like to admit. Those catalogues mean commission for the hostess. My mum does the Grattan catalogue, a seasonal encyclopaedia of aspiration with a section on women's underwear that is boldly educational. The street has a communal carpet cleaner. Every couple of months, by rote, the shampoo Hoover is delivered and the carpets soaked with soap. We stay outside until they are almost dry, returning at dusk to find the living room foggy with the smell of damp wool.

❋

Here is where the second of my first memories returns as trauma.

At the age of four, with a slight Geordie accent, I go to school. The accent is most notable on the word 'Ford', which will be problematic later, when talking about cars becomes a thing that boys are required to do. For now, at the age of four going on five, everyone is more or less lost, entirely unsocialised. There is no pre-school or nursery. Primary one is a sudden plunge. We each have a desk, entire of itself, with a hole for an ink pot. Teaching is done to us, not with us. It is a matter of rote and discipline. What do I feel? From this distance, re-entering the moment, I feel like an outsider, small and lost. Is that how it was?

My teacher is Mrs McAllister. I do not like Mrs McAllister. Possibly I do not like being in primary one but having an opinion about school is not on the curriculum. Mrs McAllister is the school. I do not like how the other children mock my name, chanting 'Alastair McAllister'.

On the first day a boy in my class wets himself and the sense of his shame spills across the classroom floor. What is it about Mrs McAllister? She seems ancient and unsympathetic. Does she even like children? If she does, it's a secret.

But wait, here is a fun thing. The Happy Smile Club is a health initiative designed to promote the habit of good dental hygiene. We are given cards to take home and encouraged to record the brushing of teeth twice a day. There is a song by Larry Marshall, who hosts a light entertainment show on STV. The verse is a grimly cheerful thing that manages to rhyme morning with warning, night and bright with sleep tight. 'If we have teeth that look like pearls,' Larry sings, 'then we are really wealthy/They masticate our food for us and help to keep us healthy.'

You have to wonder what kind of light entertainer it is who thinks it is a good idea to lecture young children on the health benefits of mastication. Larry is that entertainer. Did I ever hear that song? I can't be sure. Certainly, I have stronger memories of my dad singing the punchline from an ancient toothpaste commercial: 'You'll wonder where the yellow went, when you brush your teeth with Pepsodent.'

In Edinburgh, where I am not, the Happy Smile Club has razzle dazzle. It is launched with a guard of honour: twelve pupils of West Pilton Primary School dressed as toy soldiers, with giant toothbrushes instead of guns. Mr Happy Smile, who has an outsized papier mache head, hands out toothpaste samples and delivers dental hygiene advice. During the campaign Mr Happy Smile takes his outsized head to schools across the capital accompanied by officials from the Department of Health for Scotland and the director of the Oral Hygiene Service. At the end of the campaign the class with the highest standard of dental hygiene and a perfect record of tooth-brushing is given the prize of a bus tour and a visit to a Glasgow television studio. A class from Stockbridge Primary wins that, while five runners-up are given a giant toothbrush. Official records record the Happy Smile campaign as a success. A dental examination of 1,000 children shows that they have absorbed the rules for good teeth, and tooth-brush sales have risen. More fruit is being eaten in playgrounds, 'although the campaign had followed a poor fruit season, apples particularly being scarce and very dear'. The report concludes that 'continued propaganda will be maintained especially in the case of five-year-olds'.

There is none of that hoopla in North Berwick. We are given cards and encouraged to tick off the tooth-cleaning events. The prize at the end of this feat of heroic industry is a Happy Smile Club badge.

Not for me.

I have cleaned my teeth at the appropriate moments. My boxes are ticked. It is not enough.

Mrs McAllister calls me to the front of the class and orders me to perform a happy smile. I do my best, though the conditions – fear, extreme self-consciousness, the urge to dissolve into a void of nothingness – make the occasion feel less than joyous. 'Try again,' Mrs McAllister commands.

The teacher's words are drowned by the sound of hot blood rushing into my face. Why is this happening? I am smiling so hard my jaws ache.

Still not enough. Mrs McAllister speaks again, this time with a sense of threat. 'Smile with your eyes!'

Smile with your eyes. How does that work?

I try to pull the sides of my mouth up towards my eyes. The wax in my ears creaks. My smile betrays me. I want to be invisible. I want to be someone else. What have I learned in the Happy Smile Club? Self-consciousness, mostly. There is the stuff about teeth and mouths, and rinsing after eating, and how apples and raisins are more joyous than lollipops, even if they are scarce due to the Scottish weather and the failures of local farming. But this thing about eyes . . . What kind of teacher tests a child on the quality of their smile? Instead of being rewarded I have ended up questioning the concept of smiling. What is it anyway? A stretching of the mouth. A baring of teeth. A smile is what happens when a photographer says 'Cheese!' and you laugh because saying the word cheese means shaping the lips in a facsimile of happiness. That's a trick of photography, of making memories seem brighter. It's not something four-year-olds need lessons in.

I am learning something about school, about a Scottish education. Everything is about regimentation. It is about being obedient and staying silent. It is about knowing your place.

15

I go home in tears. I am the only person in the class not to be rewarded.

The next day my mum marches into the school and berates Mrs McAllister. I am given the badge. I know I have not earned it. I have learned that smiling is an act of propaganda. I have learned how to be shy.

3

Primary School: First Thoughts, As They Occur, As If to a Therapist

Rats in the hall. Fainting during assembly. Maybe it was Easter. Getting punched in the stomach by Billy Two-Times, whose trick was to hold a fist in your face and say 'See that?' while thumping you in the guts with his other hand. The punchline? 'Didnae see that.'

Carbolic soap in the toilets, to be used after swearing to wash out the mouth. Football with a tennis ball in the back playground, endless games. The year the clocks didn't change and we wore luminous armbands so the cars could more easily knock us down. Being asked to demonstrate the Green Cross Code to the whole school on Law Road and mixing up left and right out of sheer embarrassment. Tubby's Chopper. Tubby's Targetland. Tubby's Mouse Trap. Tubby's KerPlunk. Performance anxiety. The tiny chairs. The puddle beneath the tiny chair. Conkers. Winning a cow's tooth at conkers. Losing a welly boot in a sci-fi cowpat vortex on the school trip to Congalton farm. Mr King talking about Orange Bicycle. Mr King getting the whole class to belt anybody who forgot their activity money. The Jacobite Rebellion.

'Popcorn' by Hot Butter. Mr Marshall's long hair. Jimmy Savile. Handiwork in Mr Marshall's class, making a flower pot decorated with varnished shells. I put it in the bin when I got home because it was a disaster. My mum fished it out and told me it was beautiful. 'Son Of My Father' by Chicory Tip. Lovely Miss Thorburn and the interpretative art class. There was classical music. We were asked to draw what we heard. I drew a dripping tap and Miss Thorburn cuffed me gently on the head, just where the bandage was. The arrival of Adidas trainers, like a message from space. The lollipop man. The election posters on the trees. Miss Draffan's green Morris Oxford. Kevin Hughes drawing a perfect Mini. The time I got to ring the bell at four p.m., and the surge of power and freedom and alarm.

Going home slowly.

School is where you discover you are shy. School is where you discover other people are not. School is about knowing things and not putting your hand up.

4

Brigitte Bardot Came to North Berwick and Nobody Noticed

Brigitte Bardot came to North Berwick and nobody noticed. There is a great deal of evidence of her visit, mostly stills from the shoot. She was filming *Two Weeks in September* (aka *À Coeur Joie*). The visit took place in August 1966 and the pictures show Bardot in a number of striking poses. She sits on the shoulders of Laurent Terzieff in front of the Bass Rock. The angle of the Bass suggests that shot was taken at Seacliff, a couple of miles to the east of the town. Getty Images mentions a windy beach in its caption, though there is no evidence of a breeze in the picture. Bardot's hair is very blonde and a bit ruffled but she seems more concerned with the challenges of looking pert while sitting with her legs around the neck of her co-star. Her feet are bare and pointed like a dancer's. She wears a tight sweater. Terzieff has a dark Aran jumper, as if dressed for autumn. In another shot, captioned as Dirleton, Bardot is wrapped in a knitted cardigan and sitting on a deckchair with a tartan scarf covering most of her face. In this picture, she does look cold. The Dirleton shots, which must be on

Yellowcraig beach, are dated 5 September 1966, which may account for the chill. Another shot from the same day shows Bardot on the beach, surrounded by the crew, alongside a Citroën van. The crew wear coats with collars upturned, headscarves for the women. The most dramatic image from the visit shows Bardot on the rocks in front of the Bass, her hair blowing slightly. She wears a dark sweater and sea boots that leave her upper thighs exposed.

Two Weeks in September catches Bardot in the full bloom of her beauty. She plays a model in the film, so there are plenty of excuses for her to be gratuitously prepossessing. Promotional materials for the film are full of optimistic possibilities, inviting readers of local newspapers to 'Judge the holiday moods of Brigitte Bardot'. Suggestions include photographic competitions for the best holiday pictures taken during the month of September ('Quality, composition, lighting, etc.' should all be taken into account).

'Most male filmgoers will agree that gorgeous Brigitte Bardot would be the ideal holiday companion,' the promo materials continue, proposing 'an attractive competition block' in which readers are asked to study six portraits of BB in the film and place them 'in the order they consider would win her the title of the ideal holiday girl'. The correct ranking should be determined in advance by the newspaper's Beauty Editor. 'To avoid a tie, ask the entrants to add an adjective of their own which best suits Brigitte's mood in the six pictures. Or ask them to choose from the following: "PLAYFUL"; "ALLURING"; "COY"; "ADORABLE"; "STUNNING"; "DESIRABLE"; "BREATHTAKING"; "CHARMING", etc.'

For newspapers with a zoo nearby the possibilities are more exotic. 'Parallel the film scene by having a number of pretty model girls in way-out fashion outfits . . . photographed against empty cages, posing with animals, etc. This would be certain to provide a novel photo-feature of the type all newspaper picture editors would find especially welcome.'

Two Weeks in September proves to be no more than a footnote in Bardot's career. Biographer Barnett Singer suggests that 'Scotland gave Bardot pleasant feelings' whereas filming later at London Zoo proved a depressing experience after Bardot saw a gorilla going ape in a cage. The film is 'just silly', according to David Bruce in *Scotland: The Movie*. Another critic suggests Bardot 'is clearly fed up with playing ravishing idiots'. She would soon meet Serge Gainsbourg, prompting him to write the orgasmic chanson, 'Je T'Aime . . . Moi Non Plus', later made famous by Jane Birkin.

But still, the evidence exists of an impossible thing.

Brigitte Bardot came to North Berwick, wore sea boots, was playful, alluring, coy, adorable, stunning, desirable, breathtaking, charming. And nobody noticed.

5

Calum Kennedy: Kilty By Suspicion

My first-ever concert is Calum Kennedy. It is traumatic. It is Montrose.

I don't blame Montrose entirely but the town must take some of the blame. Montrose is where my dad comes from. It is where my gran lives. In terms of family visits my gran's comes second to my mum's parents, Grandma and Grandad in Brechin, though you can never have one without the other.

Partly the hierarchy is practical. Grandma and Grandad have spare rooms. There are books – shelves and shelves of Agatha Christies – and a busy stove on which the tea is always stewing. It boils away all day long like the tar pit in *Quatermass*. Grandma and Grandad have a speechless budgerigar called Budgie who goes to bed with great ceremony at nine p.m. They have a serving hatch that links the kitchen and the living room. It is luxury. They have a tin full of sweeties, boilings mostly, always full. The beds are warmed with a hot-water pig. They have a ticking clock on the sideboard. Auntie Elsie, who isn't my auntie but must be somebody's, lives across the back green. She washes the strips for Brechin City football club. On the day after a game her washing line is a semaphore of anguish, a whole team of red strips waving in apology. As a team Brechin are a model of consistency. They have their own joke. Q. What's the strongest team in the Scottish football league table? A. Brechin City. They hold the rest up.

Visits to Brechin are sociable and loud. Montrose is sombre. True, there is a swimming pool, and that is fun, although I can't swim. There is a field at the edge of town where my dad takes us for golf practice and we hack away silently together. There are amusements, occasionally, and the beach, sometimes, though less often than you might imagine. Early childhood visits to Montrose involve being sent to the corner shop to buy a lucky bag, though our luck does not extend beyond infancy. Latterly we are holed up nervously in my gran's flat. Time passes, every second registered by the ticking clock on the mantel, every quarter-hour marked by the Westminster chimes.

Gran has some interesting stuff. She has a vibrant print in a frame in her hall, rumoured to be a work by the artist Rolf Harris. She has a print of a Turner painting showing a stormy harbour. There are souvenirs of my dad's travels, notably a ship that is also a lamp, fashioned from a clog. The ship's sail is the lampshade.

Gran's fireplace is guarded by a plaster statuette of Little Miss Muffet on her tuffet, accompanied by an ominous spider.

For entertainment Gran has a box of implements, not all of them broken. The best is a mechanical whisk. We spend hours with the whisk, stirring the sour air from the chemical factory as it wafts through the flat.

Gran does not cook. She prepares a Scottish salad of ham, or hough, a lettuce leaf, half a boiled egg, a sliced tomato and ready salted crisps, warmed in the oven. On leaving the house Gran will press a Milky Way into our hands as compensation for the long journey south. The chocolate will be eaten quickly because a Scottish salad is not filling, even when supplemented with tiger bread and a Simmers butter biscuit. By the time we get to Dundee I will be vomiting the sweet you can eat between meals over my father's head. He will drive on patiently, his hair suppurating in the sickly fondant until a lay-by can be located. Then, suddenly barefoot, he will dismount the Vauxhall Victor and sponge his features clean with his socks.

I know little about Gran. She is a quiet woman, and slight. My middle name is her maiden name, Herschell. It sounds exotic, or Jewish, or German, or something. I am embarrassed by it at school. I learn to keep it quiet. I ask my dad about the name and he replies: 'There were a lot of Herschells in Arbroath.'

The other thing I know about Gran is that her husband, my dad's father, my grandfather, died suddenly the week before I was born. I inherited his Parker fountain pen and a bottle of Quink.

Years after my gran died I am given a letter she had written to my parents. It is dated the day after I was born, with the words 'Sunday morning' below Gran's wharfside address in Montrose. It is a beautiful letter, a masterpiece of autumnal stoicism. The language flits between colloquial and formal, the tenses between now and then.

Isobel is my mum. Geo is my dad. Colin is my brother. Vi remains a mystery. Gran's 'Granny' is a chimney cowl.

I was so happy indeed to get your call with the glad news of the safe arrival of another wee grandson. You were well ahead of your time yesterday Isobel, and I have no doubt you will be feeling 'gie glad' that it's a' ower again.

Don't be too disappointed about the baby not being a little girl. I think little boys are so nice and couthy. You'll just have to have patience like me. When you, my third bonnie lad came, Geo, I was quite pleased and just consoled myself with the belief that there wasn't to be a girlie for me. I was always very thankful to see a bonnie healthy lad, and was, and am, still very proud of you all and have every reason to be. However, the very unexpected happened and I am very thankful for the blessing I had in having such a fine loving family.

I was so glad that you had a pleasant journey back, after the terrible soaking you must have got going to the station. I can't tell you how vexed I felt at you having to go and face yon terrible morning. How I wished I had ordered taxis in spite of your protests. Your Dad would definitely have had them ordered.

It's very comforting to me to know that I have you all behind me if I need you. I am trying very hard to keep going, but there are times when I feel rather sorry for myself. I went to see the Doc on Monday morning and he gave me several different tablets, sedatives etc etc. So I'll soon be 'rattling'. Vi comes every evening after eight and we just have a cuppa and prepare for morning and then off to bed. Of course she doesn't sleep at all well so I have somebody to speak to during the night.

I hope to go the cemetery sometime today. It's a fine mild day for a change. We've been having awful weather the past week, and terrible gales. Our new 'Granny' came down one night and fell into Wharf House, so we were nearly 'reeked out'.

I've had lots of visitors the last week, so I've been well off for company. I got the Death Grant and put it into my account. I also had to take up the Co-op book and Div (due this week) as well as they were in Dad's name. I can't think what little thing I could bring for my new grandson so I will enclose just a small gift and I would like you to buy something he needs, Isobel, please, with my love. I'll have to see about some breakfast now. I've been up with the lark with the change of clocks, Trust you are all fine, love Mam xxxx

None of this is anything I knew or even suspected about my gran. I wasn't curious while she was alive and my dad never explained. It had always seemed unfortunate that I hadn't met my grandad but nothing more. Yet here was my gran, in the depths of tragedy, keeping everything together and reassuring my parents that they might have better luck next time. I was a boy. Too bad.

So, Calum Kennedy.

This time we don't leave Montrose after lunch. We go to see the Golden Voice of the Highlands. Is it the Locarno Ballroom or the Town Hall? I have no way of knowing. It is bright and noisy and intimate and most of the things I don't enjoy, all at once. I am old enough to understand that the event, with its blend of forced charisma, morose melody and exhausted ritual, is not aimed at me. It is to be endured. It is church, with ungentlemanly accordions.

Can I get back there? All too easily. The flavour of it – acrid, peaty; salt tears and shortbread crumbs – is captured beautifully in Michael Begg and Ian Wooldridge's 1982 documentary, *Calum Kennedy's Commando Course*. The film follows Kennedy and his ever-decreasing band of entertainers on a tour of the Highlands and Islands. As a documentary it is years ahead of its time. The tone is what is later known as 'mockumentary' and it's hard to observe the travails of Kennedy's diminishing troupe without concluding that they are in on the joke. As the entertainers approach Wick, Wooldridge's voiceover suggests that the town is Scotland's last exit to the North Pole. 'By local standards, it's almost spring-like. Temperature not much below freezing. Sea rather calmer than usual.' Kennedy, who seems to be slightly less aware of the joke than others in his company, suggests that the locals in search of entertainment might visit the butcher's shop to watch the bacon slicer.

Reportedly Kennedy was unhappy with the film and succeeded in delaying its broadcast for a few years. Today he would have been advised to lean towards the mockery and embrace it in the way that his own act had repackaged traditional music with a voguish cocktail of ventriloquism and racist jokes about the Irish. As the voiceover suggests: 'Calum Kennedy is hugely popular with older audiences . . . even if his stage style does remind you of Rob Roy taking ballet lessons.'

What do I remember about seeing Calum Kennedy in Montrose? One thing hits me like a fork in the eye. At a certain point in the show Kennedy addresses the audience. 'Are there any English people here tonight?' he says. His manner is like that of a teacher. Or maybe a policeman. I raise my hand. 'Och, well,' Kennedy says, with mocking sympathy. I hear nothing after that except the thump of blood in my couthy wee face.

6

A Poem

In primary seven I have a poem published in the school magazine.

Some talk of Gary Glitter
And some of Francis Lee
Some talk of flashy sports cars
But no one talks of me

7

The Music Period
'Sing soft, man, y'know I mean like wow.'

Mrs Turner is our music teacher. Music class never changes. Primary one and fourth year at high school are the same routine. Mrs Turner has a piano. It is upright, like her.

Mrs Turner's husband, Mr Turner, is the technical drawing teacher. He has a musical approach. Techie drawing is terror with pencils. The classes come in double periods, to allow time for the drawing to go wrong. I can't do technical drawing. It requires neatness and conceptual understanding. There are front elevations and end elevations and rear elevations. There are elevations from every direction. Sometimes there are dissections too. You have to draw things as if they had been cut in half. This is not something my brain can comprehend. It is engineering. It makes me cry.

My dad is an engineer. The loft is full of hardbound notebooks from his night-school classes, with spidery drawings and equations worked out in fountain pen. But Dad has gone beyond drawing. He is a charge engineer and also a mechanical engineer. The mechanical engineers' journal piles up unread by the front door.

Dad works at the power station. He has a white boiler suit. All our bathroom towels have SSEB on them. We are kept dry by the South of Scotland Electricity Board. My dad works nights sometimes and then he works days. There is something called back-shift that he is often on. When he is on nights we have to creep around all day, trying not to wake him. Waking Dad during the day is the worst thing that can happen. You hear the rumbling upstairs and he will emerge bleary-eyed. He never says anything. We just know. Sometimes he will leave his ear plugs on the arm of his chair during the day, a warning in wax. The best thing about nights is when Dad drives home at breakfast time. I can detect the thrum of the Vauxhall Victor as it approaches and Dad will come in with his piece box, his face on backwards, caught between day and night.

My mum helps with the techie drawing and the applied mechanics. After I have run lines with her, for her starring role in the Abbey Church Drama Group production of *Blithe Spirit*, she takes an apple and asks me to imagine what is inside. I am confused. What is inside an apple apart from apple? She cuts the apple in half and holds it forwards, backwards and sideways. I can just about understand. This is technical. This is engineering. This is music. If Mr Turner had diverged from the techie drawing curriculum and asked us to draw a child's impression of a Cox's Pippin, I would have known where to start.

Mrs Turner's approach to music is technical. It is rules-based. It does not involve apples. It involves bananas.

There are two elements to the music class. The first bit,

which is the only bit if things don't go well, is about the ears. It is the 'higher or lower' bit. Mrs Turner plays a note on the piano. She pauses for effect. Then she plays another note. 'Was the first note higher or lower than the second?' she asks. This process is repeated around thirty-five times, depending on absences and acts of insurrection. We all get a turn. Higher or lower? How hard can it be? It is multiple choice, a coin-toss. You have a fifty per cent chance. If you get it wrong, Mrs Turner might repeat the experiment.

The higher or lower game is followed by 'the teeth, the lips, the tip of the tongue'. After the terrible jeopardy of the higher or lower challenge, this is easy. It isn't singing. We are warming up. We have to chant in unison while Mrs Turner assaults the piano. Pianos have it tough. This is a period in history when summer entertainment in the town might consist of grown men smashing pianos with hammers then dressing as babies and riding from pub to pub in a Silver Cross pram. 'The teeth, the lips, the tip of the tongue,' we chant. 'Roast beef, your hips, the whiff of your bum.' The point of the teeth, the lips exercise is never questioned and never explained. It is singing reduced to its technical essence. There is no need for melody or rhyme. The pleasure is to be found in the rhythm of the mouth. It is singing as physical education.

Sometimes, often, the class gets stuck. Doing higher or lower followed by vocal jerks takes time, and there are up to forty of us in the class. Sometimes in a music lesson, we graduate to music. It is quite a leap. There is more to think about. There are words, which have to be read in a loud monotone from a printed sheet, and there is volume. How loud can you go?

There are two songs, and I love them equally. The songs are 'Marie's Wedding' and 'The Banana Boat Song'. In 1974

Billy Connolly recorded a routine about the music classes of his childhood, in which 'Marie's Wedding' was accompanied by an order from his teacher. 'Appreciate! Appreciate! Appreciate!' In my class we are not obliged to appreciate anything. Mostly, the lesson is about draining the joy from a celebratory song. We ignore the wedding. We concentrate on the grim gratitude of the third verse: 'Plenty herring, plenty meal, plenty peat to fill her creel.' How many herring was plenty? Not many.

Was Mrs Turner religious? I have seen her at the kirk but that is not the same thing. There is certainly something Church of Scotland about her punitive approach to a tune. The attitude of the Church to music is similar to its view of fun. It is a serious business.

The churches in North Berwick are territorial, with almost imperceptible social codes and micro-snobberies. There is dark talk about the comings and goings at 'the English church'. These include rumours of guitars and clergymen in leather jackets. My mum has a word for this sort of nonsense. The word is 'happy-clappy'. Happy-clappy is as bad as things might reasonably be expected to get, outside of Hell.

Then there is the other tune. The other tune is 'The Banana Boat Song'. There are numerous versions of this composition. The first was recorded by Edric Connor and the Caribbeans on the 1954 album *Songs From Jamaica*, when it was known as 'Day Dah Light'. Edric Connor's version is a sombre worksong with mellow piano, almost churchy in its cadence. That is not the version we sing with Mrs Turner. Most likely we are doing Harry Belafonte's 'Banana Boat (Day-O)', which comes with an improbably robust vocal and an exaggerated call and response on the 'day-o' bits. Perhaps some of us are aware of the comedy version of the song by

Stan Freberg in which a hipster bongo player interrupts proceedings with his complains about the noise ('Too loud man, I can still hear you, would you mind leaving the room?'), because that is the sort of thing they play on Radio 1 during the dinner hour after the chart rundown. But mostly we concentrate on doing our Jamaican accents and getting the volume of the day-os up to an unreasonable level.

Cultural appropriation has not been invented. Sing soft, man, y'know I mean like wow.

8

The Marconiphone E1

There is no music in my house. This seems accidental, rather than malign. It is as if the question of music hasn't come up.

Certainly, there is no record player. A musical instrument would have been viewed with suspicion. The car does not have a radio, so there is little to distract from the serious business of swallowing vomit. Occasionally, as if to signal he is aware that music exists in another world, not this one, my dad will sing while driving: Tom Jones songs with the words twisted slightly for comic effect. Mostly, I lie flat on the back seat of the Vauxhall Victor trying to tune out the traffic. 'Oh,' my mum will say as the Victor judders towards autumnal Angus, 'the trees are bonnie.'

My dad is methodical. He arrives home with a giant box. Inside the box is a machine. As he often does with technology, Dad has surveyed the evidence and decided that while a record player might have its uses, a Marconiphone E1 is a more versatile machine.

The Marconiphone is a chunky reel-to-reel tape recorder with its own microphone. The microphone is a beautiful thing. There is a *Star Trek* simplicity to its design. The tape reels look like science but the Marconiphone is more than that. It is the future. It means you don't have to buy records. You can record them yourself, direct from the television, and when the novelty of the songs wears off they can be wiped and replaced with fresher hits.

To get the party started, the Marconiphone comes with a pre-recorded tape of the soundtrack from *The Sound of Music*. Is that part of the package, a gift to demonstrate the high fidelity of the machine, or was my dad persuaded to buy it by an over-zealous salesman with a penchant for singing nuns? We never find out. *The Sound of Music* stays in the box. 'Edelweiss', 'Climb Ev'ry Mountain', 'My Favourite Things'; these songs are never played. There is no room for a lonely goatherd in our house.

The Marconiphone is a serious piece of technology. It is heavy. It has heft. It has its own quirks and foibles. It has a personality. It is stubborn, if not aloof.

You can't just turn it on. There is a lengthy foreplay. You have to wait for fifteen minutes while the valves and coils that lurk beneath the silver and grey exterior come to life. The Marconiphone hums and purrs in expectation. It can record at different speeds, so a reel can last for as near to forever as is practically possible and recordings can be played back at the wrong speed. This never stops being hilarious. We can all be Pinky and Perky. It is a technological wonder.

There is a flaw in the plan, of course. In order to record the music, silence is required. When *Top of the Pops* comes on, the Marconiphone is stationed in front of the TV and powered up. The microphone is propped up and the room silenced, as if observing a religious rite. In between songs there is a scramble for the pause button; an attempt to delete the DJ.

There is one other way of getting the nation's pop hits into the house on-demand. This is Dial-a-Disc. It is the musical equivalent of the speaking clock. It is like setting fire to money.

Ringing the speaking clock is viewed by my parents as an act of supreme decadence, so doing Dial-a-Disc from home is impossible. The phone itself – a Trimphone in two shades of purple – is viewed with great wariness. It is quarantined on the hall table. Sometimes a call relating to work or golf will be taken by my dad. He will address the Trimphone in an alien voice, as sternly polite as a British officer under interrogation in Colditz, never using two words when none will do. I absorb this formal phone behaviour, beginning with a deeply suspicious delivery of the number – 'North Berwick 3272'. The implication is clear. The telephone is an impertinence. It is a machine with ways of making you talk.

We have a radio, of course. Radio 1 is launched in 1967, so there is some of that. Certainly later, when chart positions become an important piece of information in the global debate about whether Slade are bigger than The Beatles, listening to the chart show on a Tuesday lunchtime is an important ritual. Who were The Beatles anyway? They were ancient history, long gone, almost forgotten. They couldn't compete with glam rock.

I'm getting ahead of myself. Before Slade, before Mud, before Lieutenant Pigeon, before 'The Streak' and 'Seasons In The Sun' and Showaddywaddy and Darts and The Rubettes and Suzi Quatro and Sailor and Hello and a hundred other bands in denim or tinfoil and feathered hair working out ways to remake rock 'n' roll as a dense and aggressive stomp of teenage lust; before The Sweet and Queen and Elton John brought confusing news about masculinity; before everyone's big brother had *Band On The Run*, before Chuck Berry's 'Ding-A-Ling'; before 'Convoy' and truck songs and CB slang and suicidal folk soundtracks and Deep Purple playing 'Smoke On The Water' for seven hours without stopping, and the coloured girls going doop-de-doop on 'Walk On The Wild Side'; before dope-on-the-fingernails introspective folk; before Hipgnosis sleeves and Pink Floyd being boringness viewed through a prism; before private-school prog; before Marc Bolan saluting The Damned; before Bobby Crush and Hughie Green's clap-o-meter, and Tony Hatch and Mickie Most telling it how it was on *New Faces*; before *Rock Follies* and Julie Covington and 'It's the buzz, cock'; before *Lift Off . . . with Ayshea* or Flintlock naked on *Pauline's Quirkes*; before Alvin Stardust's come-hither glove and the campification of black leather; before the never-ending tragedy of Lena Zavaroni, the tight fit of David Dundas's airbrushed jeans; before the tantalising warmth of Noosha Fox's 'S-S-S-Single Bed' . . .

Before all of that, a couple of records sneak into my mind.

My first favourite record is 'Storm In A Teacup' by The Fortunes. There are things to know about The Fortunes. They are a harmony group from Birmingham, originally called The Cliftones and briefly (wearing green tights as the backing group to Robbie Hood) The Merrie Men. They flirt with Merseybeat, tour with Peter & Gordon and The Moody Blues, and their manager Reg Calvert is shot dead in a dispute over pirate radio. They record the Coca-Cola jingle, 'It's The Real Thing', and have a surprising revival in the 1970s when they switch labels and adjust their musical style.

I do not know this when I hear 'Storm In A Teacup'. What I know is that 'Storm In A Teacup' is an extraordinary thing, a swirl of pop soul, jagged strings and a lyric that begins with an impersonation of rain. After the pitter-patter the song swings between the simplicity of a nursery rhyme and the comfort of a sermon. Ron Roker, who composed the song with Lynsey de Paul (credited as Lyndsey Rubin), also wrote the theme to *Rupert the Bear* and *Pipkins* – a puppet show dominated by a narcissistic hare called Hartley – so it's possible he had a knack for a childish melody.

Why do I like it? It is not a technical question. It must be an instinctive thing, though the imagery – the crockery tempest – has an Alice in Wonderland feel to it. Why do I remember it? Because it is playing on the day I decide it would be fun to run through the house with a red-hot poker and stab it into the plastic hull of an Airfix battleship. The ship is holed beneath the water line. The grey plastic melts. It smells terrible. As I inhale that noxious odour I realise how stupid I am being and how terrible the punishment will be. I return the poker to its place beside the fire and bin the destroyed destroyer. On the radio The Fortunes are making light of their meteorological differences. Then comes some coded stuff about gossip and betrayals of a more adult nature. Never mind. The tune has done its work.

Another record, another moment of childish terror. I am riding my bike. My bike is a red Moulton Mini, which is not the coolest thing. My dad has chosen it because it is a wonder of British engineering and design. But I am a child. I am not an engineer. I grow to like the Moulton Mini, taking pride in its ruggedness and the fact that no one else has one, but my initial feeling is that it isn't a racer or a Raleigh Chopper. It isn't fast, and thanks to its brilliant design – the balance of weight on the low frame, the revolutionary suspension – it cannot be coaxed into doing a wheelie. The only irresponsible thing I can do with the Moulton Mini is to trigger the brake by back-pedalling suddenly, which will cause the back wheel to skid across the tarmac. It is less satisfying than a wheelie but it is my contribution whenever I am required to summon a moment of stupid boyish danger.

So there I am, pedalling industriously down Lady Jane Gardens, enjoying the sense of exhilaration. The wind is in my hair, freckles are on my face. Life is good, or at least neutral, which isn't bad. Being carefree is a moment to be treasured, and as I power downhill I feel my self-consciousness lift to the point where I start singing.

Singing? Singing what?

Singing the chorus of 'Jumpin' Jack Flash'.

Of course I have no idea what it means. Still don't. Does Mick Jagger even know? It doesn't matter. Somewhere in the space between the first 'gas', the second 'gas' and the third 'gas' I forget where the brakes on my bike are and crash into the garage wall of number 12 Lady Jane Gardens.

9

The Man Who Put the Bang in Gang

I buy a record before we have a record player. It is a matter of urgency. It has to be done. The record is 'I'm The Leader Of The Gang (I Am!)' by Gary Glitter and it is beautiful. The record comes in a maroon paper sleeve with a silver label, catalogue number Bell 1321. I know what it sounds like, of course. There has been an outbreak of technological detente in the house and my dad has sanctioned the purchase of an FM radio. The FM part is of limited use but we are able to access Radio Luxembourg, Fab 208, on the medium wave. Fab 208 manages to sound more relaxed than Radio 1, though the signal is often weak. The songs drift out of focus, the melodies fog. We are listing to Radio Luxembourg in the living room while Gary Glitter is interviewed. The singer blows in and out but in the audible bits he sounds detached and playful. Not taking yourself seriously is a feature of the glam rock period, but this feels like something else, as if Glitter is playing along with an image of himself. My parents, eavesdropping on that distant signal, are dismissive. I am hurt and confused. It is as if my loyalties have been challenged. The interview ends with a competition. The prize is Gary's glitter shirt. It has not been washed, the singer notes. The sweat is still in the fabric.

This is it. I have chosen Gary Glitter. Gary Glitter has chosen me.

Owning the record and not playing it is almost enough but it is not a speculative purchase. My brother is getting a stereo. My dad has done his usual survey of all the available options and settled on the Alba 642, a Dansette-style record player fashioned from heavy-duty plastic in two tones of grey. The 642 is a modest machine, built for portability with a handle on the side. It has a speaker on the front of the plastic box that contains the turntable and another that can be stored inside the lid. If it were a building, the 642 would be a brutalist coal bunker. There is something brilliant about the functional design. There are four sliding controls on the front of the box, like you'd find on a mixing desk, for volume, treble, bass and balance. Under the lid the turntable allows for six records to be stacked on top of each other. This is thrilling, though there can be slippage when you get to record number six. I only have one record. That is a problem for the future.

The time comes. The Alba 642 is set up in the bedroom near to the window. I open the window wide and click the record on the spindle, shifting the controls to 7" and 45 rpm. The record drops down, plastic onto plastic, and the needle hits the groove.

Gary Glitter is not a subtle artist. 'I'm The Leader Of The Gang (I Am!)' starts with a revving motorcycle and descends quickly, like Evel Knievel crashing into a Pepsi truck. Why a motorcycle? The early 1970s is a good time for bad biker films, cashing in on *Easy Rider* or *The Wild Angels* or *The Wild One*, and Marlon Brando rebelling against whatever. It's a rebel kink.

What does this have to do with Gary Glitter? Everything and nothing, except that the panto tinfoil excesses of glitter rock, like the effeminate hod-carrying of glam, are variations on a formula that has already been recalibrated several times. Glitter alluded to that in his first hit, the almost instrumental 'Rock and Roll Parts 1 and 2'.

What kind of gang is Gary Glitter leading? You can take it literally and conclude that a self-satirising showman such as Glitter will be aware that his audience of teens and pre-teens is unlikely to join a motorcycle gang, even as they ride the streets on their Raleigh Choppers. Few of us are even aware that the design of the Chopper – dropped handlebars, mismatched wheels, genital-threatening gear-stick in the shape of Kojak's lollipop – owes anything to the cinematic imagery of biker gangs.

Even so, 'I'm The Leader Of The Gang (I Am!)' is not a song that repays close examination. There are the exaltations. Come on, come on! The way the tune speeds up, the implied applause of the handclap rhythm. Glitter, hiding in open sight, is a cross between the Child Catcher in *Chitty Chitty Bang Bang* and a post-panto Elvis, without the redeeming features.

I push the slider on the Alba 642 up to 10 and let the record play out over the back garden. When it finishes, I let it play again. Come on, come on! I feel like a king!

10

What Fruit Grows on
Telegraph Poles?

In primary seven I make a magazine. There is not much that is notable about this publication except, perhaps, the fact that it is done at all. It is hand drawn with felt pens, running to sixteen A5 pages of graph paper and tied together with a shoelace. I am no artist. I have trouble drawing badly.

The cover reveals the most impressive thing about the publication. As a handmade magazine, *Ali's Assortment* has a print run of one copy, available for rent at a cost of a penny per reader. Nobody gets rich. The inside back cover reveals only one reader signing up (in purple felt pen) for a subscription.

The cover also has a badly rendered drawing of a glam rock singer in platform boots, purple flares and a turquoise t-shirt with a smiley face and the slogan *Shame On You*. He wears sunglasses and has a nose in the shape of an inverted heart.

Inside there is a page of Snoopy cartoons drawn by my classmate Grant, 'copied from some pictures my sister got from Germany'. Overleaf, Grant explains who Snoopy is.

'I bet you didn't know Snoopy is famous in Korea,' he says.

There is a page of gonks, with Vikki Viking and Pesky Mo beating Big Jock in a popularity poll. (Total votes cast: six.)

There is a page of jokes, including my all-time favourite, stolen from a *Beano* annual.

Q. What fruit grows on telegraph poles?

A. Electric currants!

Also this:

A boy comes home from school, much earlier than usual. His dad says: 'You've been sent home, haven't you?'

'Yes.'

'What for?'

'The lad next to me was smoking.'

'So why were you sent home?'

'It was me who set him on fire.'

Page six has a forgery of the Celtic footballer Bobby Murdoch's autograph.

There is a pop quiz.

Question one: What is Noddy Holder's tarantula called?

Question two: What pet does Alice Cooper keep?

Question three: What was David Bowie's last single?

The centre pages have pop photos Sellotaped from magazines. They are the usual suspects: Gary Glitter, Elton John, Rod Stewart, Wizzard and Slade, minus Dave Hill, who has been cut out by mistake. The oddity here is a photo of Jook, who pose around moodily in skinhead clothes in front of a graffitied wall. 'From Edinburgh', the caption explains. Jook make an appearance on a later page, with the shock news that they have thrown aside their skinhead image: 'Photo maybe next month'.

'By the way,' the text on the next page says, 'Rod Stewart and Elton John were at Hampden to see Scotland v

West Germany.' This observation is straightforward investigative reporting. The Gullane Under-14s football team travelled to Hampden for the game and Elton and Rod were in the enclosure behind us, along with the West German striker Gerd Müller. This was more memorable than the game, though the Scotland team included Kenny Dalglish, Billy Bremner, Danny McGrain and Denis Law. West Germany were captained by Der Kaiser, the great Franz Beckenbauer. The game finished 1–1, with Manchester United's Jim Holton scoring for Scotland and Uli Hoeneß equalising near the end.

It was a friendly and didn't matter much. Except for the fact of Rod and Elton.

This is a strange thing. Actual evidence that famous people exist in real life.

An Engineer Answers the Telephone

My dad appears on television. It is an episode of *Tomorrow's World*, the magazine programme that makes science accessible. *Tomorrow's World* is Reithian television in the raw. It is a programme designed to entertain, inform and educate, not necessarily in that order.

Tomorrow's World does all of these things, though the emphasis between the education and the information seems to shift depending on who is presenting. When the former Spitfire pilot Raymond Baxter is on, the science of tomorrow sounds like a bulletin from the Ministry of Dreams. The programme becomes more accessible when it is presented by Michael Rodd, a student of Glenalmond, the downmarket public school in Perthshire. From 1974 onwards the show is helmed by Judith Hann (described by Clive James as the 'intelligent and extremely presentable presenter' at a time when the intelligence and presentability of a female broadcaster are suitable subjects for appraisal).

There is no way of knowing who is presenting on the day my dad appears. Before video, television comes and goes. It only exists as now, even when it is predicting the future.

What is the story? Why is *Tomorrow's World* filming at Cockenzie power station?

Possibly it is reflecting on the optimistic certainty that a future powered by fossil fuels will be warm and glorious. That memory, that tomorrow, belongs in the past. Coal is gone, Cockenzie is gone, my dad is a blush of fond memory who existed, when he did, in the present tense.

What I do know is that we close the curtains to appreciate *Tomorrow's World*. That's what people do when they are watching television formally. The blacks and the whites are deeper and more convincing if there is no interference from the outside. Plus, nobody can tell you are watching television, a faintly despicable pursuit, as Lord Reith understood.

In my recollection of my televised dad in the fabulous future there is a control room, like a mixing desk, somewhat *Star Trek* but closer to *Dr Strangelove*. There is a telephone. The telephone rings and my dad picks it up. There is no sound on this bit of film, and in my memory there is a jolt, some interference, a splice, and I hear my late father's voice answering the telephone in the way he always did, like a charge engineer intoning magick. 'North Berwick 3272,' he laments, as if by casting the number slowly he will dissolve the threat.

12

The Princess and the Tree

Lady Jane Gardens is strange. The street isn't finished when we move in, so there is building work all around. The street is a cul-de-sac. There is no one passing through. The road lies in the no-man's land between the council scheme and the pretty bungalows of St Baldred's Road, bordering the Lodge grounds. It is neither here nor there.

The houses in Lady Jane Gardens are not quite semi-detached. They are semi-attached. The street is a nervous queue, with each home built slightly back, or forward, aloof from its neighbour. The gardens are small, with a driveway, a coal bunker and a space for a rockery at the front and a parcel of garden at the back. The houses are less imposing than the council blocks on Brodie Avenue behind and more off-the-shelf than the little castles of St Baldred's at the front. We watch in amazement as a slurry of smashed shells is hosed onto wet cement on the walls of the unfinished houses. The look is seaside pebbledash. In the sunshine it gleams like a coral reef. In the wet, the street is a rainbow of grey.

My brother and I are friends with two boys who live at number 5. There is a community spirit. These are homes for

48

young families. Many of the dads also work at the power station. There are a few teachers, like Mr McAlpine, the high school PE teacher who lives down the hill towards the Boys' Brigade hut. The McPhees, down the other end, host the odd soirée. At one of these the parents discuss the sex scenes in the Peter Benchley novel *Jaws*, which is everywhere because of the film. I have a *Jaws* poster on my wall. In the High Street, John Menzies has a *Jaws* window display. At other times the John Menzies window has celebrated the moon landing and the publication of *The Gulag Archipelago* by Aleksandr Solzhenitsyn. The Cold War is played out in the John Menzies shop window. But *Jaws* is the big event. When the parents talk about the sex in *Jaws*, my brother and I do our best to look uninterested, if not invisible. Then the conversation turns to the genius of Frank Spencer in *Some Mothers Do 'Ave 'Em*. About this, there is no debate. Funny doesn't get funnier than Frank Spencer.

At some later date I am asked to compile my memories of North Berwick in the 1970s for the parish records. My entry in that austere journal reads like the minutes of a meeting with a disqualified psychiatrist. Perhaps that is what memory is. I remember more now.

On 8 June 1971 the sports centre is opened by Princess Margaret. I am there without a flag to see the queen's sister plant a tree. It is one of those non-event events. In royal terms, planting a tree means turning some earth with a brand-new spade into a hole that has already been dug. It is life as ceremony. I understand now that Margaret was probably being sent to dig the dirt at the sports centre as a punishment for the dirt that was being dug about her sexy life. On the day, the event is all about her presence, and the fact that it is witnessed. If a princess plants a tree in an isolated car park and no one sees it, does the tree exist at all?

Margaret is not doing sexy at the sports centre. If there is any excitement, it is restrained. Standing some distance away by the wall of the Law Hotel I overhear someone describe the sports centre as a white elephant. I am unfamiliar with the metaphor but it could be a description of the architecture. The building is a harled box with no obvious relationship to design at all.

But the sports centre is brilliant. It has bar billiards and five-a-sides. My team, the Fireballs (named after the Gerry Anderson space puppet show *Fireball XL5*), wins a tournament. The referee, Mr Vineyard, aka Grapes, has the patience of a volcano. Also in the sports centre, two men play squash for several days, hallucinating grand pianos, and win a paragraph in the *Guinness Book of Records*.

It is outside the sports centre that my head is split open. It is not a serious head injury – it is not yet a serious head – but there is blood. The wound happens during a routine stone-throwing game; boys from here versus boys from there. Because of the blood and tears I am taken to the cottage hospital and made to lie down for a nap while my parents are alerted. Embarrassed and fearful of punishment – yet proud that I have achieved a disfiguring wound – I fall asleep. My mother takes a while to arrive because she has been in Edinburgh on a shopping trip. When she does get to the hospital she is not angry. She is worried and gentle. She presents me with a pair of purple underpants to cheer me up.

There are other things in my official report of the decade, though nothing as exciting as the purple pants. In 1972 Arnold Palmer and Tony Jacklin helicopter into town to play the 15th hole on the west links. They are playing a round of golf at the eighteen best golf holes in Britain and the 15th,

50

'Redan', is one of them. Redan is one of the most copied golf holes in the world. It is a par three, 189 yards long, with a sloping green hidden from view and guarded by deep, unforgiving bunkers. There are many Redans around the world. This is the original. The word Redan implies a military fortification and playing this one requires a golfer to delve into philosophy, conquer the routine dynamics of hitting the ball and display an appreciation of the untrust-worthiness of the prevailing wind, which comes from the west until it doesn't. Playing a Redan means making an accommodation with failure and planning for the least worst outcome. It is a Scottish thing. It is an east-coast thing. It is very North Berwick.

There is a lot of golf in the 1970s. It is a golden age. The Open comes to Muirfield in Gullane, followed by the Ryder Cup. I watch both tournaments through a cardboard periscope designed to resemble a carton of Embassy Regal cigarettes and learn to understand the religious hush of the golf spectator. I get the autographs of all the greats: Jack Nicklaus, Arnold Palmer, Seve Ballesteros, Tony Jacklin, Mr Lu. My favourite is Lee Trevino because he keeps up a running commentary as he hits balls at the driving range. He is a born comedian. He is a Texan-Mexican. He is the most American American I have ever seen.

The *Clockwork Orange* droogs stalk the Lodge for a while but they are replaced by a more benign kind of ultraviolence when the Bruce Lee films arrive at the Playhouse. I am too young for the kung fu fighting but the influence of the films hops and jumps along the High Street. The older kids no longer walk, they glide forwards and sideways in a series of snake slaps and nut punches. Just to show willing, I learn how to karate chop pencils in half and acquire kung fu pyjamas from the Grattan catalogue. Mine are purple and lavender. My brother's come in two shades of brown.

The decade is punctuated by strikes and power cuts. They are fun. My dad gives us fair warning. He claims to be the man who flicks the switch at the power station. We are never short of candles. When the high school runs out of oil and the heating goes off we are taught in the St Baldred's church hall and allowed to wear jeans. It is more of an adventure than an inconvenience.

For 204 days the Member of Parliament for Berwick and East Lothian is a Conservative. In the two elections of 1974 Michael Ancram wins then loses to John Mackintosh of Labour. The parties have election offices in North Berwick. I go into both with my pals, asking for literature, stickers and posters. The woman in the Labour office, Mrs Milne, makes tea and sends us away with a booklet about Keir Hardie. The woman in the Conservative office tells us to skedaddle, so we grab a box of Ancram leaflets and make a bonfire of them in the empty swimming pool.

13

Yeti-Hunting at the Harbour Pavilion (Part One)

Mr Foster Grant is coming to town. Mr Foster Grant is a man of mystery. Mr Foster Grant wears sunglasses. If you see Mr Foster Grant and go up to him while holding a copy of the *Edinburgh Evening News*, he will pay you. What you have to say is: 'You are Mr Foster Grant and I claim my £5.'

No one has ever seen Mr Foster Grant. Mr Foster Grant stalks the Scottish seaside like a benign yeti.

I think about Mr Foster Grant a lot. Mr Foster Grant gives money away. If Mr Foster Grant appears, how will I know? He is in disguise. How will he be different from any other man in sunglasses? What if it isn't him? How many strange men in sunglasses can you approach before it becomes awkward or dangerous? Is it worth carrying the *News* around, just in case?

The visits of Mr Foster Grant are not random. That would be too vague. That would not be exciting. That would be Spot the Ball in human form. If Mr Foster Grant could appear at any time, people would get bored of carrying the *Edinburgh Evening News* around on the off-chance.

Mr Foster Grant is not like the football pools. The pools is a game of skill and chance. The pools is a gamble in which a Grattan catalogue family in purple polyester kung fu pyjamas might earn a life-changing windfall by predicting eight score draws from the British football calendar.

Most of us know someone who has won something on the pools. My dad won 7/6 (37½p). That was something. It was better than nothing. After a while it did change my dad's life. He gave up the football pools because it was a waste of money. He calculated the number of minutes it would take to earn 7/6 if he didn't bother entering. It wasn't many. So he quit while he wasn't behind.

The retreat from the football pools makes Saturdays less exciting because the absence of a possible jackpot makes the football results on *Grandstand* less consequential. Grandstand is interminable, an endless parade of unpopular sports, speedway and running through mud, but it comes to life with the clatter of the teleprinter, quickly followed by the classified results. *World of Sport* on ITV gets the final scores more quickly but the BBC brings the poetry. On the BBC the classifieds are read by Leonard Martin, aka Len the Lip. Len the Lip has the football voice. It is the voice that delivered the Movietone News, a voice of truth and consequence, a voice that is classless on account of being Australian. Len the Lip knows the score.

Mr Foster Grant does not have a voice. His existence is scarcely more than a rumour. He is the tooth fairy in polarised lenses. His visits are trailed on Radio Forth. That's how we know Mr Foster Grant is coming.

There is a Mr Foster Grant in *Brighton Rock*, the seaside novel by Graham Greene. In *Brighton Rock* Mr Foster Grant is called Kolley Kibber and he wafts through the town, down the seafront, into teashops, along the pier, leaving little calling cards to show where he has been. Kolley Kibber is based on Lobby Lud, the newspaper mystery man who caused a sensation when he toured English seaside towns in 1927. Lobby Lud was promoting the *Westminster Gazette*, and was five foot three, clean-shaven, with a mole on his right cheek. Lobby Lud smoked a pipe and wore a fedora. In 1927 wearing a fedora and smoking a pipe was like activating the cloaking device on a Romulan spacecraft. Lobby Lud was invisible. He travelled undetected for days and weeks, passing through crowds, thumbing his nose, puffing fine shag, until his employers, weary of the escalating prize money, sent him to meet his fate on Boscombe Pier. On that pier of doom a Lud hunter wearing 'a bland £150 smile' captured the invisible man with the precise form of words required to unlock the prize: 'You are Mr Lobby Lud – I claim the *Westminster Gazette* prize.'

Mr Foster Grant is cheaper than Lobby Lud, even without adjusting for inflation, which is rampant. But £5 is £5. A ticket to a top pop concert costs £2, maybe £3, and you'd still have change for chips.

But where to look? It shouldn't be hard in North Berwick. North Berwick is not a sprawling metropolis. North Berwick is not Los Angeles. North Berwick is not Haddington. Unless Mr Foster Grant is being deliberately perverse, he is likely to be at one of the main tourist centres. The Lodge grounds? Mr Foster Grant would stand out if he hung around the trampolines. He might enjoy a knickerbocker glory in Luca's, a round of crazy golf or a visit to the town museum to see the stuffed gannets, the rusting weathercock and the gutta-percha golf balls.

If his aim is to cause a commotion, Mr Foster Grant will be found around the harbour. It is the heart and soul of the town. Mr Foster Grant might saunter past the ruined kirk, clocking the barometer on the old granary wall, its needle stuck on 'change'. Mr Foster Grant could take a boat trip to the Bass Rock, play the puggies in the Piv or treat himself to a voyeur's ticket at the pool, where the water is a guaranteed sixty-seven degrees and still too cold for polar bears.

Mr Foster Grant could do all of these things, and perhaps he does. But nobody sees him. And if nobody sees Mr Foster Grant, was Mr Foster Grant there at all?

14

Career Opportunities Never Knock

There is a careers night at school. We are invited to dream our dreams and receive practical advice on how to achieve them. Becoming a professional footballer seems unlikely, and there is no obvious route to becoming Rod Stewart, so I tell the man that I want to be a journalist. It is the only thing I have ever really wanted to do, so I pluck up all of my courage and suggest it.

'I want to be a journalist,' I say.

'You are too intelligent,' the careers man says. 'Journalism only requires five O-grades. You study it at Napier College. You don't want to do that.'

I am stumped. I do want to do that but I am confused about this intelligence thing. Up to this point I have assumed that intelligence would be an advantage. Now it is a handicap.

'Is there anything else you would like to do?' the careers man asks.

There isn't, but I say something just to show willing. 'Architect?'

Even as I say it, I know I am not cut out for architecture. I hate technical drawing and have no artistic imagination.

'You should be an engineer,' the careers man says. 'The country needs engineers.'

15

Sunglasses After Dark in a 1970s Weirdo Apocalypse (Yeti-Hunting Part Two)

The cinema is war. On matinee afternoons, when the Playhouse functions as a holding pen for under-fourteens, chaos reigns. There are whoops and jeers, running in the aisles, and it becomes fashionable to shower the screen with sweets. It doesn't matter what kind. Tooty Frooties, Jujubes, Pontefract cakes, Kola Kubes, Sports Mixtures, Victory V lozenges, Fisherman's Friends, Fox's Glacier Mints, Maltesers, Fruit Polos, Treets, Tunes, Matchmakers, Opal Fruits, liquorice pipes, Spangles (fruit or Old English), chocolate cigarettes, sherbet Dip Dabs, Fruit Salad, Midget Gems, Revels, cola bottles, Jelly Tots, Parma Violets, Anglo Bubbly, Bazooka Joe, Paynes Poppets or Mint Creams, anything from the Woolworths Pic 'n' Mix, except the coffee cream. All tastes are catered for, anything goes, including your last Rolo. It is a form of critical analysis.

Today the film is *The Omega Man*. I know nothing about it. There is no way of knowing anything. The only clues are the photos in the 'Coming Attractions' box on the Playhouse wall and they show Charlton Heston in all kinds of square-jawed jeopardy. He is in a convertible, firing his machine gun into the sky, the shots drawn onto the 10 x 8 like the trails of shooting stars. He stands, holding onto a motorcycle, a faint look of concern on his face as Rosalind Cash points a gun at his right shoulder, more sexy than threatening. He sits playing chess in a military cap while dark hooded figures pull at his arms. It is all my night terrors rolled into one.

The Omega Man is fantastic. It is very 1970s, set in a deserted Los Angeles. Charlton Heston is the last man on earth. This is not as bad is it sounds. Charlton has his choice of fantastic cars, fine wines and a decent apartment in which he can play chess with a bust of Julius Caesar while chilling to easy listening sounds from his 8-track cartridge deck. 'Hi, big brother,' he says to his topless reflection in the mirror, 'how's your ass?'

The calendar in the abandoned garage is stuck at 1975 but the action is set two years later. On the rare occasions when he isn't topless Chuck wears a safari jacket. This is because he is fashionable. This is because he is a hunter. He is a man of many guns. He has access to a cinema, where the hoarding shows that *Woodstock* is playing. Charlton screens the film for himself and mouths all the dialogue as it spools past. 'They sure don't make pictures like that any more,' he says, because the whole notion of Woodstock, that humanity could come together and wallow in the mud listening to Country Joe and the Fish, is laughable. Punk has not happened in Charlton Heston's 1977, and it has not yet happened in real life, but *The Omega Man* is very punk rock. It is paranoid and angry. It is the best film about shyness I have ever seen.

Charlton Heston is on his own in the world, not answering the phone, and that is OK. The problem is everybody else.

The phone rings. There is flying litter in the air. The ringing multiplies. A hundred phones are ringing. A thousand. A symphony of hellish bells. Who could be calling at this hour? 'THERE IS NO PHONE RINGING, DAMN IT!' Charlton Heston shouts, checking himself. 'My God,' he says, 'it's almost dark. They'll be waking up soon.'

They are the others. Nobody likes the others. The others are other. In *The Omega Man* the others are a kind of Charles Manson family of vampirish monks in the kind of hooded robes that will later become fashionable among holidaymakers in Moroccan mountain retreats. Here, the djellabas are the uniform of a mutant sub-species of human. Allergic to sunlight and living by night, they set fire to machines and try to lure Charlton Heston out of his comfortable post-apocalypse apartment by lobbing balls of flame at it with a giant catapult.

Soon enough the others capture Charlton Heston and put him on trial for crimes against The Family. His main crime seems to be that he is not an albino mutant. 'He has confessed all, brothers,' the leader of the others proclaims. 'Murder, use of forbidden tools, practice of proscribed rites. He admits science, medicine, weapons, machinery, electricity. He has not shared the punishment. He does not bear the marks.'

'Marks?' says Charlton Heston.

'Show him, my children,' says the terrible cult leader. 'Show him the pretty marks.' Slowly, and with awed choreography, the albino mutants remove their sunglasses to reveal their terrible eyes. They have bleached, animal irises, like germ warfare vampire cats. Even Charlton Heston contrives to fashion his wooden features into a look of concern.

A terrible hush falls over the North Berwick Playhouse. The hard rain of confectionery halts in mid-air. Scratcher, the cheekiest kid in the school, stands up in the cheap seats and announces into the void, 'You are Mr Foster Grant, and I claim my £5.'

16

Rod Stewart Came to North Berwick and Nobody Noticed

R od Stewart came to North Berwick and almost nobody noticed. In the 1974 edition of the North Berwick High School magazine Judith Laing of year 2A writes a story called 'A Very Well-Kept Secret'. It is a short report of a visit made by Rod Stewart to North Berwick on Sunday, the 19th of May, the day after he had visited Hampden Park to see a Scotland side captained by Billy Bremner beat England by two goals to nil in front of a crowd of 95,000. Rod had spent the Saturday night in Edinburgh and then popped down to Dirleton and North Berwick to meet relatives. 'The very first thing he did was to play football on the back green,' Judith Laing writes. 'He was looking as stunning as ever. After having a quick drink and chat, he gave us his autograph and then, leaving his magnificent Rolls (with colour TV, cassette recorders etc.), he walked calmly down to my uncle's hotel where he had lunch.'

After lunch at the Nether Abbey Hotel, where Rod signed more autographs, he returned for a game of football and then some photographs. 'He was very nice and was always joking and laughing,' Judith notes, 'and he seemed to enjoy himself a lot. When he left, waving his Scottish flag from the car window, we were sorry to see him go.'

17

Dave Hill Is Five Foot Three

I have a wallet. It is textured plastic, man-made crocodile, and has a picture of a Chinese pagoda on it. It is a gift from Hong Kong. Our old neighbours, the Woolleys, have been out to the colonial island and brought back the wallets as gifts, along with red and gold metallic Chairman Mao badges. I rarely have paper money, so the wallet is only theoretically practical. Until I get a ticket for Slade.

I don't understand Slade. There is nothing to understand. There is nothing to discuss. Everything about them is correct. Everything is perfect.

I know this by virtue of being young and infallible. There is nothing to explain. Slade have no ideology. They have an image, and this image is more successful than their earlier images, but it doesn't work as an explanation of their power.

I have a fan magazine from 1973, called *Slade Alive!*, which tries to explain the inexplicable.

'Noddy's snarling between numbers is part of Slade. Dave's glitter, garments and gavotting is part of Slade. Jim's bass patterns and his charging across stage is part of Slade. And Don, with his gum and Long John Scotch, battering out the back-beat is part of Slade.'

64

The group have slipped into the parody of false memory now and the knowledge is hard to access. They have been copied but not properly acknowledged. You can't have Oasis without first having Slade, and while this isn't a recommendation, it's worth noting that most of the sparkly bit of Noel Gallagher's career can be seen as an attempt to write something that could sit at the feet of Slade's ballads, 'Far Far Away', 'Everyday' and 'How Does It Feel?' Possibly, maybe, those songs were Slade's attempts to sound like The Beatles. When Oasis try to ape The Beatles, they're actually trying to be Slade. And ballads aren't even the main point of Slade.

Decades later I have watched television interviews in which Noddy Holder is coaxed through anecdotes, wild tales, their details excised for censorious modern sensibilities, and he has seemed remote from, bewildered by, his legacy. It's as if Noddy himself doesn't know how to connect with the preposterous brilliance of his former self. Why should he? It is absurd in design and execution. It asks no questions. It just shines. Is there even a convincing explanation of Noddy's mirrored top hat? It looks like a topper that has been reinvented as a glitter-ball, putting Noddy's head right at the centre of the disco. Look into it and you see yourself from many different angles. Stand back and there is nothing but bouncing light. It is a definition of pop music, an obvious exaggeration, shadowplay. It is a top top hat.

I still have my Slade scrapbook, though many of the pictures are ripped or missing, the victims of dried Pritt, stale Blu-Tack, desiccated Sellotape. They come from magazines that no one remembers or laments – *Fan, Disc, Pop-Up!, Pop 73, Popswop, Mates, Music Star, Disco 45, Fab 208* – publications with a bewilderingly democratic approach to music. Possibly they were designed for girls. That would explain their emphasis on joy rather than the strident hierarchies of criticism. In the fragments I have, everything is there, jumbled. Criticism implies a value system; bad and better. In this pop world, glittering is enough. A letter from Little Jimmy Osmond has the same cachet as the lyrics to Roxy Music's 'Pyjamarama'. Both are works of fantasy and projection. Jimmy, a child in a family where being a pop star is the family business, writes about his birthday lunch – fruit cup, the salad he loves, roast beef with mashed potatoes, green peas and cauliflower – and his presents. He gets a Mickey Mouse watch, two sports shirts, a pair of brown jeans, knights on white horses. His day is 'super-neat'. Roxy, meanwhile, are rhapsodising lust in language no child can possibly understand.

The horoscope slot on the back of particularly magnificent Slade poster (the mirrors now applied to Dave's jacket rather than Noddy's hat) features a horribly truthful interview with Jimmy Savile OBE, a Scorpio. The final question, the sting in this tale, suggests that this playful 'Mr Scorpio' is forever on the defensive. 'To him, life is a battleground. He must conquer or be conquered. How do you match up to this?' The predator replies: 'I don't know. It's a bit complicated is that. I just breeze on, minding my own business and try not to do anything wrong. I'm not always successful in that. I don't want to conquer anybody, but I don't want to be conquered. I just want to be left alone. How about that, then?' On the other side of the poster is a comic strip called 'The Black Nightingale' in which Linda Koning, a Rotterdam nurse, works for the Dutch resistance, fighting the Nazis. This is pop.

The first album I ever buy is *Slade Alive!* I get it in Asda on the old Musselburgh Road. It costs £2.13. Asda is a super-store, a new and exciting way to shop. You can buy records there without encountering the heavy energy of record shops. Actual record shops tend to be dark, intimidating places smelling of patchouli, damp leather and personality disorders. Asda is vast, practical, soulless. Asda is the future.

Slade Alive! is a strange record because it doesn't have the compressed brilliance of the group's hit records. It harks back to an earlier point in their evolution. But I am committed. I have spent my money. I enjoy it in principle. I don't really like the record but I can't afford to admit it.

I order *Sladest* by mail. The album arrives with the sleeve only partially assembled but it is perfect in every other way. *Sladest* is the most Sladey thing you can find on a record. The vital songs are identifiable by their misspelt titles: 'Mama Weer All Crazee Now', 'Skweeze Me, Pleeze Me', 'Cum On Feel The Noize' and – best of all – 'Gudbuy T'Jane'.

The words of Slade songs don't bear examination; they are all about the spirit, a kind of convulsive, sherbetty explosion of group identity, exuberance, pure joy. Slade are entirely loveable. Musicology is beside the point. Slade's biggest songs are about the Sladeyness of being Slade. 'Mama Weer All Crazee Now' and 'Cum On Feel The Noize' are defiant celebrations. 'Skweeze Me, Pleeze Me' is, Dave Hill tells *Melody Maker* in 1973, 'a very exciting non-stop domineering song'. Dave explains further: 'The record has one dominating line, when everybody goes "Whooooooh!"'

But Slade are more than just the music. They are very male, which isn't a disadvantage in 1973, and their supposed yobbishness is inbuilt. Dave Hill, the Bacofoil-wrapped guitarist, has a Rolls-Royce, or possibly a Jensen Interceptor, with the number-plate YOB 1 and a hand-made Super Yob guitar.

Other groups of the glam pop era have one effeminate member with more extravagant make-up, broader flares, a more pronounced pout. Dave represents the far borders of Slade's glam styling. In that same *Melody Maker* interview he mentions that his Super Yob image has been invented with the help of an art school student called Steve. Steve is Steve Megson, whose father runs a jazz pub in Bilston, Wolverhampton, which occasionally hosts the band. Slade's manager Chas Chandler, formerly of The Animals, charged Steve with turning Slade from a skinhead group into a glam rock outfit. The clothes are mad, all harlequin dungarees and space-age shoulder pads, though not noticeably bizarre for the early 1970s.

'My idea of a really flashy yob is to make it look butch,' Dave explains. 'Not poufy. You see big blokes looking like poufs now, they may have glitter or make-up on, but the thing is they look at it in a different way now. When I first did it, it was "He must be a queer", but people have now accepted the fact that it's not true so, therefore, the situation has matured. Personally, I'm not into make-up. Basically, what I use is sparkles and the clothes and the big boots for stamping – it's all got a positive connection with what we're doing.'

Is Dave referring to a bouffant hair style popular with women in the eighteenth century when he talks about poufs? He surely isn't. Poof is a commonplace insult in the 1970s. Pouf is a deviant spelling. Much has been written about glam rock and gender-bending but it's worth noting that its strangeness operates within strict limits.

I love Slade for far longer than I should. Just as Dave predicted elsewhere in that *Melody Maker* interview, they become more sophisticated. They learn to spell. They care less for rabble-rousing, they add strings. They tour America, fruitlessly. (America gets Kiss instead.) They make a film, *Flame*, which never comes to the North Berwick Playhouse.

In 1975 they announce a date at the Citadel Theatre in Leith. I am just about old enough to go. The first part of the excitement is getting a ticket. My pal Kendo and I journey to Edinburgh and queue outside the Usher Hall. The tickets cost £1.50 and are printed on yellow paper, with the band's name rendered in Umbra, a shadowy, thin font which makes the letters stand up on the page. This ticket is my passport to somewhere else. I carry it with me like a charm in the inside fold of the Hong Kong plastic crocodile pagoda wallet.

Any journey requires new clothes and I set about gathering a mid-1970s wardrobe for my trip to planet Slade. There are rules about these things; unwritten, well understood. Jeans must be made by Wrangler; the same for denim jackets. By virtue of novelty, and easy availability at East Fortune market, Brutus high-waisters are just about permissible, though they carry a taint of soul-boy. All other jeans are derided as 'Bobby Washables'.

In real life a Slade stage outfit is not an achievable look. Close inspection of fan magazines shows that even Slade don't maintain their Dickensian space urchin look offstage. The achievable things about the Slade look are the Day-Glo stripy socks and – to an extent – the shoes. This isn't an exact science. An article in *Disc* ('Putting the Boot in Pop!' by Lynne Thirkettle) offers a thoughtful survey of the footwear of the glam era and reveals a surprising lack of uniformity. Unsurprisingly, Elton John has a hundred pairs of 'ankle-breakers' in his dressing-room wardrobe, and while some of these are bespoke, similar footwear can be found at the King's Road shop of Terry de Havilland, also favoured by Steve Priest, the glamorous member of The Sweet. (Terry's rock and roll shoes are also available at Baffies of Morayshire.) Roy Wood of Wizzard favours boat-style clogs similar to those sold by Olaf of Sweden. Rod Stewart dislikes 'silly' shoes, preferring Fred Astaire patent leather and finely-made lace-ups 'with a subtle brogue look'.

And Slade? Mixed messages. The offstage photograph shows Noddy wearing three-tiered high white lace-ups on a wood heel. ('Noddy has been known to wear plimsolls off stage.') Dave has knee-length white leather boots with red leather dollars and red triangles on the platform and a high heel. ('They make me feel taller, says Dave, 5'3".'.') Jim Lea wears beige leather lace-ups on a wood heel with a blue snake strip running through the platform with an 'almost Paisley' print. Drummer Don Powell's feet are in shadow in the photograph but are clad in knee-length black leather boots on a three-tiered platform and wood heel. 'Two inches is about my limit,' says Don, talking about the size of his platforms, 'otherwise I find I can't play the drums.'

North Berwick High Street is not the place to find fanciful footwear. There is a shoe shop, lined with boxes and posters of Polyveldts, and there is the Co-op, where the foot-measuring is done on a fluoroscope, an X-ray machine which brings science and unnecessary radiation to the awkward business of buying sensible shoes. Stupid fashions are not available. For those, you have to go to Haddington.

It is not a stressless task, trying to buy glam rock shoes in Haddington with your mum. It's even more troubling when the shoes you are looking for do not exist and the town in which you are searching has also been the scene of an unpleasant incident in which you and your pals have been chased by neds, eventually taking up refuge in the police station until a parent can be summoned with a getaway car.

Eventually a compromise is struck. My mum, exhausted by my glam rock tantrums, sanctions the purchase of a pair of plastic brothel creepers with an elevated heel. There is a question about whether they are actually girls' shoes but I try not to worry about it. They are good enough, which is better than embarrassing. What I don't know at the time of purchase is that the 100 per cent plastic uppers will give me terrible athlete's foot. Never mind. They go well with my brown polyester bags, which are broad enough to hide the creepers and generate enough static to power a static caravan.

We are in the car, leaving Haddington, when I notice that the Hong Kong pagoda wallet is not in the pockets of my Bobby Washable denim jacket. I search in the pocket with the Super Slade patch and then in the pocket with the Union Jack peace sign. Nothing. The wallet is gone, and with it, the ticket to my adolescence. Did it drop out while I was trying on a succession of bad ankle-breakers? We retrace our steps; to the coffee shop where we had the early bird lunch, the shoe shop, the wool shop where my mum looked at knitting patterns. We scour the pavements and gutters. It is hopeless. In a final desperate flourish, I suggest the police station. I know where it is. Out of habit, I start to run.

A miracle! The wallet has been handed in. The Slade ticket is inside! All those desperate calculations in which I have to phone the venue and persuade them that the empty seat – W21 in Stalls Block C – is mine . . . all of them are unnecessary.

There is one further humiliation. My mum takes down the address of the person who has handed in the ticket and we drive there in her Harvest Gold Mini Clubman estate, up a rutted track to a farmhouse cottage. On the doorstep, staring at my PVC feet, I mutter a reluctant thank-you. My voice is inaudible, my sincerity painful.

The concert is the best. It will always be the best. Nothing can compare. It is a riot of noise and chaos, a blush of joy and incredulity. Slade exist and are in the same room. They are right there on the stage of the Citadel and the entire audience is up on the seats, wailing and moaning, untameable. It is a teenage yobbo apocalypse. I buy a 30 x 20 poster, which I wave around my head. I feel liberated.

Looking at the songs Slade played, I can see now that the band was evolving, or de-evolving, into boogie woogie and heavy rock, and the glorious unity of their biggest hits had been replaced by something less shapely. Slade were no longer at their Sladest. But that is the critic talking, and I wasn't a critic then. Music in that moment was all about affirmation, being in the room, being part of the gang. It couldn't have been better.

It isn't a long show. It goes by in a flash. Kendo and I float out of the Citadel onto the alien streets of Leith, pausing only to liberate album covers from the merchandise stands in the foyer. The scene on the streets is one of joyous mayhem, though the crowd thins out quickly. There are a few policemen looking the other way. Standing on the kerb, waiting for our lift home, we are surrounded by skinheads. There is a bit of jostling, a flurry of grabbing and punching, then the skins of Leith make off with our merchandise. Kendo phones home, to be told that his father will pick us up in thirty minutes. By the time he arrives we have made a pact to say nothing about the violence.

In Kendo's dad's car we stick to our story. Everything is all right. My face is grazed, my ears are numb. I have a pale blue Slade badge in my pocket, a souvenir of the best night of my young, stupid life.

18

(Never Listen to) Electric Guitar

My brother has an electric guitar.

The guitar lies on his bed, like a tiger at rest, daring someone to pick it up. There is no amplifier, no speaker, no electricity. Just the guitar.

No one plays the electric guitar.

My brother cannot admit that he has an electric guitar. That would be 'a lot of nonsense'. He pretends he has borrowed it and is letting it have a rest on his bed.

It is my brother's second guitar.

His first guitar was an acoustic, from Woolworths. It had a spruce top and mahogany sides and a mother of pearl inlay, and it lay on the bed in the same accusing manner until it disappeared, like a kitten in a bag in a lake.

The Woolworths guitar did not work. It needed tuning. There was a tuning fork but no instructions. How do you get the strings to sound like the fork? It is impossible. No wonder it disappeared.

My brother has a book: Bert Weedon's *Play in a Day*.

It is a fucking joke.

The electric guitar disappears. It is as if it never existed.

The electric guitar is a lot of nonsense.

19

Oral History: An Ultra-Year-Zero Moment

There is a version of punk rock history in which the movement explodes, and is over, in 1976. It is and it isn't. It was and it wasn't. The glorious aftermath takes longer and did not happen in London. In this version of punk – we can call it long punk – the consequences spiral in different directions. This is not punk as a straitjacket from Sex on the King's Road. It is punk as a catalyst to break the rules, have a go, find your voice. It is punk as permission to speak.

In Scotland the year-zero moment is the 7th of May 1977, when The Clash's White Riot tour appears at the Edinburgh Playhouse. As much as The Clash, the show is about the support acts: The Jam, Buzzcocks, Subway Sect and The Slits. Anyone who aspires to be anyone is there.

Seventeen-year-old Edwyn Collins is there, with Steven Daly and James Kirk, who will later band together in Orange Juice.

'I went to the Playhouse in the afternoon,' Edwyn tells me, years later. 'The Jam were there, Paul [Weller] and Bruce

[Foxton].' Edwyn offered to carry The Jam's gear. 'I was a stage-door Johnny. It was sneaky: "Carry your gear, sir?" The Slits were there, Ari Up was talking to me. I was seventeen, and the Subway Sect and the Buzzcocks were mesmerising.

'I liked Vic Godard, and Rob [Symmons] the guitarist couldn't play, and the bass player couldn't play, and the drum player, debatable, but so what? I liked the position they took. It was exciting and unusual. From the beginning of Orange Juice, I wanted to associate myself with that strand of punk rock.'

Davy Henderson, who will distinguish himself in a series of punk inspired groups – Fire Engines, Win, The Nectarine No. 9, The Sexual Objects – was also at the Playhouse.

'I went with my school friends, Willie Kirkwood – who eventually played bass with Another Pretty Face – and Murray [Slade] from the Fire Engines. We never had anything like an idea that we wanted to be in bands, although Murray had an electrical guitar. Well, we always wanted to be in bands, but we thought there was no way: you had to be a divine virtuoso to even pick up a guitar. The thought of writing songs wasn't even on the menu. There was no menu. Prior to that, seeing bands, they were treated like divinities.

'But when The Slits came on, Ari Up walked to the front of the stage and asked if anyone had a comb. She walked down off the stage into the audience and started backcombing her hair. That was an ultra-year-zero moment: one of the performers came into the audience. In subsequent reading, it was Brechtian. Someone had broken through the curtain. That was a jawdropping moment – that someone the same age as you, or even younger, had done it. I was sixteen at the time.

'Then the Subway Sect came on and they were just incredible. The singer kept going into his pocket, and singing, and ripping up paper. It reminds me of subsequently reading about Hugo Ball and his first Dada performance in 1921. The singer was standing on the stage tearing up bits of paper – it was almost like he was tearing up what he was singing. It was this otherworldly performance, yet these people looked exactly like you. They had what looked like their school greys on, like their grey school breeks and blazers, and white shirts, and the V-necks. They looked exactly like where you'd just been – at school.'

❄

I am not at the Playhouse. News of the ultra-violence at the Slade show two years earlier has scuppered any possibility of a parental taxi to punk rock hell, and the last bus home is too much of a risk. But the tremors can be felt twenty-five miles away.

20

Readmore Books

Punk comes in spurts. My brother Colin is the messenger, though John Peel is also involved. Colin listens to Peel in bed and I drift in and out of sleep. It isn't an immediate conversion. It is messy. The wall on my brother's side of the room is still decorated with a square poster of Nils Lofgren at Coney Island but it is being squeezed on one side by Elvis Costello's 'Less Than Zero' and on the other by The Rezillos' '(My Baby Does) Good Sculptures'.

I still have record-buying mishaps. I buy *Frampton Comes Alive!* because you get two albums for the price of one. Peter Frampton's gimmick is a talk box, which makes his voice sound like a drowning man trying to make a phone call with a cocoa tin. It is horrible. I buy *Animals* by Pink Floyd because it gets a five-star review and has a cool pig on the cover. It sounds like a headache interrogating a radiator. On both occasions I return to the Melody Centre and sheepishly persuade Mr Stewart to take the records back. I have no legal case. But my argument that the records are unlistenable, if not injurious to public wellbeing, is persuasive. Mr Stewart can only agree. Mr Stewart is kind and decent. Mr Stewart knows that, eventually, I will buy the copy of *James Brown:*

'*Live' At The Apollo Volume II* which he has been trying to sell at a reduced price for some years, even though I will give it to my brother for Christmas (having taped it first). Mr Stewart, I know, has tacitly agreed never to mention the Status Quo album I ordered and then never collected. North Berwick is a Status Quo town. It will not have gone unsold.

At the same time, records that I used to like are going off. Queen now sound ridiculous, so I loan out *Sheer Heart Attack* to my friend Robert and never see it again. I start to accept that I never really liked Nazareth, even though I got their album for free and it has a fantastic gatefold sleeve, by Hipgnosis, of a photo taken from the inside of a limousine, with fans crushing onto the windows. It feels passé, moaning about your fame. About Rod Stewart, I feel conflicted. He was everything. He was football and music in one package. He was George Best. He was conspicuous success. And now?

The good news leaks in via the music papers. Colin buys the *NME*, I buy *Sounds*. The music papers are telegrams from a more exciting world. The writing is spiteful, urgent, cruel, cynical, petty, ill-informed, insecure, postmodern, pretentious, precious, too stupid, too clever; just like the voices inside my head. At the time of punk, *Sounds* is better than *NME*. *NME* still wants to be elegantly wasted, like Keith Richards. *Sounds* has Jon Savage, Jonh Ingham, Jane Suck, Vivien Goldman, all of whom are more or less on the spot when the bomb drops. The music papers are an argument. To me, they are also a way of relating to other people. Abstract people are easier.

Radio is starting to crack, too. With Radio Forth, there is a local connection. One of Forth's disc jockeys is Jay Crawford, who does a show called *Edinburgh Rock*. His parents run a hardware shop on North Berwick High Street. He is a star DJ but he is all about the rock and not about the punk. He likes 10cc. He probably wears a blouson tour jacket. Still, Forth bleeds around the edges. It does not discriminate against strange information.

At school my terrible fanzine *Blow Your Nose on This* reports on rumours that the Sex Pistols are planning to play in Haddington. There is no truth in the story, and nobody knows where it comes from, but the possibility is enough to excite. By 1977 my brother is at university in Edinburgh, living the life. He dyes his hair black, he wears my dad's white boiler suit as his formal attire, he goes hillwalking in Craigmillar wearing a homburg as a helmet. When my brother visits home, he brings music and fanzines. He gets my records signed when the Ramones and The Rezillos do an in-store at Bruce's Record Shop. He takes The Clash, I get The Jam. But because punk rock is a mess that nobody understands, I also get Eddie and the Hot Rods, The Boomtown Rats, The Boys, The Damned, the Sex Pistols, Siouxsie and the Banshees, Generation X, The Gorillas, The Valves, The Slits. I get the Buzzcocks, I get the Subway Sect.

One day in 1977 I find a copy of Caroline Coon's book, *1988: The New Wave Punk Rock Explosion*, in Readmore Bookstore in North Berwick. Readmore does for books what the Melody Centre does for records. It is a small shop with secrets. It sells diaries and birthday cards and novels by Nigel Tranter. It smells of potpourri and furfural. Seeing the Caroline Coon book in this setting feels like an interruption of normal service. The cover has a beautiful photo of Johnny Rotten (by Ray Stevenson), his hair spiked red, a safety pin in his jacket, his lips distorted into a snarl. Only Johnny's right eye is sharply in focus and it glares into the lens like a laser. Later John Lydon, née Rotten, will reveal that this uncompromising glare is the result of childhood meningitis, but he projects defiance beautifully. He is the president of the Unhappy Smile Club.

The title is confusing. Why 1988? The book's conclusion suggests an answer. 'Whatever happens now, the force of punk rock will be felt in society at least until 1988 . . .'

In 1977 longevity is not an issue. Everything is about currency. Everything is now. In 1988, there is a quote from Derek Jewell, the music critic of the *Sunday Times*, lamenting 'the latest musical garbage', a phrase that betrays the critic's habit of disappointment. There are photos of the queen with Elton John, of Princess Margaret with Mick Jagger.

Caroline Coon's prose is excitable, tantalisingly obscure. The Sex Pistols' manager, Malcolm McLaren, is 'the Diaghilev of Punk'. The Slits are described as deporting themselves 'like lofty viragos storming through life with the lusty abandon of stage hands at the Folies Bergère'.

What does it mean? I have no idea, though I love The Slits and am aware of the Folies Bergère. The Parisian cabaret has previously been discussed by my elegant English teacher Miss Taylor, who spent an age exploring the phrase 'couldn't pass muster at the Folies Bergère'. By the end, we understood things that were not on the curriculum.

We knew about the can-can.

We knew about John Donne and his erotic flea.

We understood tumescence.

21

Sex Pistols: 'Who's Oor Wullie?'

There is an advert on Radio Forth for the *New Musical Express*. It is read in an edgy street voice. 'Heavy metal came and stayed,' the advert says. 'In 1971, David Bowie came and tossed glam rock into the arena and his Diamond Dogs came back to haunt him as punks. "Your generation don't mean a thing to me," they say. So are we to believe that the Seventies have only just begun? Starting this week, New Musical Express puts the Seventies straight. An ambitious assessment of a decade's changes by some of the best writers in rock. Only in NME.'

The Sex Pistols album *Never Mind The Bollocks* is released on my sixteenth birthday. I buy it at the Melody Centre as a present for myself. It is fantastic if you ignore the terrible bits, like the song 'Bodies', which I do. Six weeks later the Sex Pistols, minus Sid Vicious, travel to Edinburgh to do a signing at Virgin Records and an interview at Radio Forth. I miss the signing but I record the interview on the Marconiphone and play it over and over, diving for pearls.

It is not illuminating. Forth has fielded a team of three. There is Christopher John, who broadcasts the interview on his rock show, *Cruisin'*; North Berwick's own punk sceptic,

Jay Crawford; and Mike Gower. In so far as they have a plan, it seems to be based on getting the Sex Pistols to say something outrageous. Steve Jones tries, girning something about running a brothel, but the group seem tired of outrage.

The most notable bit is the start, when Johnny Rotten asks: 'Who's Oor Wullie?'

'He's a cartoon character,' says Christopher John.

'I keep being told I look like the [censored] cos of my spiky hair, when it was bright orange,' says Johnny.

Oor Wullie, as all Scots know, is the star of a comic strip in the *Sunday Post*. He has jaggy hair, wears dungarees and tackety boots, and sits on a bucket. He has a pet mouse called Wee Jeemy and gets embarrassed when he is asked to hold a bunch of flowers, hiding them behind his back, where they will invariably be eaten by a passing milk horse. Oor Wullie is anarchic but loveable. There used to be a waxwork of Oor Wullie in the now-defunct Edinburgh Wax Museum on the Royal Mile. It was the spitting image of Johnny Rotten.

The interview starts with a question about whether there is a vendetta against the Sex Pistols. There is, Johnny Rotten suggests, though he claims that the terms of the vendetta have shifted and it is now based on claiming that the Pistols are 'nice boys'. Rotten declares himself uninterested in politics because it boils down to Communists versus the National Front. 'They both wanna destroy, they're both wreckers,' Rotten says, as if he has never heard the lyrics of 'Anarchy In The UK'. There is a discussion of whether the Pistols would like to own their own island. Not really. Christopher John mentions 'chicks like Caroline Coon' writing in the music papers, and Rotten replies: 'I was grossly pissed off by people like that. Believe me. That kind of socialist implication kind of writing bores me, it's, like, tedious. It doesn't mean anything.'

Rotten continues: 'The music press, to me, stinks. My personal ambition would be to blow it all up, destroy it.' He suggests that instead of having failed musicians writing about music, the journalism should be done by the bands themselves.

The Clash are dispatched as 'completely condescending', 'naïve and silly', though Rotten admits to liking The Slits and Johnny Moped. 'I hate the Banshees,' he says.

In the commercial breaks there are ads for Emerson, Lake and Palmer, Gumley the estate agents, and Buf-Puf non-medicated soap, which will cure acne when used once a day. The luxurious delights of plump and delicious Del Monte pear halves are contrasted with suet pudding. Christopher John mentions Cliff Richard, which prompts Johnny Rotten to mention another vintage rocker. 'Alex Harvey – now he went down in the press saying as soon as he'd seen a band do what he was doing, but better, he'd give up. He's just given up. Who that band is, it's not for me to say. But . . . you know what I mean?'

If the Radio Forth team had asked the Sex Pistols about David Bowie, they might have received an interesting answer. Moments after the interview is adjourned the band repairs to Mathers bar on Broughton Street, where drummer Paul Cook answers questions for the local listings magazine *City Lynx*. Bowie, he says, 'moves with the times, he's not stagnant'.

Rod Stewart is selected as an example of the kind of rock star who should not be copied. 'When I was young I was into the Faces,' Paul Cook says, 'just like everybody is interested in us today. If I was you, I'd be interested in us as well, but the Faces have turned sour now.'

22

Salad Days

Mrs Turner holds auditions for the school show. It is a terrible process. We are lined up next to the piano and she is listening to our singing. The songs are terrible. Musicals are terrible. But everyone wants to be in the show. I hate musicals. I want to be in the show.

It is all quite routine. The popular extroverts and solidly middle-class people are found to have excellent voices.

When she gets to me Mrs Turner looks worried, then appalled. It is like the Happy Smile Club all over again.

'Yes, Alastair,' she says. 'It's the chorus for you. And it would be best if you just mouthed the words. Do not attempt to make a noise.'

It occurs to me months – possibly years – later that I have missed the point of ten years of Mrs Turner's music lessons. Despite all that time spent trying to identify whether a note is higher or lower than the previous one, I have not applied this in practice. I have not realised that, in singing, the voice has to aim for different notes, going up and down. Instead I have varied the volume, going from a whisper to a scream, a mumble to a moan.

23

The Body in the Boot

At lunchtimes I go home from school. Sometimes my dad is there. Sometimes we have mince. Today my dad has news. 'Your friend Johnny Rotten has left the Sex Pistols,' he says. It sounds odd, coming from my dad. 'Johnny Rotten' is not the sort of thing he says. He has to make an effort with 'Sex Pistols'. But it's true. It is on the lunchtime news. I eat my mince quietly and feel bereft.

After school I buy the *Evening News*. It is a big day for North Berwick on the front page. The main story is all about the strange case of the body in the boot, in which a motor car containing a deceased man (37) was found in the car park of the Blenheim House Hotel. This is unusual for the Blenheim, a polite establishment with a cocktail bar over-looking the putting green.

The body in the boot is famous. The television news films the corner of the Blenheim's car park. On this day, 19 January 1978, a person of no fixed abode appears before the sheriff in Haddington charged with theft of property in England. The report tells how the man arrived in an unmarked car, handcuffed to two police officers and with a grey blanket over his head.

That is the splash. Oddly, the story continues on the right of the page. Now, it seems, there are three bodies: the North Berwick boot man (37), a former Labour MP (82) found in a rhododendron bush thirty miles from Inverness, and a woman of indeterminate age, 'dressed in men's clothing', who was found in a burn at Waterbie near Dumfries on Christmas day. The woman in men's clothes is understood to be a cleaner from Kings Cross in London. Heavy snow has halted the investigation.

I don't care much about the body in the boot. The thing I care about is at the top of the page under the headline 'Sex Pistols Come To A Rotten End'.

'Johnny Rotten, the British punk rocker who has been known to vomit on stage, squirt beer at his fans, and indulge in other anti-social behaviour with the Sex Pistols, will be doing things alone from now on.

'Interviewed in New York today, Rotten said: "As far as I'm concerned, the group doesn't exist at the moment. That's about all I can say." He added that the group will not perform "in the original format".

'"It means I'm carrying on and the rest are quitting," said Rotten (21) after he left the rest of the group in Los Angeles. The apparent break-up could explain a last-minute cancellation of the Sex Pistols' tour of Brazil, scheduled to start last Monday.

'When a reporter asked why the group were dissolving, Rotten said: "I don't care what you want to know. I'm not going to say no more."'

I feel cheated. I feel confused. This ending feels like a beginning.

24

Alone Here in My Half-Empty Bed

Early in 1978 Pete Shelley and Steve Diggle from Buzzcocks appear on Radio Forth. The programme they are interviewed on is *Cruisin'*, hosted by Christopher John. Chris is a typical mid-1970s DJ. He has a mocking, crazy tone in his voice, as if he has swallowed, but not yet digested, Kenny Everett. But he has an open mind about music. He likes '2-4-6-8 Motorway' by the Tom Robinson Band, a trucking song in new wave trousers. The interview is amazing but not because of what Christopher John asks. What makes it amazing is what Pete Shelley says in response to questions that are almost meaningless.

First, there is some joshing about coming from Manchester and how the city has previously been seen as 'a second division Liverpool'. Pete Shelley ignores this and suggests that being remote from London might actually be an advantage. A question about being branded 'punk' follows, which Shelley defines as being an 'upsurgence from the blandness of the music at the time'. Talking about the formative season of the formative year, 1976, he says: 'There was so much concentration on things from America, everything was either disco fodder or the remains of the hippie-dippy days where everybody was into peace and love and everything, and things started changing and becoming . . . exciting again, and exciting on your own doorstep.'

Pete Shelley talks about Buzzcocks' new single, 'What Do I Get?' The song is a rush of energy and is distinct from the usual idea of a punk song because of its mocking introversion. There is none of the filth and fury or stencilled defiance of punk cliché. 'What Do I Get?' is a hymn of self-pity.

'It's an attempt to actually make fun of the plight of the person, i.e. myself,' says Shelley. 'It's showing that there's a basic desire in every one of us to actually make contact with another person, another person of another flesh. It's a basic desire, which we put down to love but it's a lot more than that. In the lyrics which I write I tend to become extremely naïve about things, because . . . I assume that people are naïve in things like love because nobody takes an O-level, or an A-level in love. Everybody's got an opinion but if you have the wrong opinion you end up leading a really awful life.'

Christopher John misses the point and drifts off into a reverie about songs being banned. Shelley indulges this politely. Then he says: 'I've got this dream and this hopeless ideal that somewhere, there will be one person . . . if there's one person in the whole lifetime of that record who will actually be able to listen to it and see the same things and feel the same feelings from those words which I can, well, then it's all worthwhile. It's basically a communication. Communication needs two people.'

25

Who Are the Poofs?

It's not all great. I record the John Peel show and Radio Forth on the Marconiphone, pausing and erasing as I go. What remains is the good stuff, the crème de la crud. What remains is a double-glazing advert by Peter Cook and Dudley Moore ('single-glazed twit!'), live sets by Ian Dury and Dr Feelgood, and a lot of music in which lack of expertise is worn like a badge and comedy obscures emotional reticence. The Proles, Visitors, Johnnie and the Lubes, The Jolt, Protex, The Tea Set, Tubeway Army, Métal Urbain, Squeeze, The Clash, The Jam, The Clash again, Wreckless Eric, Devo, The Flys, Patrik Fitzgerald, Patrik Fitzgerald, Patrik Fitzgerald.

I like Patrik Fitzgerald. He sings 'Safety Pin Stuck In My Heart'. He is the punk Bob Dylan, or at least the punk Richard Stilgoe. Richard Stilgoe is everywhere you don't want him to be. He is on *Nationwide*, he is on *That's Life!*, the consumer programme with Esther Rantzen's teeth and the dog that says 'sausages' and Cyril Fletcher squirming in a chair. On live television Richard Stilgoe, with his tan suit and his deputy headmaster's beard, sings the 1979 general election results – in which Margaret Thatcher triumphs, heralding the end of everything – with a plink of his baby grand and a tiny smile. 'Well, thank you very much, Richard,' says Sue Lawley, sounding super posh and politely amused, 'well done.'

So that's Richard Stilgoe, the frivolous harbinger of Thatcherism. Sorry, Patrik.

To be clear, Richard Stilgoe is not on my tape except as an absence, because punk and all that follows is about rejecting the brain-crushing tedium of the news magazine shows with their middle-brow whimsy and the consumer shit where pensioners are invited to laugh at phallic tubers during hilarious vox pops at knees-up-Mother-Brown vegetable markets. I hate *Nationwide*. I hate it every night. I write a song about it. The Instant Whips record it. Nothing happens. The Instant Whips split up. The Whips record a less instant version but not with me singing. It appears on the B-side of their three-track EP *Walking In Circles*, the sole release on the Flying Headbutt label. The chorus is 'crisis, what crisis' because that was the phrase the *Sun* used to undermine the Labour prime minister Jim Callaghan, even though he never said it. The phrase comes from a sex scene in *The Day of the Jackal*. It is also the title of a Supertramp album, and I hate them, obviously. The Whips' record is on the jukebox at the Quarterdeck, and it is always on, not least because James Quarterdeck, the son of the landlord Jimmy Quarterdeck, is friends with the group and has access to the switch where you can pick tunes for free. Sadly the record is badly pressed, and plays very quietly, while the other bikers' favourite, 'Free Bird' by Lynyrd Skynyrd, is loud enough and stupid enough to induce its own microclimate, a misty torpor that swirls out of the bar and along the High Street, where it hangs in front of the Golfers Rest like a mocking spirit. One night, when leaving the Quarterdeck, The Instant Whips are assailed by a group of youths from the year below. The leader of the youths, whose father is a local bank manager, steps out of the 'Free Bird' smirr and starts a chant. It is the 'we are the mods' chant from *Quadrophenia*, except instead of singing 'we are the mods' he turns it into a question. 'Who are the poofs, who are the poofs, who are, who are, who are the poofs?'

In a moment of levity, I reply. 'We are the poofs, we are the poofs . . .'

Soon enough the banker's son is punching me in the poofy face and I am hovering above myself, baffled and not fighting back.

But these are febrile times. Politics is infecting everything. I am perhaps North Berwick's only active member of Rock Against Racism and the Anti-Nazi League. I receive many letters from Irate Kate at the RAR headquarters suggesting I form a cell, and enquiring whether I have met any like-minded souls at the disco in Aberlady Community Hall. She encloses Day-Glo stickers and badges, one of which celebrates the reggae group The Cimarons, and has the slogan 'Racism is a Dirty, Mucky Schism' printed over a red, gold and green RAR star. Miss Dodd, my Modern Studies teacher, takes an instant dislike to this badge and hauls me to the front of the class to explain the meaning of the word 'schism'.

I also spend my evenings flyposting Anti-Nazi League stickers along the lampposts of Old Abbey Road. To my knowledge there is only one black person in North Berwick and he resides in the Redcroft Old People's Home, singing to himself on a tuneless guitar. I do know a Nazi but he lives in Gullane.

'Woof,' says John Peel after playing Johnnie and the Lubes. 'If not tonight, maybe tomorrow night,' he says after playing 'Maybe Tonight' by The Jolt. 'Pleased to hear a mention in there for Prince Far I,' he says, on playing The Clash's 'Clash City Rockers'. 'I'll probably play all three sides of that, and there are only two, on tomorrow night's programme.' Sure enough, the next night Peel plays 'Jail Guitar Doors', the B-side of The Clash single. 'Is this power pop?' he says. 'Door bangs open, enter Joe Strummer breathing heavily.'

26

Gary Don't Need His Eyes to See

Finally, I get out of North Berwick.

I go to Aberdeen.

I go to Aberdeen because it is far away, and because it was sunny on the day I first visited, and on a sunny day the granite in the Aberdeen buildings makes the whole city look like shimmering silver. There is nothing more beautiful than Aberdeen on a sunny winter's day, with frost and blue sky and silver granite. This is worth keeping in mind on the other 350 days of the year. Aberdeen in the rain is like a headache encased in concrete.

I have high hopes.

There is no university accommodation available, so I get a room with two friends from school and a Stranger. There are four of us in the room. It is not a huge room. There are four uncomfortable beds and a gas fire. We do not have access to a kitchen. On a cold day, and Aberdeen has nothing but cold days from October to December, the condensation runs down the walls. We have to keep the window open to let the air in and the cigarette smoke out. The Stranger in the fourth bed is a smoker, a trainee alcoholic and a congenital liar. He claims to be 'resting' because his university studies were cut short when he was run over by a bus. He also says that the runaway bus flattened his career as a footballer for Celtic.

The Stranger is certainly resting. He barely leaves his bed. The Stranger has a terrible cough. In the night, as we lie sleepless in our dampened sheets, he sputters endlessly, to the point where it seems as if his lungs are about to explode, and then there's rustling, followed by a fizzing sound and then a series of desperate gulps. The Stranger in the fourth bed keeps a large bottle of Irn-Bru by his bedside, as medicine. When the gulping stops, he has a cigarette to dampen the sugar rush. During daylight, the Stranger sleeps like a pub carpet.

We are not the only people in these lodgings. It is a house of many rooms. It is hard to say how many people are in residence because no one makes any attempt to socialise except at nine p.m. every night, when the landlady delivers tea and fig rolls to the television room. At these times there are around sixteen of us, all silent, all hoping for something less medicinal than a fig roll. We are all boys, technically men. Girls are not allowed. One of the boys manages to break this rule. He has a single room. He does not bother with the fig rolls.

Food is a problem. On Sundays me and my two pals treat ourselves. We cycle to a shop a mile or so down the road and buy baguettes and Primula cheese spread. Back in the room we toast the baguettes on the gas fire, occasionally pausing to set light to a fart. At lunchtimes and in the evenings I enjoy an Olympian diet of pie, beans and chips from the university refectory. We live like kings. It is brilliant.

On the Friday of Freshers' Week, The Adverts play at the university Union. The Adverts are a proper punk group.

Their first record, 'One Chord Wonders', is an ironic manifesto and they have enjoyed an actual hit record with 'Gary Gilmore's Eyes', in which the singer TV Smith narrates a horror tale about an eye-transplant patient being gifted the vision of the convicted killer Gary Gilmore, whose death by firing squad was an international pop horror incident. Gilmore inspired Norman Mailer to write *The Executioner's Song*, was played by Tommy Lee Jones in a TV mini-series, and his last words, 'Let's do it', provided the inspiration for the Nike slogan, 'Just Do It'.

Time will make Gary Gilmore more famous but no less dead. The Adverts, two years on from their moment of inspiration, are almost defunct. Still, they are amazing.

The Adverts have an actual punkette, Gaye Advert, on bass. Gaye is beautiful. One of the music papers has printed a topless picture of her, which I have had photocopied because we are still in that post-hippie moment where naked women are a symbol of liberation, at least for men. This will change with the invention of sexism but that moment is yet to arrive. (A mere three years later my then-flatmate will express his disappointment that Lesley Woods, the singer of the Au Pairs, is 'a hack'. By then I will have received enough education to know that he has missed a meeting.)

I go to The Adverts on my own. My attempts to make friends during Freshers' Week have been thwarted by my refusal to join any clubs or societies and my inability to strike up a conversation without wanting to evaporate. I do have one Freshers' Week chat, in which I try too hard, making the bold and unprovable claim that *All Mod Cons* by The Jam is the best album of all time. At that moment I also pledge that I will never again attempt to measure the value of a piece of recorded music against forever.

The Adverts are great. They are supported by Visitors, who I love. Visitors are austere and confrontational. They dress in grey and their songs are like cinematic vignettes. The singer, John McVay, shouts as much as he sings. They are like Wire, if Wire came from Oxgangs.

The Adverts are fierce and dynamic. They are almost exciting enough to persuade me that the university life I have dreamed of will actually come to pass. There is a bit of violence in the crowd but I leave the Union exhilarated and hopeful.

I am about halfway to my digs when it happens. I am almost aware of footsteps behind me. I feel a blow to the head. I am knocked to the ground, kicked in the stomach, booted in the face. Nothing breaks, except for my spirit. Two men run away laughing. They are wearing suits. They look like businessmen. They say nothing. I am not robbed. It is pointless, absurd.

I drag myself along Clifton Road to the lodgings and realise I have missed the curfew. The front door is locked. I have to clamber through the garden to the back door of the house and creep through the landlady's quarters to get back to my bed. As I open the door of the room there is a carbonised hiss. The Stranger is taking his medicine.

27

A Different Kind of Tension

The next day, on my way to the Other Record Shop to buy the new Buzzcocks album, I bump into the Adverts singer, TV Smith, on Union Street. I approach him warily and tell him I enjoyed the show but got beaten up afterwards. 'I'm sorry,' he says, signing an autograph on my copy of the *Evening Express*.

A few days later Visitors return to play a show at the Aberdeen Music Hall. During the spoken-word section of 'Acrobat' John McVay talks about the violence at the Adverts show.

'Who were the guys that were fighting? That was very nice. It was really sickening. We came all the way up last Friday with The Adverts and all you did was fight amongst yourselves. Pretty sad, isn't it? Wankers! Just arseholes, the lot of you! Apart from one or two, maybe. You don't even justify it. You were fighting students. You were fighting yourselves. You gave our roadie a doing. Tried to trash the gear as well. Very good of you. Thing is, none of you stopped it. There was about ten people at the front who were fighting, and not one of you, not another person in the crowd, tried to stop it. Didn't matter what you did. That's not a nice reputation to have, 'cos that's what you've got down South. Just fighters. "Aw, you ken Aberdeen crowds, they're really heavy, man. You shouldnae go up there. They're really heavy." And you just proved it.

'Tonight's relatively quiet. but that's probably because they don't sell bottled beer like they do in student unions, which is a mess. Have you ever had a bottle flung at you? Well, come up here one day and you can try it. Does anyone want to come up and say something about that? That wanky incident. I don't know if you can even hear me, the echoes in this place are that bad. One-two-three-four . . .'

At the start of my second week at university I receive a postcard from my brother in Edinburgh. It has a painting by Beryl Cook on one side, an image of cheerfully pneumatic working-class stereotypes having a cartoonishly great time in a pub. On the back my brother has written a thoughtful message. 'By now you will have discovered that 99% is shit. Hope the other 1% is available.'

The languor of youth, how unique and quintessential it is.

28

A Non-Sexist Night Out

The Commercials do not sound like anyone else, though this is by accident not design. We are, at best, a half-musical group, and I am in the non-musical sector. I am a singer who does not sing but does something else. There is an honourable tradition of singers who do something else. They get away with it because they have the artistry to push their non-singing voices into interesting shapes. I do not do this. I am stuck with not-singing as my means of expression. Lou Reed can sing, and very sweetly, but often his delivery is conversational. It has intimacy and menace, occasionally at the same time. Mark E. Smith does not sing. He barks like a tramp. I speak a bit more urgently. I do this because much of the concept of singing has passed me by. This becomes clear early on, when The Instant Whips attempt to fashion a novelty punk version of 'Sugar, Sugar' by The Archies. As with many great pop songs, the simplicity of 'Sugar, Sugar' is trickier than it seems, especially to a non-musician reading the lyrics from sheet music. The main part of the song is OK, though it's hard to access the correct dosage of saccharine. But there is a little moment of release in the song when the singer breaks loose, which baffles me entirely.

The Commercials have been arrived at by a process of elimination and refinement. After the drama of The Instant Whips' implosion at the high school dance, various bands have formed, collapsed and mutated. The Instant Whips' guitarist, James Bondage (real name: Ian), liberated himself and went to play with The Whips. They were a real group. Some of them came from Haddington, which was almost the same as coming from Glasgow. They were tough, and popular with the local motorcycle gang, the Baader-Meinhof. One of the Whips' songs celebrated a lewd act in the cludgie of the Haddington Corn Exchange. I slide through various group line-ups, some of which never amount to more than a name. I don't think God's Golfballs ever reach the stage of becoming legends in their lunch hour but the concept flickers briefly. The Creatures of Doom play more than once, and while we are rarely as cheerful as our name, the glum cacophony does attract the attention of Jane, the one punk from the year below, who will eventually be persuaded to join The Commercials as co-vocalist. Jane has a jacket with *Creature of Doom* painted on the back and we take this to be a sign of devotion. It isn't. She just likes the song by The Only Ones. The Corselettes play a party at the Mallard Hotel in Gullane. During my performance I wear a Heinz soup apron similar to the one Paul Weller had (inexplicably) worn on *Top of the Pops*. At the end of our set Jane, the Creature of Doom, marches forward and says: 'I hate mods.'

Ultimately, everything flows into The Commercials. Ian brings his guitar back and agrees to play with both us and The Whips. This means there is a skirl of Stuart Adamson in the guitars, because we all like the Skids, and this evolves into the pealing guitar sound of U2, because we mostly like U2 and The Edge has copied Stuart Adamson. (I stop buying U2's records after '11 O'clock Tick Tock' because I am an elitist bastard and allergic to popular things.) Maybe there is a rumble of Joy Division in The Commercials' bass. We have exploding drummers, so there is no consistent drum sound. We have boy–girl vocals, an effect which is supposed to be discursive, a contrast, beauty and the beast.

Something like that. But then music changes. We evolve. We copy new things. The same new things as everyone else. As punk recedes, the floral psychedelic flourishes of the guitar become more pronounced, people start suggesting that Duran Duran and Spandau Ballet are appropriate influences to have. Then there's Depeche Mode, and before you know it someone has acquired a Casio VL-1 and we have solved the exploding drummer problem by employing Bobby Washable da-da-da electronics. (The musical sector of The Commercials will eventually drift into new romantic territory as The Assassins of Hope, later losing the hope, but that is not a hairstyle I can follow. Also, nobody asks me.)

I am also entirely ignorant of stagecraft. Punk in its more inept formulation appears to be a rejection of performance. It trades in honesty. But something happens to honesty when you put it on a stage, and the successful punk bands are actually full of theatre. The Clash have stencilled clothes and an oppositional stance, The Jam have Mod suits and Pete Townshend leaps. The Ramones are a high-concept art statement. Johnny Rotten is Ian Dury doing Richard III via Max Wall. Somehow, with punk, the theatrical artifice is rolled into the broader idea that the singers are genuine. They mean it. I prefer the Subway Sect, who wear school jumpers with a rip in the same place.

The Instant Whips had a flying pig on a wire across the high school stage during our fateful first performance but that was a parody of the pomposity of Pink Floyd. As an un-frontman I have negative amounts of stage presence. I can't remember the words, even though I write them, which is why I tend to proclaim the texts from a repurposed school jotter.

Outside summer holidays we all live in different places. There is one Commercial in North Berwick, two in Glasgow, and I am in Aberdeen. Looking back at the letters I have from the time, we all contrive to have a terrible time, though maybe we are just being polite. The Commercials do play a few shows, some of them notable. We play my brother's birthday party at the old Traverse Theatre, we do the North Berwick Harbour Pavilion, Strathclyde University and Glasgow Tech, where we support The Delmontes. We play an anti-nuclear benefit and a Non-Sexist Night Out, which covers most of the available definitions of fun in the early 1980s. The shows go well. People applaud. Missiles are not thrown. For the thirty or forty minutes when The Commercials are on stage, the anxiety is completely intoxicating.

Where do we think this thing is going? We don't think about it. As long as we don't, it remains fantastic.

29

A Horrible, Truculent Youth

And then! In 1980, Orange Juice arrive in a rush. Their music is frivolous, playful, funny, arch, sincere. They are shambolic in a new and interesting way, with clothes from all over the place, the emotional softness of Pete Shelley, Chic rhythms done DIY, Northern Soul bashed out on the roof of Subway Sect's Transit van.

Orange Juice are utterly original and fresh. Orange Juice are on Postcard Records and suddenly there is not just one great group but several. There is Aztec Camera from East Kilbride, who are built around the tender songwriting of Roddy Frame. And from Edinburgh, Josef K, who are as dark and moody as the Juice are refreshing. Postcard comes with its own hype, delivered in packages decorated in scraps of Scottish kitsch. The label's logo is a drumming cat. There is a Svengali, the camp commandant Alan Horne, who knows enough about Andy Warhol to pose with his face framed inside a tambourine.

Alan Horne also suggests that the three Postcard bands represent different stages of the Velvet Underground. This is wildly misleading and not even slightly true but it sounds good.

And beyond the three core Postcard bands there are others. The Go-Betweens wash up from Australia and are compellingly strange. The Go-Betweens are am-dram Bob Dylans; The Bluebells are a pure pop rush; the Jazzateers wear Aran sweaters and sound like they've inhaled a jazz record at the youth club hop.

The Postcard thing is tiny and out of control. The gigs are exuberant, joyous events. It feels as if punk has taken root and produced a crop of wildflowers. The talk of Postcard as a new Motown is obviously absurd but there is something thrilling about inhabiting an obvious absurdity. In *Sounds* Dave McCullough loves Postcard. In the *NME* Paul Morley confects a fantasy universe in which Josef K could be number one. In these heady months, which rush past so quickly that they might actually be days or hours, everything is possible and Scotland is the place to be.

In the fable of Postcard everything happens because of truculence. When the first Orange Juice single comes out Alan Horne borrows his dad's Austin Maxi and drives to London. He goes to Broadcasting House and demands to see John Peel.

'There'd just been the Liverpool thing with Echo and the Bunnymen and The Teardrop Explodes,' Orange Juice's bass player David McClymont tells me years later. 'And prior to that the Mancunian thing centred round Factory Records. And Alan said to Peel, "That's all over now, get with the times, move further North to Scotland to hear the future." When he said these things, it wasn't all bravado. He could be very convincing but Peel said, "There was a horrible truculent youth who badgered his way into Peel Acres."

'Alan did sort of talk himself into these things,' McClymont continues. 'There'd been precedents for his attitude. It was an immediate post-punk period and I remember listening to John Peel and he was playing some tracks from The Clash's album that had just come out, and Joe Strummer had phoned in saying, "That's a very bad choice of tracks, here's the ones you should have chosen." The establishment – whether it was the London music industry or the Scottish music industry – they weren't used to being told, "Well, fuck you, this is what we're doing." They thought we were insolent or impudent or mad or deranged. But the impetus came from punk rock.

'It wasn't easy. We didn't really drink in those days. It wasn't really Dutch courage, we just had to talk up a storm.'

My dad has an Austin Maxi but London is a long way away. The Commercials decide to go to Postcard Records. The corporate headquarters is not hard to find. The address of Postcard is written on the record sleeves and everybody knows that the new Motown is run from the inside of a wardrobe at 185 West Princes Street.

We arrive with a tape. Alan Horne is there, along with Steven Daly, the drummer in Orange Juice. Steven makes some tea while Alan plays the tape. He looks as if he is being tortured. 'You sound like the Au Pairs,' Alan Horne says, reversing into the safety of the kitchen, and we know this is not a compliment.

30

Dead Letter Office
'I thought you were Aztec Camera
for a while.'

The group Wire make a remark that many bands seem to be concentrating on getting their T-shirts made, rather than their music.

The Commercials order T-shirts from Willie the guitarist's screen-printing shop. The T-shirts show a cartoon of a man and a woman. In the speech bubbles the man says, 'Is the war over?' The woman replies, 'I don't know.' The Commercials have a song called 'I Don't Know'. It is our manifesto.

We make demo tapes, splicing them together with razor blades and cheap tape which will self-destruct in five seconds, like the undercover orders in *Mission: Impossible*. We send the tapes out to uninterested parties and wait.

Letter from Johnny Waller typed on the back of a letter from 4AD records. Scored out, the note from 4AD. 'Here's a Complete Singing Fish, Try and get Col's picture in.'

Dear Alistair Commercial,
No excuses – OK, so it's been a long time, but then you can't eat it raw, can you?

As for the tape(s), well . . . you seem to be falling between various stools, neither capturing the glorious teenage trash rush of Buzzcocks, nor aspiring to the equally glorious (though admittedly calculated) pop cinerama of Kim Wilde!!! And what's wrong with Duran Duran 12"?

Some of the last tape was nearly there (all this purely subjective, y'unnerstand) – like the guitar intro to The Heroine Dies, and bits of the singing on 16 Again . . . but unfortunately (good excuse this!) the actual physical tape was slightly worse for wear when it arrived here, then my cassette machine did the rest, mangling much of the middle section of Heroine – at last, a tape machine with a built in rejection mode for tapes that lack sufficient panache. That's style!

Can't wait to see a gig, though, cos tapes are misleading for bands so young – wear bright gear, blow kisses and dance a lot, OR never play gigs with false glamour, sign away your dreams to Mickie Most OR go back to your dreary office jobs. Me? I'll just keep flirting with pop! for fun! with the Polecats! and Girls At Our Best!, but my heart is forever owned by the Fall and Delta 5.

I don't think my life is very dull, but I can always stand a little bright excitement, so further tapes, bribes and dubious letters to:
Johnny Waller
FRIEND TO THE DESPERATE + UNKNOWN!

The letter is devastating. I do not see the fact that Johnny Waller of *Sounds* has taken the time to reply and, as well as supplying his phone number and his address, has invited further communication. I see the phrase 'bits of the singing'. I see 'tapes that lack sufficient panache'. I see 'wear bright gear, blow kisses and dance a lot'.

Another tape. Another letter.

Letter from Johnny Waller on page torn from diary dated St Andrews Day (30 November). Letter dated Edinburgh, 29 March 1981.

> *Hi Commercials,*
> *Ta for the tape . . . I'm always interested in new bands/ tapes etc. and I'd heard fairly good reports of the Commercials live.*
> *As for the tape – yeah, right – as you said, the quality + songs seem a little, er, TAME? It's not a question of power-chords or vitriol . . . I just thought you weren't getting the best out of your ideas by adhering to established formats/arrangements. Both voices sound to have amazing potential but don't have the advantage of good phrases/phrasing to use. That said, Escape rolls along in better style + the phrase 'Martini smiles' in Simon is brilliant. Very few backing vocals too, I noticed!*
> *Aw hell – look, this is all sounding too hyper-critical and analytical, but you must be demanding of the band – attempt to be a little stronger in your approach (the guitar tends to sound very thin and tinny) maybe leaving more gaps, rather than attempting frantic pop. Listen to Start by The Jam, and anything by Pauline Murray for examples.*

Please stay in touch, I'd love to see a gig.
Cheers, Johnny
PS Can I keep the tape, yeah?

It is great that Johnny Waller has written another letter and found new ways to be encouraging and dismissive in the same sentence. Accordingly we are outraged and hurt, flattered and unaffected. There is some progress between the first and the second letter. In the first one Johnny was delighted that his tape deck had eaten the cassette. In the second the cassette survived to fight another day.

I make a list of Johnny Waller's suggestions.

Be more Buzzcocks, or be more Kim Wilde. Make up your mind
Don't rule out Duran Duran!
Bits of the guitar are OK
Bits of the singing are OK
But only bits
Wear bright gear, blow kisses, dance a lot
OR don't
Sign up with Mickie Most
Go back to your crap office jobs
Get more out of your ideas
Forget established formats
Learn what an arrangement is
Learn about phrasing
Learn about phrases
Be stronger
Turn it up!
Turn it off
Forget about frantic pop
Copy The Jam
Copy Pauline Murray

It all seems logical and reasonable. We have a band meeting to decide how famous we want to be. Not mega-famous is the answer. Just Echo and the Bunnymen famous.
Letter from Rough Trade Records.

> *137 Blenheim Crescent*
> *London W11*
>
> *Dear Commercials,*
> *Thank you for letting us hear your tape. We like several things about it. We feel that you might want to look into DIY as a way of finding out something about getting it right. Beyond that, it's hard to know what to do, suggest.*
>   *Try us with some new work when and if you see fit. Let us hear from you.*
>   *Yours,*
>   *RT*
>   *DIY details available with 30p & an SAE. Think about a 4-track EP?*

Letter to Dave McCullough, at *Sounds*.

> *Dear Dave,*
> *This is a letter from The Commercials. These Commercials come from North Berwick. A few months ago we sent you our demo tape. It had four songs on it, Simon, 16 Again and Again, Escape and I Don't Know. Since then we have heard nothing from you so naturally we assumed you didn't like the tape much. Imagine our surprise when, while scanning this week's Sounds (bought as a last resort – every week I swear*

I will never buy Sounds again) we saw a mention of The Commercials in your 'Groups for 1981' column. This has caused some excitement, but also some bewilderment. Are we The Commercials you meant? If there are some other Commercials then we'll have to change our name.

Hope to hear from you soon whether the news is positive or not. Get up and use yourself!

Yours,

The Commercials

Letter from Dave McCullough, at *Sounds*.

Dear Comms,

Yes, it was you. I am peeved that you are reluctant to spend 25p on Sounds – at least it's on a badness level with NME, and much less trendy.

Anyway, send me more, send me more!

Love, Dave McCullough

PS I did like your demo. I thought that you were Aztec Camera for a while.

We never hear from Dave McCullough again.

31

The Square Window

Recording the Commercials' single is exciting. It is a kind of holiday. We drive from North Berwick to Wales in a hired Transit full of equipment with a cassette player on the dashboard playing reggae and Echo and the Bunnymen at dangerous volume. It is a long journey but we manage to stay alive. The studio is Foel, run by Dave Anderson, the older brother of the Commercials' guitarist Ian. Dave was in krautrock pioneers Amon Düül II, though we don't know much about them. He was also in Hawkwind, which is impressive. Dave has recorded a number of post-punk acts such as the Young Marble Giants, Mo-Dettes, Lora Logic and Delta 5. These acts are more our thing, especially as we are now said to sound like the Au Pairs.

Recording with The Commercials is not like being in The Rolling Stones but there is a lot of waiting around, many wine gums to eat. There are hours stretching into days of trying to record the rhythm track and then the guitar. There are lambs in the fields. We see Ian Gomm on the street. There is a police raid, some backbreaking toil on the farm and a live show in which a dispute about stolen equipment threatens to undermine Scottish/Welsh relations.

The downtime is made bearable by two things. Someone in an adjacent building keeps playing The Everly Brothers and their harmonies sound like the sweetest, most magical thing. It has not yet occurred to The Commercials to attempt harmonies. It will never occur to us. The other odd thing is the presence, in and around the studio, of Lionel Morton of The Four Pennies, who had a number one hit in 1964 with 'Juliet'. It is a doo-woppy thing with intense harmonies. That is not who Lionel is to us. We do not know about The Four Pennies. To us, he is Lionel from the pre-school children's TV programme *Play School*, so we spend an inordinate amount of time asking about the wellbeing of Humpty and Little Ted, and whether we should be looking through the round window or the square one.

Finally it is time to play. The studio is ready for a vocal take. I give it everything, enunciating, emoting, breathing with my stomach, smiling with my eyes. At the end of the take there is an awkward silence, then Dave's voice comes through the headphones. 'Sounds a little flat, Ali. Are you happy with that?'

Flatness is not something I am familiar with. It has not been covered in Jessie Turner's music class. I felt exhilarated for a moment but now I am flat, with no idea how to re-inflate.

Are We Not, Or Are We Not Going to North Berwick Now?

The Commercials' record is released. It has a sleeve by Kendo's brother John, who will go on to be a film director. In an unacknowledged reference to a North Berwick summer fête of years before, the sleeve shows the *Blue Peter* presenter Peter Purves. The record is reviewed in *NME* by Vivien Goldman, who isn't keen. It appears in a classified ad for the Rough Trade shop. The records listed show the splintering of post-punk music, with The Raincoats and Wire alongside Josef K and Aztec Camera. The Commercials are jammed between 'Motorhead' by Hawkwind and the debut EP by Felt, which is about right.

The single is played once on John Peel. Peel suggests for reasons that are not clear that he owes the band a drink. Some weeks later I mention this to Peel at a roadshow at the Nite Club in Edinburgh and he is entirely baffled.

The record is discussed on Radio Forth's *Rock Report*, a shambolic show in which Christopher John and Colin Somerville discuss new releases in the manner of an old married couple. First, the A-side, '16 Again And Again', is played. 'It's a three-track single and that's inspiring enough to make me want to investigate the two songs on the other side,' says Christopher John.

'Yes,' says Colin Somerville. 'I think maybe if that lady sings on the other two songs it could get even more interesting, I would say.'

'She does indeed,' says John. 'We'll check them out next week on the *Rock Report*, Wednesday night between eight o'clock and ten o'clock.'

Two weeks later, Christopher John and Colin Somerville are discussing Louis Armstrong and the Newport Jazz Festival.

'Are we not, or are we not going to North Berwick now?' Somerville asks, making a geographic handbrake turn.

'We are indeed,' says John. 'I have a postcard from North Berwick, depicting the swimming pond and the Pavilion. It comes from, would you believe, The Commercials, who say: "Ta for playing our single the other week, glad you liked it."'

John plays 'The Heroine Dies'. 'Seen a lot of movies like that myself,' he says. 'Commercials, and the B-side of their current single, which has an A-side entitled "16 Again And Again". There's two tracks on the B-side, that's the first of them. The other one is . . .'

'Simon,' says Somerville.

'Say-mon, eh,' says John. 'Actually, I think it's got more going for it than the A-side.'

'No,' says Somerville. 'I prefer the A-side.'

'OK, fair enough,' says John.

'Sorry,' says Somerville.

'Well,' says John, 'let's just drop another opinion in here. When the single came in the post I said to young Jay Crawford, who is a native of North Berwick, I said, "Hey, local band, Jay, I wonder if you know the guuuuuys." I played it to him, he said [unimpressed Dick Dastardly mumble] "local punks". So don't expect too much support from your countryman Mr Crawford, I don't think he liked it. We like it. Reasonably.'

'Some of it,' says Somerville. 'This is enough of that. What's next?'

'Funkapolitan,' says Christopher John.

33

The Quarterdeck

Punk rock gave me a voice. What did I say?

It is not a painless process, revisiting this past. There is evidence. There is an actual book, a repurposed school jotter, full of drool. The lyrics are still legible. The handwriting looks naïve. The entries span several bands, including some which never progressed beyond being a name. The Commercials are there, and The Instant Whips. So are The Creatures of Doom and The Corselettes. There is a nod to God's Golfballs.

The lyrics are a form of teenage diary, but the songs were not written with secrecy in mind. These words were designed to be heard. They are the things I wanted to say. This was the version of myself that I wanted to share. I was giving myself permission to speak.

From this archaeology I can observe the creative genesis of 'Smoke Signals', the song I performed at the Nether Abbey after having handed the abusive lyrics to all of my peers. Before it was called 'Smoke Signals' it was known as 'Cliques', and then 'Celebrity Squares'. The dust of self-pity wafts from the yellowed pages. In the margins there is a checklist of subjects I hoped to include in the song. These include: the QD, dope, cigarettes, go-go dancers, Southern Comfort sweat-shirts, North Berwick Rugby Club, and the phrase 'Indians not chiefs'. There is also a definition of the word 'sycophant', in case of questions from the audience. 'A flatterer, toady, or parasitic person.'

The QD in the song is the Quarterdeck, a now mythical bar, once moored at the west end of North Berwick High Street, opposite the old Post Office. It was frequented by motorcycle enthusiasts and recalcitrant youths, and was believed by my mother, and all mothers, to be 'a den of iniquity'. In reality it was a place where order and good humour prevailed thanks to the widespread belief that the landlord, Jimmy Quarterdeck, had a baseball bat stashed beneath the ship-shaped counter. The bat was a kind of nuclear deterrent. The threat of it kept a lid on hostilities.

The front room of the QD housed a pool table. The back room was more mysterious. The rear wall was decorated with a lysergic space mural, painted in the style of the Haddington expressionists. The artist may have been one of the droogs who booted my brother in the balls after Scouts, though it's hard to be certain. (It was dark – the bowler hat cast a shadow over his face.)

With the invention of video recorders this psychedelic back room doubled as an impromptu picture house, screening classics of global cinema, some of them narrated on fast-forward by Jimmy Quarterdeck. One example of this hybrid of cinema and oral storytelling occurred during a screening of Walter Hill's existentialist neo-noir *The Driver*. In *The Driver*, Ryan O'Neal is assisted by Isabelle Adjani and hunted by Bruce Dern. It is a taciturn getaway movie in which destiny is characterised as a bag of cash stashed in a locker at a railway station. 'Anyway,' says Jimmy Quarterdeck, ringing the bell for last orders with more than forty minutes of the film remaining, 'he gets the bag, like, and he hands it to the cops, but the bag is empty. Another OJ and lemonade, killer?' (Jimmy Quarterdeck calls me 'killer' when he serves me soft drinks. The nickname may be ironic.)

Another song in the jotter is called 'Confinement'. It is dated 1980. The theme, as ever, is teenage misery. 'My dreams are so frightening,' the song goes, 'thank God they're not true/My life is quite frightening, thank God it's not true.' It's possible this is an allusion to the night terrors I suffered in early childhood, which were accompanied by tooth-grinding and sleepwalking. In one incident I fell down a flight of stairs yet survived unhurt. The rest of the song is whimsical by comparison, as in the spoken mid-section: 'Take me to the factory, take me to the zoo, take me to the Hoover shop, nothing else to do.'

Glum introspection is the default position for teenagers experimenting with self-expression. The North Berwick High School magazine for 1977 includes poetic works on the death of an eagle, the reason for existence, dying, death, being a worm, and being a guinea pig. Actually, there are several poems about being a worm. Perhaps it was a thing.

In that same school magazine, I attempt a poetic account of an afternoon at the beach. The essay includes references to Charles Atlas, 'top-heavy blondes' and perspiring nuns, though not in the same sentence. The geography of North Berwick also appears in some of my attempts at songwriting. One song, 'Out', which never gets as far as having a tune, records the desolation of the amusement arcade inside the Harbour Pavilion. The song's narrator puts his last 5p in the fruit machine, without reward. 'At least the beach is free,' the song concludes, 'Yet deserted and cold/Save the oystercatcher.'

Inevitably, shyness is in the songs, and not always obliquely. In 'A Simple Maze', the difficulty is bluntly stated. 'It's so difficult,' I write, 'to say the words that don't come/ And the words that escape wish they had stayed/Wish they had stayed in the films/I wish they had stayed in the films.'

Even now, with the distance of a lifetime, I feel the urge to make light of this misery. But it's not a passing fancy. 'Sixteen Again and Again' is a riposte to the Buzzcocks song, 'Sixteen Again', based on a fundamental misreading of Pete Shelley's sentiments. Pete knew that being sixteen wasn't all it was cracked up to be. I thought it was worse than that. 'Sixteen, life's a dream,' I sang, 'but you're having trouble sleeping.'

'Chicken' is about getting beaten up in a small town ('I'll swap words till you're black and blue'). 'Speeds The End' explores the monotonous dynamics of an empty life. 'His problem is an empty life/Awareness makes it worse.' The chorus, in the true spirit of the early eighties, is cribbed from a sociology book, *Working for Ford*. 'Escape' is an attack on escapism, set at the abandoned Whisky Bottle reservoir by the foot of Berwick Law. 'Nobody Talks' is about shyness and getting your head kicked in. 'The Automaton' is a superficial exploration of gender roles. 'I Don't Know' is a less than comprehensive list of things the singer does not know (including: 'I don't know what to say'). 'I Knew The Dead Man' is a lyric inspired by a conversation overheard outside John Menzies on North Berwick High Street, following a local plane crash in which two men died. The second verse reflects on the exploitation of the dead Sid Vicious ('They make the stiff a martyr/show him posing in his coffin'). And the near hit, 'Nationwide' (as covered by The Whips), is an early audition for a job as a television critic.

A moment of levity occurs on the final page of the jotter, with the lyrics to the Instant Whips' novelty effort 'Acne', in which the hormonal skin complaint is cured with a chain-saw. The song aims for comedy, but the scarring remains.

SIDE TWO
Listen with Prejudice

34

My Life as a Fanzine

The 1980s are an unforgiving time. There is no work, particularly if you have no idea how to get it. I footer around getting accepted for post-graduate courses in post-structuralist Marxism, secure in the knowledge that these will make me unemployable and unintelligible. Fortunately no one will fund studies in post-structuralist Marxism, so I take a post-structuralist approach to getting a job. This is long-term unemployment.

I am not alone in my ambition. Everybody is at it. As Roddy Frame of Aztec Camera tells me years later, 'My ambition when I was at school was to be on the dole and have a band. That shows you what Joe Strummer's got to answer for.'

It takes a bit of care and attention, but mostly time, to become long-term unemployed.

I plan a fanzine, to be called *Fish Pie Talks*. The fish pie will do the talking because I will write letters to artists asking for contributions. It doesn't quite work out. I relaunch the idea as *Alternatives to Valium*, a name I steal from an article in the *Sunday Post*. It includes interviews, some of them conducted with the help of Jane from The Commercials, who has the diplomatic skills that I lack.

I move back to Edinburgh but DJ in Aberdeen at a club called the Flesh Exchange one night a week. It is not strictly legal, though I make no money from the deal once I have travelled both ways on the train. It's more like a night out than paid employment and I get free 12-inch singles in the post. There is a lot of Def Jam, a bit of Bruce Willis. I do some scouting for a record company and am paid in REM albums. Money, as The Valentine Brothers warned, is not mentioned.

Music is heading in a thousand directions by this point, tangling itself in contradictions. The argument about whether it is possible to be subversive and popular at the same time is resolved in favour of straightforward popularity. The mid-1980s are the time of Bruce Springsteen's *Born in the U.S.A.* and Michael Jackson's *Thriller* but there's also room for Prince and The Go-Betweens and Talking Heads and Adrian Sherwood, and The Bluebells and Orange Juice finally having hits, and Malcolm X remixed for the electronic disco, and Public Enemy, and Simple Minds getting simpler and more popular, and heavy metal, and Tom Petty, and U2 getting lost in America, and Sade, and mullets, and Scottish bands rising without trace and falling back down when stilted literate funk is abandoned in favour of unapologetic hugeness and East German hair. Music is no longer about having a go.

There are a few areas – dance music, maybe – where a lack of musicianship can be overcome with technology but the era of knowing two chords and not being able to play either of them is clearly over. Yet, in some airily defined way, I still identify with punk. Not the Mohican heritage beggars who pose around tourist London like pigeons in the snowglobe sequence of *Mary Poppins*. It's more the principle of the thing. Or an interpretation of that principle.

My efforts at playing music end in ignominy when I buy an Omnichord – a musical instrument designed for idiots – and compose a song so sad that I can't let anyone else hear it. The tune is a lament for my musical ambitions because I have come to accept that my future does not lie in being an extrovert. I abandon that battle. It's a matter of self-esteem. Shyness is only a disadvantage when it is defined by show-offs. That's what I tell myself because I can't bring myself to tell anyone else. There will always be extroverts hoovering up the oxygen. Instead of talking, I can listen.

For a while I hang out at the Edinburgh Unemployed Workers Centre, doing the things that unemployed workers do. These things include occupying the Conservative Party headquarters for ten minutes. It's a protest about something. The something survives but everyone feels better. The police are very patient. No harm is done. I stay outside and take photos because if a ten-minute occupation isn't photographed, it never happened.

We also make videos because the technology is just about affordable and almost portable. We sit in a circle and talk about the kind of videos we might make as unemployed workers. I propose a pop video, an unemployed art student wants to make a feature film, a third un-worker proposes a hard-hitting documentary about the fact that the old water fountain on Salisbury Crags isn't working any more. An unemployed hippie wants to sing a song and has brought his guitar. 'Help me if you can, I'm on the dole,' he trills. He sounds like Dylan, the stoned rabbit from *The Magic Roundabout*.

As a compromise we make a film that none of us is interested in, because that is how democracy works. The film is about being unemployed and how we all want improved concessionary prices at leisure facilities such as museums and cinemas. This is nobody's idea of fun but we have a community worker helping us to access our potential and he has the casting vote. A punk cameraman whose nickname is the Teenage Tarkovsky agrees to help us plug the camera in and show us where to point it. The film is called *Time on Our Hands* and includes self-pitying interviews with the unemployed workers, by the unemployed workers, for the unemployed workers. In the film I note, almost audibly, that my generation has been betrayed. We had been led to expect lives of leisure and luxury, if not jetpacks. Instead here we are, in a damp Edinburgh basement, pretending to be interested in UB40 concessions at leisure centres. We also make a film about the Edinburgh festival. We corner Russell Harty in Holyrood Park, and Dawn French in the Assembly Rooms. They are not happy. The video also includes a sketch culled – with fearless contempt for copyright – from *Spitting Image*, in which the puppet Prince Philip can be heard complaining about his lot. It is very punk.

The lads at the Unemployed Workers Centre are impressed with my fanzine. Thanks to a few friendly mentions on the radio and in the music papers, *Alternatives to Valium* now has a print run of 1,000 copies. I have an *Alternatives to Valium* cheque book and the look of the fanzine is transformed by Les Clark, from the ferocious and frightening Aberdeen punk-goth group Nervous Choir. Les is a graphic designer. He brings professionalism to the headline fonts and designs the covers. We are beyond Letraset now. A positive review from broadcasting geezer Gary Crowley prompts a few problems when he urges prospective readers to 'make your 50p postal orders out to Jock rocker, Alastair McKay'. Within days I receive dozens of postal orders made payable to Jock Rocker.

At the Unemployed Workers Centre I hear of a job going as editor of the *North Edinburgh News*. I get the job for two reasons. Both of the reasons are the fact that the other candidate was drunk. Plus, I meet the criteria, which state that all the staff must have been unemployed for six months. My idleness has become a qualification. I write for the *NME* on my days off. I go to gigs, often at the Venue. The shows finish after midnight, I walk home and bash out a snide and prejudiced review then walk back to the station to meet the photographer and put the copy and the pictures on the first train to London. After these all-nighters I breakfast on scrambled eggs and grilled tomato at the Carolina Cafe on Bread Street. It tastes great.

This is how I become a journalist. There is no apprenticeship, no test. I have a typewriter. I type. Years later I watch a reading by the author James Kelman. A woman sits at his feet, gazing up adoringly. She asks a question, perhaps hoping to receive a fragment of mystical knowledge. 'How do you become a writer?' she says. 'I get a pen,' Kelman replies, 'and I get a piece of paper.' It is very punk rock.

I see some great shows: Tom Waits at the Playhouse, with his armchair and his giant fridge. I see The Fall. I see Townes Van Zandt, though he turns up very late and very drunk, and says he has been unavoidably delayed at a Thunderbird wine-tasting. I also annoy many of the local bands by giving them bad reviews. I bump into Finitribe in Princes Street Gardens and we stand by the fountain beneath the castle while they hold an impromptu band meeting to decide whether my reservations about their performance were warranted. I survive because Finitribe are honourable men. In the Doric Tavern an outraged drummer (nickname: Psycho) accosts me to discuss a review of his Beefheart-inspired blues-punk combo, and when I tell him I tried to be fair he replies: 'My fucking granny didn't think it was fair.' Harry Horse, the singer of cajun-thrash poseurs Swamptrash, tells me that I have destroyed his band by expressing reservations about their speedy cover of 'Ring Of Fire'. I can only reply that he has overestimated the power of a single opinion. I give a bad review to a record by a leading pop-soul singer and when I meet him months later on a radio programme I say I am glad to see that he doesn't hold a grudge. 'I do,' he replies. 'You're a cunt.'

Explosions of enthusiasm are, regrettably, less frequent. Occasionally something amazing happens. The Proclaimers, blending Merle Haggard, Al Jolson and Jimmie Rodgers with the unembarrassable honesty and bloody-minded certainty of Kevin Rowland, are entirely original and unstoppable. I still have an early demo by Craig and Charlie Reid, and it remains as fresh as it is ferocious. The harmonies, the call-and-response, the bongos. Very punk.

I start to write for *Cut* magazine, which is changing shape from being a Scottish music paper into a music magazine for Britain and the world. I sell them an interview with the comedian Jerry Sadowitz but by the time they get round to running it I have had it published in the *Scotsman* under a false name. I get a job at *Cut*. The wages are terrible and the employment contract requires me to rent my own desk but these are the best of times. The editor, Allan Campbell, is an inspiration. He knows everybody. He knows most things. The desk I rent at *Cut* is next to the turntable. Allan's hip-hop selections are interspersed with my own nervous dabbles into country music. I play a Lucinda Williams record. Allan informs me gravely that 'it lacks the Gram factor'. He loans me a Gram Parsons album. It is the best kind of post-graduate study.

All of my journalistic opportunities arise from cracks in the fabric. Punk leads to fanzines, unemployment leads to community newspapers, community newspapers are made practical by the invention of Apple Macs. The designer of *Cut* (and guitarist of TV21) Ally Palmer uses a Mac at the Wester Hailes *Sentinel* and brings visual dynamism to the magazine. The new publishing technology leads to new newspapers, including *Scotland on Sunday*. *SoS*, as it is nicknamed after a faltering launch, employs Andrew Jaspan, a listings-magazine editor from Manchester who almost made it in the music business when managing The Smirks but signed them to the doomed UK branch of an American label. Andrew tells me he witnessed the first performance by Magazine, after which he presented the singer Howard Devoto with a bunch of flowers and said: 'You passed the audition.' It is very punk.

I write about music and television because, in the spirit of the age, I have monetised my enthusiasms. Increasingly I do interviews. Interviews are a form in which shyness can be a secret weapon. If you are familiar with awkward silences, you can use them. If you worry about having permission to speak, the interview is your friend. You have an excuse. You can't say the wrong thing because the reaction is all that matters. If making friends is awkward, it doesn't matter. Interviews are not about friendship. The worst thing you can hear when transcribing an interview is the sound of your own voice trying too hard to be pally. You can ask things you would never ask your close family or friends. You must. You can drill into your obsessions. You can meet your heroes and pinch the flesh. You can keep asking why.

Why do they matter? Because interviews are an interrogation of the great 'what if'?. Interviews are shy autobiography.

35

Fish Pie Talks

Instead of having failed musicians doing all the writing, Johnny Rotten had asked on Radio Forth, why can't you have the bands themselves? This, more or less, is the initial idea for my fanzine. It is to be called *Fish Pie Talks*. The title is taken from a misheard Captain Beefheart lyric.

Getting the bands to do all the journalism has another advantage. It means I don't have to speak to anybody. I can write letters. In the age of the stamped-addressed-envelope, that is what I do. It doesn't work. It turns out that musicians are not the best people to write about the things they are doing. If things were that simple, they wouldn't need to write music.

Fish Pie Talks does not happen.

In a folder alongside a leaflet announcing the new express bus service between Aberdeen and Glasgow (£7 weekend return) I have a note written after the first issue of *Fish Pie Talks* fails to materialise. It is not short on self-importance. It is written on lined foolscap paper, like a university essay on the subject of irrelevance. There are multiple scorings-out.

This Fish Pie has failed – but the next one could be better. Too many established names – not enough new blood – briefly – to mention smaller bands – some impressed, but not enough. The Presidents Men from Aberdeen are polished and touching on something good, but often too traditional, try their two singles. Visitors (see New Order) are mighty. Their single is the best this year.

Too many live reviews, which are just one person's opinion. A mixture of shyness/conscious decision means there are no fan-to-star interviews.

Any future editions should still strive to escape traditional rock journalism and rely more on articles written by individuals/bands on any subject.

If you are an individual or a band with something to say, contact ———. Any tapes, poems, anything, are obviously welcomed.

This note is not even typed up. The sentiment makes the short journey from foolscap pad to manilla folder without being seen by anyone else.

As cries for help go, it is lacking in self-knowledge and a bit of a non-event.

I was even shy of talking to myself.

※

But still. I waved at Mike Scott and Mike Scott waved back. Later Mike will roam and conquer the world with The Waterboys, but at this point, his career is in flux. His band, Another Pretty Face, has been spat out by Virgin Records after one single.

To me, Mike Scott is pure punk. Punk in this definition means he does whatever he wants, dresses to his own design and is in complete control. Mike might argue with this. He's not keen on being defined. But it remains true that, in punk Edinburgh, Mike Scott saw the possibilities from the start, along with The Rezillos and The Valves. None of them were punks in the restrictive sense of the term: all three groups were fresh and alive to the possibilities of music.

Mike is a fine and passionate music writer. He produces *Jungleland*, one of the great fanzines, and the musical taste is all his own. Mike has inhaled The Clash but he's also a classicist. He likes John Lennon, Bruce Springsteen, Patti Smith. He likes Blondie. He likes the beauty that lurks behind the music but he also has a great passion for the transformative power of a tune.

Mike's reply to my speculative letter takes months to arrive, by which time *Fish Pie Talks* has been muted. When I refashion my fanzine into *Alternatives to Valium* APF are over and Mike Scott has gone wandering to the sound of a different drum.

Here, after a delay of forty years, is that spiky exchange.

Fish Pie Talks: Judging by the last single and the recent John Peel Session (18 February 1981), the music has changed. It seems more mellow, less Clash, more traditional rock music – like Patti Smith. Is this a fair reflection?

Mike Scott: I would agree that the direction our music is going in is definitely more along the lines of Patti Smith than The Clash but I would deny vehemently that it was entering the realms of traditional rock music. Obviously our definition of that label differs quite extremely from yours. To say that what Patti Smith does is traditional is totally ludicrous to us. Smith innovated with *Horses*, *Radio Ethiopia*, *Piss Factory*, etc. She was using poetry set to an anarchic thrash backing. There was no way Smith's music would get played on American AM radio; she only received mass exposure with the release of the uncharacteristic 'Because The Night'. On the other hand, The Clash's *London Calling* fitted, quite easily, AM radio's commerciality. This is not a judgement on The Clash, merely an observation. OK, The Clash were a punk band, and punk rejuvenated the whole scene, but they never really took risks in their music, like Smith did, they still worked within the confines of traditional rock 'n' roll, which is why they were so popular.

So, by our reasoning, if anything, we are moving out of the realms of trad rock music in that The Clash's influence on us has now been exorcised and we are taking more risks. I think the Peel session was evidence of this. After all, how many bands these days use instrumentation of piano/violin/solo acoustic and mesh jazz with rock 'n' roll (not jazz rock)? I'd agree we are traditional in the sense that we write actual songs (as opposed to chord structures with convenient lyrics superimposed) but it's the way in which we execute them, and the lyrics, which make all the difference. To use a comparison: Lou Reed writes essentially traditional songs but his interpretation of them makes them utterly unique, transcending convention. As for being mellower, slow songs are not synonymous with mellowness. The lyrics to 'Heaven' are as potent, if not more, than anything we've done in the past.

FPT: Are you bitter about the rock process? From *NME* single of the week and *Sounds* front page to total indifference.

MS: I do feel a certain amount of bitterness but it's mainly a case of sour grapes. Every artist has an ego to contend with. I am concerned more, however, with the rock press's power, or more specifically that of individual writers, to literally make or break a band. It seems that few writers these days possess objectivity; sycophancy is all too dominant. All it takes is one journalist to gush forth every conceivable superlative in a review and previously unheard-of bands are in the limelight overnight. Whether the bands in question deserve such attention is not the point; some of them undoubtedly do. But this lack of objectivity puts incredible pressure on a young band to deliver the goods quickly instead of allowing them the time to mature musically. The journalist now has the power to create a fad as opposed to just witnessing and commenting on it. The result is a change of fad every six months or so, with little or nothing of lasting worth evolving. So what's wrong with constant change? Nothing, but not when it's change for the sake of change. Nothing can grow under that pretext. The press should stop focusing on just a few bands (who wants to read the same Stray Cats article every second week?) and broaden its scope. There should also be more emphasis on grass-roots culture.

FPT: Do you hope for mass popularity?

MS: Yes, in that we want our ideas and songs to reach as many people as possible. What we don't hope for is that to achieve this we will have to water down our music and creativity, which is something we're not prepared to do. We do want mass popularity but on our terms, which means that we want to take the control over the music away from the middleman/the entrepreneur. I should add that rather than simply popularity, we would like mass ATTENTION or mass thoughtful response, if such a thing is possible.

FPT: Will APF categorically not sign to a major label, no matter what the terms, or would you settle for a 2 Tone-style autonomous agreement?

MS: When we left Virgin last year, our first reaction was 'We'll never work with a major label again', and up till now we haven't, but we realise that to dismiss something without even hearing the terms would be a blinkered thickhead thing to do. But we are so sceptical of the majors, and aware of the pitfalls and pratfalls, that it is extremely unlikely that we would work with them again, other than if it was a licensing deal for our Chicken Jazz label, which we would consider more favourably. That would give us not only the autonomy we demand but also the money to be able to put all our plans into practice.

FPT: *Jungleland* 9 seemed largely a promo exercise for APF. It used to be strong in that it was dedicated to the music. When it was unfashionable you stated a love for rock 'n' roll, Patti Smith, Springsteen, Brian Wilson, along with punk bands about whom you remained objective. Now it seems like just another fanzine. Is that fair?

MS: Quite honestly, I think the answer is NO. Isn't *Jungleland* still dedicated to the music and to creativity? Number 9 includes pieces on or to do with John Lennon (before his death, I should add), Patti Smith and TV Smith. None is particularly fashionable in the fanzine world. Taking into account the extent to which my life is involved with

Another Pretty Face, it would have been impossible to keep APF and *Jungleland* totally separate, but nowhere is there a rave review, a press clipping, an advert, a discography, a photo, or anything remotely promo-esque about APF in *Jungleland*. Just a lyric and a vague piece of info about the projected next APF single – at that time. The TV Smith, Lennon, industria, Sounds/Sid, existentialism, Sheena/Kelly, Springsteen, Patti, famine, jail guitar doors, etc. pages had nothing to do with APF at all, other than I wrote or laid out the pieces. Consider for a while how we could have filled *Jungleland* with APF news and history, reviews and photos and then ask yourself if it really WAS like a promo.

The opinion that *Jungleland* is now just another fanzine certainly isn't mine but everyone to their own; but the promo suggestion HURTS.

FPT: What do you feel about what has happened since John Lennon's death (Yoko's message to John being used as an advert for her new single)?

MS: I don't consider Yoko's message, and the use of it, cheap in any way. It's a message to the public as much as to John. No Lennon ad is placed without Yoko's permission and only the most callous observer could suggest that she of all people is cashing in on the man. Think about it – Yoko and John have regularly taken ads in world newspapers and magazines in order to communicate with the people. Did you see the one in the Sunday *Observer*? The 'Walking On Thin Ice' advert message was communication – not hard sell.

On the other hand, most of the Lennon glossies stink. But anyone can see that. What really needs said is that *Sounds* needs knocked on the head for their incredibly patronising self-righteous attitude to anyone who publicly expresses sorrow for or tribute to Lennon. I saw [Garry] Bushell stuck three Lennon songs in his godforsaken playlist for one week, the one week in the year when his tastes rose above abject thuggery and musical crap. Seventy-five per cent of *Sounds* writers should pack it in today and get jobs as bus drivers or something, they have no right to criticise. Lennon wouldn't shit on them.

FPT: Why do you do it?

MS: Because if I watch *Top of the Pops* and see such talentless no-hopers as Toyah, Duran Duran, Spandau Ballet, Adam and the Ants, etc. I feel sick and empty that people are content with such trash that has neither passion nor meaning nor even excitement. We do it because things need changed. Music needs communication, humility, hilarity and honesty. If people say to us that 'Ho! You're quick to criticise and moan! ,'we'll reply 'Yes, but we're offering an alternative and a solution.'

36

Edward Heath
'What on earth are you going to do with all these geographers?'

I graduate in 1983. I can't get a job. Some of this is due to lack of preparation. Some of it is a failure of imagination. I want to be a journalist. I don't know who to ask. I don't know any journalists. I am not going to phone anyone up and ask for help. I am the definition of someone who should not be a journalist.

But it isn't just me. There are no jobs. The university starts a scheme in which graduates can enrol for undergraduate courses and attend lectures. There is no qualification at the end of it. It is something to do. You can sign on the dole at the same time and get your rent paid. It is bloody luxury.

I sign up for Russian Literature. I read Gogol. Gogol is very good. I buy *War and Peace*. That is very heavy. The class is not taxing. After one lecture some homework is handed out. We have to place the home cities of Russian authors on a map.

The course is terrible. I stop going. But technically I am a student, so I do what I should have done four years earlier and write for the student paper. I stand for election as editor. It is a democratic process, and nothing to do with aptitude, so I team up with my philosophical friend Sean, who is charismatic and plays the guitar, and has won my eternal loyalty by giving a tolerant review to a cassette release by The Commercials. Sean is bafflingly intelligent and funny, so instead of making a speech we sing a song. Later, when seeking a second term, I find another guitar-playing co-editor, Allan, who plays in the group He's Dead Jim.

In May 1984 I do my first in-depth interview. It is with the former prime minister Edward Heath. The interview is an extraordinarily boring experience and not because of anything I do, because I hardly do anything at all. The best thing about it is the photograph I take of Heath. In the picture he sits awkwardly in a bland university room with a bare light bulb glowing above his head. His finger is in his ear, as if he is trying to dislodge a troublesome memory. On top of this I write the headline 'Did Someone Say Miners' Strike?' It is almost funny.

Why isn't the interview interesting? Because politicians. Because Edward Heath is a peculiarly old-fashioned member of that tribe. Because, unbelievably, Heath makes it a condition of the interview that he should have advance approval of the questions, to reduce the chance of anything interesting cropping up.

The in-depth interview is scheduled to last for fifteen minutes. The first of my pre-approved questions is an open invitation to the former prime minister to speculate on his greatest achievement. Something strange happens to time while Heath weighs up his options. There is so much for him to choose from. He talks as he thinks. He keeps on talking. He talks like a man in a job interview whose only flaw is his ruthless perfectionism. Time goes by and it happens quickly because I notice that I can't breathe. All the oxygen is being sucked out of the room and in my weakened state I am unable to gather the energy to interrupt the old bore.

Those minutes last for years. I observe Heath dissolving in front of me, his tireless record of accomplishment dancing past in stop-motion then reversing jerkily into further elucidation. Heath is talking into my Sony cassette recorder but I hear his words droning from the speaker of the Sanyo portable television I have in my student room, then dissolving into a crackly wireless signal, then a newsreel. I see them rendered as a poignant daub on the wall of a cave. Is he still talking? He is. We are nine minutes in and it is already 50,000 years BC.

It isn't my fault. Not entirely. There was a press conference before my meeting with Heath and the red-pudding-eating attack dogs of the *Press and Journal* had failed to prise even a hint of a news line from the old sailor. Heath was asked: 'Do you think Mrs Thatcher should intervene to help settle the miners' strike?' His reply: 'Well, I don't think it's my place to interfere on that issue.' And then the punchline. 'I do, however, think that Government should play a part in settling disputes of this kind.'

Heath does make a joke. At least it seems like a joke. He says that the answer to the nation's problems is to put him back in No. 10. It's a joke any former prime minister might make.

What does he talk about while I am having waking daydreams about Mike Yarwood's impersonation of his vibrating shoulders? The 1984 stuff, which remains The Stuff.

There is nationalism. 'We're passing through a rather bad phase where nationalist sentiments and utterances get a response,' he says. 'You can't live on a diet of this sort of thing.'

There is education. Heath said there was a limit to the number of geographers a country could actually use. 'I've got nothing against geographers but I think there is a limit.'

There is media bias: the dividing line between news and views. 'Now the whole of news is coloured by views.'

But what about those achievements? Becoming president of the Oxford Union was an early success. Holding the Conservative Party together through the Suez crisis ('a political problem, one of the things that will be noticed by history'). Winning the 1970 election: most of Heath's Conservative colleagues said they would lose. 'In fact, all of my colleagues said we were going to!' Heath is inordinately proud of abolishing Resale Price Maintenance, which led to the growth of supermarkets and perhaps fuels the ire of the grocer's daughter Mrs Thatcher. 'People have an inordinately greater variety of products open to them,' Heath says breezily.

And number one in the Heath hit parade? Taking Britain into the European Economic Community (the forerunner of the European Union). As long as Europe can overcome nationalist impulses, he said, it will thrive. 'We're passing through a rather bad phase at the moment.'

I have one question that isn't on the pre-prepared list. I chant it in my head in case I forget to ask it. Ask the question, I keep repeating to myself, as Heath defrosts in front of me. 'Do you accept that, from one election to the next, the political process is a largely unaccountable and elitist charade?' I ask.

That, says the Right Honourable Member, 'is a rather extreme view'.

37

Black
'Don't worry, there's too much time, too little of you.'

Another person who writes back to my non-existent fanzine is Colin Vearncombe, who records under the name Black.

'Nice to see something different emerging,' he writes. 'About time a lot of theoretical musicians had the chance to arise from the murk of inaudible song lyrics and see how they stand. (I don't know if I could!) Have you tried contacting Mark Smith? Do – it'd be great/grate.'

Eventually Colin sends 'The Gospel According to Black', written in marker across a sheet of stave paper.

What should the new BLACK do?
Give shivers. If it doesn't, forget it.
Make you wary of what Black should do.
Letters are good and wholesome things.
Bring you out of yourself.

A process of letting things happen – reckless in the small
things. Change is inevitable and nearly always good.
No absolutes (itself an absolute). Bright sunny smiles
(unCalifornian).
Newness, and if not, freshness.
Go for it. Don't worry, there's too much time, too little
of you. Kick once and hard (?). Let the other start it.
Everything is equally important/unimportant.
WRITE YOUR OWN BLOODY BIBLES!
Fragments leading up to something : –
Ask me in 50 years.
So much for articles.

I become pen pals with Colin for a while and watch as his career stops and starts. Ultimately Colin's work is defined by the song 'Wonderful Life', a global hit prompted by a period of unhappiness. No one notices that the singer is being ironic when he sings 'It's a wonderful, wonderful life'. The song takes on a life of its own. Black is filed alongside Sade as one of the smooth, well-produced sounds of the 1980s but if you listen hard enough Colin lives up to his manifesto. 'Wonderful Life' has everything going for it. The song lopes elegantly through a summer afternoon but it wears a false smile. Colin's best songs are as self-coruscating as anything written by Morrissey but the production emphasises something else. It hides the unease. If Colin had used different producers, he might have ended up in a different place. His early single 'More Than The Sun' sounds massive and the voice is pushed into the area of high drama once occupied by Scott Walker. Colin could have done that. But he did something else. He sent shivers. There are smiles – more sly than Californian. And 'Wonderful Life' remains a great record, though Colin came to view it as a hindrance that he had to accept. Every song that he wrote would be compared to his hit. 'You can live with a stone in your shoe,' he once said, but that doesn't mean you would choose to.

We lose touch over the years. Colin gets married, moves to Ireland, grows his hair, shaves his head, makes lots of records. I always feel shy about getting back in touch because he has had a global hit and I haven't. It's as if he lives in a different space.

In 2014, out of the blue, Colin sends me a text message. 'Loops of time, life and experience being what they are, I find myself recording the vocals and some stuff for my new album in North Berwick! Have thought of you so much from all those years ago, I couldn't NOT wave and say "Hello, old friend, how are you? Thank you for all those years ago." NB has changed much since I was last here (1988, I think, to visit some friends who were recording with Calum Malcolm and staying at the Marine Hotel!!! Lovely.) Indeed, it seems to be prospering.'

We have a brief flurry of messages. I tell Colin to ask Calum Malcolm about producing the early Postcard records because although he is famous for his work with high-sheen artists such as The Blue Nile, the producer's work with Orange Juice and Josef K often goes unnoticed.

'Asked Calum about Josef K,' Colin replies, 'and he reckons they rejected the album he made with them and made it again in Belgium. He enjoyed "Poor Old Soul" with Orange Juice the most . . . this astonished me; I'd no idea he was involved in all those Postcard records. "Poor Old Soul" was my disc of choice to sing along to as I washed dishes . . . and oh, remember "Just Like Gold" and "Mattress of Wire" before Aztec Camera became (for me) a lot less interesting?

Perhaps not glory days but worth the remembering.'

There are a few more messages. I tell Colin to look out Roddy Frame's *Surf*, for proof that the fire never went out, and we make vague, unhurried plans to meet in the future.

It doesn't happen. In January 2016 Colin's car skids on ice as he drives towards Cork airport, en route for Edinburgh, where he is planning to work with songwriter Gary Clark, of the band Danny Wilson. He never comes out of the coma.

After Colin's death I listen to an interview he did with Pete Paphides about being a one-hit wonder. He is sanguine but not entirely relaxed about the way his career was dominated by one song. He talks about trying to return to a more innocent frame of mind: 'Trying to get back to the feeling of freedom you had, when you're a boy in a sandpit. Nothing that needed doing, except building a castle.'

38

The Fall
'Hu-mil-i-a-tion! *NME* Blacklist – Number One – the Scotch guy!'

I write to The Fall. I don't know what I write. It would have been the usual thing, asking an artist I loved or respected to contribute, create, say something.

After a while Mark E Smith writes back. In the package in the stamped-addressed-envelope there is a handwritten note on a torn piece of paper: 'Would love to write a piece but have huge back-log from other promises.' Smith encloses a Xerox of some materials designed to accompany the album *Hex Enduction Hour*, saying it is safe to reproduce them 'as not many people get to see it due to Manchester regarding photocopying machines as Space-craft'. Given that the information sheet advises anyone writing to The Fall not to expect a reply, I have done well. 'The Fall are not a condescending French resistance type group,' Smith writes. 'Nor do they have warehouses packed with info kits on themselves.'

I must have sent Mark E some gifts. He thanks me for a photo of Buddy Holly on the screen of my Sanyo 12' television screen: 'received with GLEE'. In return he encloses cuttings from *Titbits* magazine. On one *Titbits* page Smith has written in block capitals 'HEREWITH COINCIDENTAL "LIE-DREAM" COME TO LIFE ALMOST'. It is a story about a robot store dummy. There is a photograph of a shop mannequin with its back cut open to reveal surveillance equipment. The story begins: 'A shapely young girl called Bionica is all set to do battle with store thieves. She looks like any other attractive store dummy. But under the latest fashions she hides a TV camera and a microphone that can pick up a shoplifter's whisper at a quarter of a mile.'

Reading *Titbits*, its prose ripe with prurient urgency and truncated grammar, the grim speculations of the supermarket tabloid come alive as pulp fantasy rendered in the voice of Mark E Smith. If MES read *Titbits* over a rumbling bass and tumbledown drums, it would be a song by The Fall. But what was that voice? What was Mark E? Not a singer, exactly, more of a proclaimer, a bingo master reading the runes. If Carlsberg made William Burroughs, and he had to shout to be heard above the din in the Wheeltappers and Shunters club, he might have sounded like Mark E Smith: urgent, fractured, certain and precise in his poetic obfuscation.

Was Mark E Smith inspired by *Titbits*? Well, the fact that he was a *Titbits* man is clear but maybe this warped reality unfolds in the other direction and *Titbits* was inspired by The Fall. The 'coincidental lie-dream come to life almost' is to be found in the song 'Lie Dream Of A Casino Soul', in which the narrator has an awake dream. 'I was in the supervision dept./Of a big town store/Security floors one to four/They had cameras in the clothes dummies.'

What about the other stories on that *Titbits* page? There's another shoplifting story, though this one is more high-rent:

'A jewellery firm's bosses have launched a counter-attack on shop thieves by using a piranha fish as a security guard'. Next to that there's a photograph of 'a well-known figure playing King Canute'. 'Normally he prefers to have a good laugh, though he's made some melancholy records too. If you're baffled, turn to page 38.' Below that: 'IT'S A FACT: An elephant's trunk can hold more than 12 pints of water.' And: 'ANGELS WHO GUARD THE TERROR TRAINS. SEE PAGE 8.'

How about the press release for *Hex Enduction Hour*? In an oddly factual sentence, the photocopied sheet promises a record 'packed with typical Fall appreciation of the good things in life, plus the usual annoying BITTY observations that keep the group well away from the over exposed minds of our time'. And: 'Satirical, humorous element of past Fall work v. underplayed because 1. they've wrung it dry 2. t.v. is riddled now with liquidified "satire" in most cases inferior to what the "satirists" are trying to take da piss out of.' There are other scrawled bits in the handwriting of Mark E Smith. There is an unexplained mention of 'Billy Bardo', which is a strange song by Johnny Paycheck. And the sentence, randomly appended: 'He explodes, then the thought was VAST IST?'

This is my best encounter with Mark E Smith. Perhaps he is better written down. There are a couple of occasions when I am supposed to interview him face-to-face but neither of those events go as planned. The first time, at Buster Browns discotheque in Edinburgh, Smith is flat out on the floor, either asleep or unconscious, it's hard to tell. I speak to the band, who are keen to say nothing. The second time, at a Glaswegian university, I am due to talk to Smith for the *NME*. Smith appears only to excuse himself, saying he has a cold. I speak to the band; they don't want to say anything. A week or two later Smith does talk to the *NME* and is briskly dismissive of keyboardist Marcia Schofield and guitarist Martin Bramah for talking to me. 'I haven't seen it,' he tells *NME*'s Andrew Collins. 'So it was Martin and Marcia, oh no! Embarrasso! I've got to see this! Marty and Marsh – oh yeah – DISASTER for the public image! Hahaha. Get me a copy quick. Hahahaha. Hu-mil-i-a-tion! *NME* Blacklist – Number One – the Scotch guy!'

There's something else.

I must have written to The Fall again. Chronologically it must have happened after Mark E Smith's letter and before the Scotch guy blacklist humiliation. I have no memory of the letter. It kills me to think about it. I can only imagine I was trying to be provocative. The Fall's bass player, Stephen Hanley, writes back. The letter is on lined paper with a margin, as if ripped from a jotter. There are five pages. 'I thought your views were naive and very misinformed,' Hanley writes. 'Probably due to reading Dave McCullough's articles too much. In his lyrics Mark points out what is wrong with the Music Scene. If people listen to what he says, how can this make it more important than it is? It's only the "STARS" who think they're important.

'Just because the people where you work haven't heard of The Fall, that doesn't mean anything. The only way they would get to hear is if we had big advertising campaigns and pushed it down people's throats. We want people who are interested enough to find out for themselves so in this aspect we are an Alternative band, but we haven't got anything in common with bands like the Banshees or Joy Division. As far as ideals go, groups like Dollar and The Nolans are entertainment for the people who want it. The Fall are obviously trying to do more than that.'

The bass player continues in this vein and the rage does not lessen. There is a slight change in the handwriting on page four, almost as if Hanley has paused before returning to the tedious task of dismissing my idiotic bleatings. 'How much money we make is none of your business,' he writes, before signing off with a flourish: 'Public Image are one of my favourite groups. Am I prolonging the preconception? THAT'S ALL. It's taken too long already.'

39

Robert Smith
'I literally despise most of the things which are possible in the world of music.'

I write to the BBC asking whether I can come and witness the filming of *Riverside*. It is a naked attempt to infiltrate the world of popular television. I feel confident that the producers of the magazine programme will quickly understand that they have a vacancy for a reticent introvert with an inflated sense of self-importance and an as-yet unpublished fanzine which demonstrates critical acuity and an acidic wit.

Or not.

Riverside is an interesting show. It is very 1980s. If *The Old Grey Whistle Test* was mid-1970s' *Melody Maker*, and *Top of the Pops* was the wild aunt of *Smash Hits*, *Riverside* is a hat-check girl at the Blitz Club reading *The Face* while Philip Glass plays a toy piano in a soundproofed kitchenette. The opening titles have a girl with burning hair emerging from a lake. She seems happy enough.

I travel to London not knowing what to expect. The filming is routine, verging on boring, until the appearance of two dancers from the Royal Ballet performing to the Cure song 'Siamese Twins'. The bonus, as *Riverside* is very much a multi-media youth club seminar, is the fact that The Cure are in the room too, playing live while Sharon McGorian and Stephen Beagley dance, and 'guest woman' Dorothy Williams watches on from a chair at the side of the stage.

What does it all mean?

Happily, or to be more accurate, unhappily, Robert Smith is to be found drinking beer in the cafe after the show. Bass player Steve Severin (on loan from the Banshees) is there too, hiding beneath a broad-brimmed hat. Severin seems to be concentrating on impersonating Lee Van Cleef in *Death Rides a Horse*. Siouxsie Sioux flits around looking spectral and intimidating.

There is something quite communal about the long tables in the canteen and Smith agrees to talk.

He has dramatic news, delivered without excitement. 'I'm not bothered about releasing records at all now,' he says flatly. 'I suppose I've begun to realise that The Cure as an idea, or as an instinct, has probably finished its useful life.'

In another time, with a different me, this would be big potatoes. The Cure Split! Hopeless Singer Abandons Hope! Old Ham Cured! At that rustic table in that performing arts corner of Hammersmith it barely registers. The combination of Smith's demeanour (weary, troubled), his persona (tortured enigma with a voice like a mating fox) and my own journalistic incompetence (dry-mouthed, deferential to the point of self-harm) make it just another downbeat observation. In the spirit of the age I wait several months to publish Smith's detonation of his career, by which time he has begun to backcomb his decision.

The *Riverside* performance is a strange diversion in the story of The Cure, to be filed alongside The Fall's collaboration with the dancer Michael Clark. What Smith meant when he suggested that his band had run its course was that the departure of bassist Simon Gallup had disturbed the ecology of the project. Gallup and Smith had fallen out as a consequence of the draining experience of playing The Cure's fourth album, *Pornography*, on tour. Years later Smith will describe his ambition to make *Pornography* 'the ultimate fuck off record'. Curators of narcissistic rock will likewise classify it as the third part of The Cure's 'gloom trilogy' – after *Seventeen Seconds* and *Faith* – though the implication that The Cure only made three frowsty albums seems oddly optimistic.

Yet here Smith is, performing in a version of The Cure that includes Severin of the Banshees and Anne Stephenson and Gini Ball of The Venomettes.

'About four months ago a couple of people from the Royal Ballet came and said they wanted to do a dance using modern music,' Smith explains, 'but not to actually put a classical ballet to it. They'd seen a lot of bands and decided that The Cure was the most adaptable to dance, and they asked if I'd be interested in writing a ballet for 1984. We were going to do a piece from it here but I thought it wouldn't work out of context because it uses a lot of dancers. I knew what this would turn out like – you never get enough time – and I didn't want it to look badly done. We had this spot anyway, so we just decided to do 'Siamese Twins' with a couple of dancers. We just did it to be a bit different. We didn't want to do it as The Cure because it isn't really The Cure, it's only me and Laurence . . .'

The Cure have many miserable songs but 'Siamese Twins' is one of the most abject, with its deathly imagery of fallen angels and worms eating flesh. On the page the words have the self-immolatory tone that would provide Morrissey with his entire oeuvre, though Robert Smith just about avoids the implication of comedic self-parody by aspiring to be Jean Cocteau rather than Jean Alexander.

'Your words are depressing,' I say to him. 'Are you really that depressed?'

'At times,' Smith replies. 'But I think so is everybody, really. The thing is that most of the music reflects just one mood, just one aspect, but it just happens that that's when I write songs. It was like a release rather than bursting into tears or drowning myself.'

'I suppose when you feel normal, you don't write songs?'

'Well, no, I think people do other things. Probably a lot of people either just retreat completely into themselves or they seek communication with other people. It's the same thing, really, just like writing songs, like I would never go up to somebody and say, "Oh! I am unhappy". I didn't used to get depressed in the normal way, I still don't. I just didn't think there was any point writing about things that I had no control over, like things that happen in the "real world". I realised again that there was little I could do about the big things that people were always talking about. I was never depressed thinking "Oh my God, life." I mean, that's so obvious there's no point singing about it. No, the bizarre thing is that I've probably had more fun in the years that I've been in the group and been able to make records than I ever had before but I would never write a happy song. I mean, probably in the last year for about seventy-five per cent of the time I've been in a really good mood but those are the

156

times when you don't write songs. Because you're happy you don't sort of think "Oh, I must go and write it down", you just get on with being happy. But when you are sad you just think "Oh God" and you do tend to write it down.'

In the aftermath of the *Pornography* tour Smith and drummer Lol Tolhurst had released the single 'Let's Go To Bed', which was considerably more playful and lightweight than anything they had done previously. In a 2004 interview with *Rolling Stone* Smith framed the record, and the subsequent series of singles that brought them international success, as an attempt to do something cheerful, and 'go from goth idol to pop star in three easy lessons'. That's not how he explains it on that day in 1983.

'I'm not sure that we should carry on – change the line-up and carry on with the name of The Cure – because it would just be trading on the name. With anything that I'm involved in I don't see why we should have trade on a name. Like that "Let's Go To Bed" single, that wasn't supposed to be a Cure single. I haven't spoken to the record company since that was released. It was supposed to go out under the name Recoil. They put it out as The Cure without telling us. They said, "Oh, we've got all the sleeves printed, we were sure you said The Cure." I hated that single.'

'Why did you bring it out if you didn't like it?'

'Because we wanted to do a Christmas single but under a name that nobody had heard of, just to see if it would get airplay. It was just an exercise in writing a pop song, really. The Cure's always been built up with what we've done before in mind. Very few people see it like that but there's always been a continuity, since *Seventeen Seconds* anyway, in what we've done. The single was so wildly out of line, plus the fact that because it was by The Cure it was immediately disregarded because people expected it to sound like The Cure. I suppose it did because of my voice but there's not a lot I can do about that.'

'Did you expect Cure fans to buy it?'

'That's why I hated it coming out under the name of The Cure, because I expect that a lot of the people did buy it because of that, and because they probably liked the majority of the stuff we'd done before. The reasons that people liked The Cure, and the reason I liked a lot of the stuff that we did, was for elements that were contained in the music that weren't there on "Let's Go To Bed". "Let's Go To Bed" was a song that The Cure would never do. It was a really cheap, tacky disco rhythm and sort of like "do do do do" and the words were completely meaningless. I was glad it never got anywhere. The record company were saying this was going to be THE SINGLE, "You might not like it but this is the one that will take you into the Top 20", but it didn't even get as high as "Hanging Garden", which was an uncommercial single.'

Smith goes on in this vein for a while, viewing an uncertain future over a half-empty pint glass. Success doesn't bother him, he says. 'I'm not bothered about releasing records at all now.' The immediate future includes playing guitar with the Banshees in Japan and on their UK tour, and he hopes to appear on a Banshees single. There is a solo album with Severin (later released as The Glove), and maybe The Cure can be revived, possibly even with Gallup. 'The whole idea of being in groups or not being in groups, it doesn't strike me as really relevant.

'If we do anything, if I did anything, it would be just to record, because I'm fed up being in a group. It's not that I'll devote my time to other things like writing a book or making a film. I just want to do normal things, which I haven't been able to do for years because I've been stuck in Australia or somewhere playing. I just want to sit at home.

'I haven't done an interview for so long I've given up trying to itemise things, trying to work out why we did them. People think you start out with some kind of ulterior motive or some kind of plan. But to be really honest, when The Cure started it was just because I didn't want to work. I just thought I could do better than most people who were making records. I would hear records and scream, so I thought "Well, I'll go and make some" and it just so happened that they sold enough for me to go and make some more. I suppose I'm losing the urge as time goes by to go and make records but when people say, "Why do you bother, why do you keep going?", I say if all the people I liked, most of whom don't sell a lot of records anyway, if they stopped I wouldn't have anything to listen to. I'd be forced to listen to whatever's number one. Men at Work.'

As cheerless conversations go, it is cheery. Smith is an amenable host, reflective and personable. Later interviews, with these events reshaped, will see this moment less onanistically – more of a rebirth than a little death.

'I literally despise most of the things which are possible in the world of music,' says Smith that day at Riverside. 'It would be a real freak if The Cure had ever had a hit single. "A Forest" was about the closest. If we'd released it two years later we could have been Tears for Fears.'

He doesn't have to spell it out. Even for a man in the midst of abandoning ship, being Tears for Fears is not an aspiration.

40

Billy MacKenzie
'We wanted to be part of a beautiful world.'

B illy MacKenzie didn't have a manager. 'I looked after myself,' he said. 'I was unmanageable.'

I interviewed him twice. On both occasions he was coming back. Coming back from record company shenanigans, easing himself into the light, biting his tongue about the compromises he had been forced to endure. On both occasions he gave the impression that there were things he could say, things which would make matters clearer, things that might make things worse. 'That's for another time,' he would chirp. 'I could say more.'

This reticence was surprising because taciturnity was not one of MacKenzie's more obvious traits. In conversation he was always reaching, always trying to charm, mostly succeeding. In 1988, coming back from a four-year furlough, he said he had 'hit a few curves, where I thought I was going mad with inactivity, like Henry VIII'. The reason for the delays was his record company's insistence that he wait for the right collaborator, the right studio, the right whatever.

It was like being Boris Becker, Billy said, and being told you couldn't compete for another three Wimbledons.

In 1992 the singer was finally freed from the record deal he compared to an eight-year sentence in an open jail. 'Can you imagine [Rangers striker] Ally McCoist not being able to play football for three months of the year and sitting on the sidelines while all his pals are out there playing?' he said. 'It would drive you demented. I used to get this inner rage. I didn't ever want to take it out on anyone, it was more out on myself. Because I thought, "You make your bed, you fucking lie in it."'

There were other similarities between 1988 and 1992, notably MacKenzie's hope that his music would finally speak for itself. But the truth of the years after MacKenzie split from his musical partner in The Associates, Alan Rankine, was that he had struggled to find a foil who could make full use of his mercurial talent. Boris Blank of Yello came close, adding majestic electronics to MacKenzie's voice. Others satisfied the singer's competing instincts, whether they were jazzy, poppy, experimental or camp: or more likely a mélange of all of that, jumbled.

MacKenzie had recipes, mostly with ingredients that other musicians hadn't dared to mix. Billie Holiday, Ennio Morricone, Sparks, special sauce. Why not? At the core of his arguments with his record company was MacKenzie's idea of the music inside his head. 'I'm much more Kraftwerk than Simply Red,' he told me. 'I don't make music for bored housewives, I really don't, and they shouldn't be bored in the first place.'

I mentioned a remark made by Bono of U2 that Kraftwerk were a great soul band. 'Well,' Billy replied, 'he said that ten years after everyone else came to that conclusion.'

Lyrically, MacKenzie suggested he was 'a space age cowboy'. What was he singing about? That was disguised but also obvious. It's there in the title of The Associates' best song, their biggest hit, 'Party Fears Two', which manages to be a joyous celebration of one man's fear of engaging with another human. The singer is the party. The singer is the fear.

We met at MacKenzie's grand apartment in a converted hospital in Auchterhouse, outside Dundee. It had been a respiratory hospital for children and now it was a respite. The building was shielded by trees, bombarded by birdsong. Most obviously it wasn't London, because Billy had been there. He had done that. It wasn't Dundee either. The MacKenzies were a notable clan in Dundee but Billy's attitude towards his hometown was on the cool side of ambivalent. Auchterhouse was geographically nowhere, a place defined by its distance from everywhere else.

This was the pre-mobile phone era. The singer, famously, didn't have a landline. Which didn't explain the telephone in his lounge. 'Heh heh,' Billy said with a smirk. 'The thing is,' he explained, 'after the Dundee experience of laying myself open . . .'

Just like that, Billy MacKenzie started to talk. Evidently he had things that he wanted to say and only some of them were about his new record, the sampler of which had been withdrawn at MacKenzie's request. (The four songs sounded like the album the record company wanted. The songs not on the tape sounded like the album MacKenzie had in mind. 'I've had to compromise,' he said, with reflexive dismay.)

'All through my twenties,' Billy MacKenzie said brightly, 'I was working towards [becoming] somebody that I thought I knew. Money couldn't have given me that. I could have stayed the night with a few people and made it all right for myself.' He laughed. 'That sort of thing happens. In music.

'Sometimes it was hard. Sometimes I felt like knocking myself out, like throwing myself down an escalator in a shopping mall. I could get that frustrated at times. I didn't have a partner throughout the 1980s to help bear the frustrations. Annie [Lennox] had Dave [Stewart]. Siouxsie had her band [the Banshees]. Ian McCulloch had his band. [Echo and the Bunnymen]. I was a bit on my own.

'A lot of people didn't understand the mood swings. Hence, that's why I'm here. If I would ever get wound up, I would just come to the country. I'd stay here and walk it off. I wasn't wanting to project that onto anybody. And I wasn't wanting to be in a relationship. I wasn't like a tortured artist at all but I certainly know what frustration's like. And it's given me an understanding of people who haven't got that release and run away. I can see why they're taking drugs, why they're violent, because frustration brings that out. You want to just crack up.'

On this second visit to Auchterhouse, in 1992, I have arrived with Adam, the *Scotland on Sunday* photographer. Adam is a no-nonsense snapper. His sessions rarely last longer than a sixtieth of a second. He had Charlie Watts of The Rolling Stones in a room and was given fifteen minutes. He left with fourteen minutes to spare. But it is potentially awkward. There are two of us, and one Billy, sat in a triangle around a salver of sandwiches. For a confessional, it is odd geometry.

I ask MacKenzie what he means when he talks about laying himself open in Dundee.

'Not being macho and secretive,' he says. 'Being a human being and speaking about normal things, like how

I felt, emotions. That was the thing: you weren't meant to be emotional. You were meant to be an emotional retard if you were to survive Dundee in the seventies. You were allowed to exist on a physical level but not on an emotional level. I would have got on better if I had got six girls pregnant, battered a few of them and basically was an ogre. I think I would have fitted in.'

He suggests that music is a form of therapy, 'seeing that I come from the type of background that I do: a working-class Dundonian who basically thought he was thick and couldn't do anything just because I was dictated to by people who had a more fortunate education. That was my main thing, I thought I was a failure because I didn't get an O-level mathematics.

'Of course, when I was twelve or thirteen I always thought that to write music you had to be intelligent and it's really nothing to do with that. It's mostly intuition and feel, and experience gathered.'

By the age of sixteen Billy had decided that music was his future. He moved to Los Angeles on 'a kind of odyssey'.

Even in retrospect this seems like an extreme move. Why did he do it?

'Well, why not, you know? I just thought, phwoah! I have to go there because I was attracted to entertainment. Not in a Butlins's fashion! It was mostly about music and I was going to do the trek throughout America. Really, I was forced to because there was nothing here for me. I was an alien. I was out of my depth with the college set and I wasn't about to go roaming the streets in gangs looking for some poor victim to pummel. I just hated it. It made my life a misery. It was hellish. I had a lot of older friends for company, even grannies. I used to go to the pub with a couple of older women, about fifty. They were hilarious. I didn't like a lot of the young people. I was forced to leave. I was so claustrophobic and so upset not to have teenage years that were just relaxed, without having to look over your shoulder, without having to put on a front psychologically and physically. It was really difficult. Plus having this opinion of myself that I was stupid because I didn't have a mathematics O-level.'

Did he sing in America? 'No. I had a wee band and we were doing great Gary Glitter covers. It was kind of the Gary Glitter stomp and the glam thing. It was very glammy. Tinged with soul. And the background was kind of jazz. It was quite a strange mixture. So that was that.'

He also got married in Las Vegas, an event he plays down as 'teenage frivolity, frolicking nonsense'. The marriage lasted 'about four and a half months. It was an education. I mean, some people's marriages only last three days.

'It was all kind of wild and Tarzan and beaches and hot nights. And just hilarity. I must admit I wasn't a very serious teenager. I didn't have acne spots, erection problems. My teenage years were wonderful to a certain degree. The only thing that marred them was living in that violence. It's akin to what's happening in Glasgow now. I had friends carved up and it just really blew my mind. Especially when you were a fun-loving type of teenager and didn't like seeing people either psychologically attacked or put down. People that had these inbred superiority complexes. Basically they were brainwashed by their parents but they believed they were better than people from the wrong side of town. I was from the wrong-est side of town.'

When Billy returned to Dundee he fell back in with his own 'wee gang'. They were mostly girls. 'I had girl friends.

I mean friends. There wasn't any slap and tickle. I cherished their opinions and they had a certain aesthetic. We didn't know what it was at the time because we dressed nice and we liked nice things. We liked gabardine. We were considered oddballs and if it was the sixteenth century they would have been burnt at the stake for being witches. It was that cruel.'

Musically, things were developing. 'Sparks came on the go. The American group who everyone thought were from Europe. I just thought they were fantastic. A real breath of fresh air. We kinda Sparksed out for a while. We used to go downtown but before we went downtown we planned our escape routes. The way we used to dress had a Deaf School/ Roxy Music element. The girls would be movie starlets, not quite Jane Russell. But they were very exotic. We used to have to flee places and we had our backs up against the wall. We had to learn how to be very agile, to avoid missiles.'

There is a pause. Some birdsong. Adam takes a sandwich. 'These sannies,' he says, sensing the void. 'I can't help myself.'

'But once again the violent thing soured the event,' says Billy, oblivious. 'It should be an event, your teenage years. It should be everybody's big event. So that was that.'

MacKenzie and two of the girls fell in with a couple of older musicians from the college set. The girls were Angie and Pat. 'One was like Twiggy, the other was like Marie Helvin. So it was not bad, one on each arm. Of course, there was all the slights about "You're a sissy" and all these things. One to one, I could manage myself, but I just wasn't into it.

'We wanted to be part of a beautiful world. We really did.'

MacKenzie went to London and 'bounced around' for a year before returning to Dundee and starting to trade in vintage clothes. 'I advertised for opera clothes, fans, silver-fox capes, and I got a little shop and I started selling that to what would be, eight years on, new romantics, but they were new romantics in 1975, in Dundee.'

The shop was called The Crypt, based on *The Addams Family*, with coffins, and piranhas in fish tanks. It closed with a champagne party when MacKenzie discovered dishonesty among his staff. By this time he had met his musical partner, Alan Rankine. 'He was like me, he was fun and hated coarseness. We weren't sissies or anything. We liked people to enjoy theirselves but we were not . . . aggressive types. He couldn't come to Dundee 'cause he used to come off the train and say, "Oh, the Dundee eye." He used to go through the town not wanting to look at anybody 'cause he thought they were Gorgon-ish. If you looked at anybody, you'd get turned to stone. They used to pierce you: the Dundee pierce. And the way that he looked, he was ready for the guillotine too. He used to bring his girlfriend through and she used to outdo Madonna. She used to wear swimming costumes with ripped Greta Garbo-like dresses, and beads. She used to flounce through the town. So we were setting ourselves up for it.'

The glory and the excesses of the MacKenzie/Rankine-era Associates are well documented but the mood of hedonism seems entirely in keeping with the opulent unpredictability of the music they made together.

I ask MacKenzie: when you were working with Alan, did you live to excess?

'We always used drink as a laugh, you know? It wasn't melancholic. It was more exuberant. Before we went down to London we used to go to this pub and drink these space-age cocktails. We used to put two measures of crème de menthe, a measure of vodka, two Bacardis and all these other things so that it would bubble up like something from a science lab. It was more of a laugh. So when we went down there [to London], there was still that wild carry-on. We didn't fit into the London set up, it was all reserved and stiff upper lip and all that kind of crap. We were kind of revellers. We were ravers. We did take some drugs but I always viewed them not as drugs . . . Drugs to me were things that got you out of yourself. Drugs made me look inward. And I didn't like that. So to me they were toxics. Someone would say, "Do you want to do this or do that?" I used to say, "Don't do drugs, drugs do you." "The high's a lie."

'It was more the drink. And drink's really dangerous when it's overdone, isn't it? There was really wild parties and there were rubber-clad women with whips, and all that kind of stuff.'

'Magic!' says Adam.

'And some rock and roll element. We could be as wild as anybody. Although I didn't like the carcass that got left. I didn't like when I had to sweep myself off the floorboards. I've not got a very strong constitution, plus at that time I had a dodgy ileocecal valve. What it means is that it doesn't get rid of toxins very easily. I was going around in a poisoned haze. It wisna very nice, actually. I was a bit of a human ashtray for a while. To tell the truth, I was disgusted by myself. I never used to eat, I was two stone lighter than I should have been. Some people loved it when you were twenty-two and you had these dark circles like you were really sort of glamorous . . . but I just thought, "What a dog."

'When Nick Cave would take drugs and maybe get a bit smacked-out and that would give him credibility, I always thought: "I want it to come from me, not via something else." I always thought it was cheating. I wanted to use my own magic.'

MacKenzie stopped working with Alan Rankine, "cause I was getting really destructive. If I'd carried it on, potentially . . . we didn't know what could have happened. Also, seven years. Late '75 to '82. If there was another cycle, I don't think we could have carried it off with the same generosity. Also, all through that period we really, really liked each other. I didn't really like Alan carrying on in a self-destructive manner, so I had to stop it.'

It's difficult, listening to MacKenzie talk so openly about his inhibitions, to marry the image with the version of the charming man who dazzled so effortlessly on *Top of the Pops*. For longer than a moment Billy was a brilliant pop star. I ask him whether had a showbiz streak in his character.

'If I was more confident in my twenties, possibly. But certain things I was quite shy about. I feel that I wasn't able to say the things that I really wanted to say because I didn't have the experience that I thought I needed. I thought that, musically, I was quite advanced.' He pauses. 'You had to intellectualise in the seventies and eighties. Having this opinion that I was a thicko and was silly, and I never went to Gordonstoun so I must be an invertebrate . . . a lot of people did think that, if they just went to a normal comprehensive school.

'You had to talk about these things. You had to be political. You had to know obscure Russian literary geniuses. I just knew Oor Wullie kept me happy. Saying that, I love programmes about abstract art and European theatre. I do. But I was a wee laddie brought up on a housing scheme. Although, I never lived there in my head. I lived in the subways of Paris.

'I hated it, I intensely hated it. I wasn't a snob . . . when I went to the housing estate I stayed in for four years. My life

169

from when I was eight until I got the first tickly sensations would have made Morrissey's look like a BBC light entertainments programme. I would get up an hour early to go to the other end of town to my old school. I wouldn't go to the school down the road. Emotionally I was in suspended animation. Even then I was wanting to change everything. To beautify things. I thought, "It's ugly, the architecture's boring." Things in the house, I hated. It was kind of this inner balance that was put out of synch. And I had that as a child. I had a visual equilibrium. I suppose that's why I wanted to escape to Hollywood because I saw it through films. I thought, "I'll maybe get it back if I go there."'

The conversation swirls round for a while, with MacKenzie kaleidoscoping between memories of past slights and the dizzy feeling of optimism he is trying to project. 'What brought me to the attention of the public in the first place was the element of surprise,' he says. 'I don't want to be innovative to be different, I want that because I never dream the same dream twice.'

I ask him to define what makes a great song. 'Heightened . . .' he says. 'Listening to a track and getting a natural high. You don't need to take ecstasy, you don't need to take cocaine. I get high from music. It's naturally narcotic. When I was about four or five I used to believe in magic. There's that kind of element – it's kind of magic-y. I used to think that the leprechauns that were on *Bonanza* were real. I wanted one and I used to look in the coal cellar for them every night. The leprechauns would come into my home. Every night between five and seven I was enchanted. And I still thought I could hear Santa Claus on the roof of the house when I was twelve. I knew but I still heard reindeers.'

Billy's voice has dropped to a whisper. Music, he says, has 'been my salvation. It sculpted me. I'm back again to what I was like before I started off on this odyssey. I'm like a fourteen-year-old with wisdom. I was a really gathered guy and I hadn't had the corruptions of adult life. I was a kind of man-child. I think I've always retained that. I'm not going to be a forty-year-old who has a menopause and has to grow up. I don't think I'll ever grow up. I don't want to grow up.'

41

Red Wedge
'You're not bothered by the answer unless it's the one that you want.'

I have a promotional photograph somewhere of Billy Bragg brushing shoulders with Neil Kinnock. It's hard to say which of them looks more delighted. The photo of the Bragg–Kinnock alliance was handed out with the press kit at the Edinburgh concert by Red Wedge, a collective of musicians attempting to mobilise what used to be called 'the yoof' against prime minister Margaret Thatcher.

The press conference at the Edinburgh Playhouse was a starry event in a dull room. Bragg was there, of course, flanked by Paul Weller and Mick Talbot of The Style Council, along with Tom Robinson, Junior Giscombe (number 7 in 1982 with 'Mama Used To Say'), plus Jimmy Somerville and Richard Coles of The Communards. The running-dog lackeys of the global media were in attendance. The BBC filmed a couple of quick questions and departed. That left me, representing the *North Edinburgh News* (the newspaper of the Greater Pilton area), the man from the *Gorgie-Dalry*

172

Gazette, the pop critic of *The List*, the man from the Wester Hailes *Sentinel* (aka 'the bard of Wester Hailes') and a few others I didn't know personally but whose circulations were modest, if not imaginary. Was the *Tollcross Times* there? It surely was. The *Tollie* never missed a trick. The *Leith Leader*? Possibly. None of us was skilled enough at press conferences to follow the protocol whereby questioners introduce themselves.

How did it end up with Mick Talbot and Paul Weller standing up to forcefully discuss the wisdom of my questioning before being physically restrained by Billy Bragg? Would I have been assaulted by the knitwear-loving poseurs if not for the strong arm of the Bard of Barking? Perhaps. A detailed study of the events reveals that I emerge with less saintliness than I once imagined. But I am not the only wanker in the room.

The event begins, as well-intentioned but futile left-wing events must, with a torrent of procedural tedium. The chair is a man from the Labour Party, or possibly the unions, but certainly an individual well-schooled in the modest business of holding the floor at consciousness-raising events. Throughout the meeting he will interrupt by announcing a 'point of order'.

First, the Man from the Party delivers a short history of Red Wedge. What is it? The famous supporters in the room will all have different ideas but the organisation grew from Billy Bragg's Jobs for Youth tour. It worked alongside Labour's Jobs for Industry campaign, from which came some informal meetings and some frank exchanges . . . and so it goes on. There are sexy namedrops for Labour general secretary Larry Whitty and Tom Sawyer, the deputy general secretary of the National Union of Public Employees. 'No act on the tour is getting paid,' says the Man from the Party righteously, 'everyone is getting £10 a day out-of-pocket expenses.'

On the political content of the evening, the Man from the Party notes: 'There is not one single act who will go onstage tonight and indulge in crass electioneering and go out here and say "Vote Labour". What they're asking young people to do is to get involved in politics and to look at the issues. Let's face it, politics is peripheral to most people's lives but a lot of people realise that the left has failed to communicate their ideas to people.'

To summarise: Red Wedge is an organisation backed by the Labour Party and NUPE with the aim of getting young people to elect a Labour government but it is not part of the Labour Party and its supporters will not urge people to vote Labour. Instead they will urge them to 'get involved' and 'look at the issues'.

The floor is opened for questions.

A woman asks: 'Are there any women on the tour at all?'

'Yeah,' says the Man from the Party, unfazed. 'There's Lorna Gee, who for some bizarre reason has not appeared in a lot of the press. She's a black reggae artist.'

'Is she performing tomorrow?' asks the woman.

'Oh yeah,' he says. 'She's performing on the whole of the tour. And also Sarah Jane, who sings with The Communards. Women have been approached and . . .'

'But when I saw the billing it was all men,' says the woman.

'I'd just like to make that clear,' the Man from the Party says to the woman, 'Lorna Gee is on the bill. All press material coming out from Red Wedge office had Lorna Gee on it. For some reason people printing posters locally for whatever ridiculous reason have actually not put her name on there. We're actually a bit annoyed by that.'

It is not the best start but at least we have clarified that any mistakes will have been made by the press and local organisers. Another man emerges from the shadows to point at 'Tiny, over there, who has press kits with all the biogs on them'. She is also, it transpires, a woman.

Now that the woman's question about women has been sorted, the press conference proper begins with a question from the Bard of Wester Hailes, who wants to know whether Red Wedge is part of a tradition, or a new phenomenon. Billy Bragg suggests it is 'a continuation of popular music helping out socialism'. He mentions Victor Jara in Chile.

The Bard of Wester Hailes is sceptical, noting that pop 'has the stereotype of rebels without a cause'.

'Well,' says the Bard of Barking, 'I've always been disappointed that popular music has traded on being very radical while not actually coming up with anything apart from a few postulations.'

'What's that mean?' says someone in the rear.

'Postulations,' says Billy. 'I'm not sure. I think it might mean something that grows on your barnet. It is a step in the right direction. It's been coming for a long time. I don't see why we should be afraid of following the folk tradition.'

The Bard of Wester Hailes, in the folk tradition, holds the floor. Eventually he fixes on Paul Weller. 'Paul Weller,' he says, leading into a leading question. 'You'd be considered a pop star. Would you say people should aspire to be pop stars or build up the Red Wedge community from the bottom?'

'I don't understand the question, to be honest,' says Paul Weller. 'You mean what should they be? I don't get that part.'

'The John Lennon thing,' says the Bard of Wester Hailes. 'A working-class hero's the thing to be. People of my generation would look to John Lennon, or people aspired to be that. There seems to be a bigger groundswell of talent getting hived off. You can go to a local pub any night of the week and see somebody that can sing as well as yourself or Billy. But their dream is to become that sort of pop star. Are you trying to do away with that image?'

Paul Weller looks grumpy. Grumpier than usual. 'It depends what you do with it, really,' he says, cheerlessly. 'I don't know about the whole thing of being pop stars. It sounds a bit funny to me, really. A bit antiquated. I dunno. I think most people here just consider themselves to be musicians, really. I don't think any of us consider ourselves pop stars.'

'I suppose we've had some amount of success,' says Jimmy Somerville of The Communards, a pop group named after the revolutionary supporters of the 1871 Paris Commune. 'And I suppose we've actually been allowed to become pop stars. None of us act like pop stars. We don't actually think of ourselves as pop stars.'

The Bard of Wester Hailes's attack on pop stardom has soured the mood a little. I want to ask a question. The question I want to ask is: how can an organisation named after a Soviet Constructivist lithograph in which the red wedge symbolises the triumph of the Bolsheviks in the Russian civil war, in which the only criterion for membership is fame, hope to inspire the disenfranchised, the disillusioned or the vast constituency of the merely don't-cares? Instead I ask about the ticket prices and whether the organisation is considering doing shows in peripheral housing schemes rather than city centre venues. Jimmy Somerville replies that he had wanted to do that in Glasgow but there were problems. The Style Councillors are by now quite agitated. Both Mick Talbot and Paul Weller stand up and lurch towards me. Mick Talbot looks especially aggrieved and has the look of a man about to make a Constructivist point of order pertaining to my facial features. Paul Weller's grumpiness has tripped beyond the sullen poutiness you might encounter on an album cover by the Modern Jazz Quartet into something more direct. In this moment I start to feel like the unfortunate hero of The Jam's 'Mr. Clean', whose life must be fucked up for the punk rock crimes of enjoying toast and having a job.

Happily The Style Council are hauled back by Billy Bragg and the Man from the Party interjects with a point of order, detailing the full rundown of concessions, and the interesting fact that the National Union of Public Employees has distributed tickets to Youth Training Scheme trainees. They don't even need to have a UB40 card to get a discount.

'He's not even listening,' murmurs Mick Talbot.

'You copping this?' says Billy Bragg.

'Are you not bothered about the answer, unless it's the one that you want?' says Paul Weller. 'It's not the one you want, so you're not bothered.'

'I am interested in the answer,' I say, startled by the fury of the modernist pop duo fronted by my (now former) teenage hero.

'Oh good,' says Paul Weller, perhaps sarcastically.

'My point is about participation of people,' I say, 'and if people can't afford to participate, how are they going to be approached by Red Wedge?'

It's fair to say that things are not improved by my attempts to explain. Bragg tries to calm the mood by suggesting that future Red Wedge events may be more involved in the communities. 'It's to do with refining what the Labour Party and the Arts Council – who get a lot of the money from central government – define as art. A lot of people don't think that pop music is art. I don't think it's art particularly but I think it's something that's worth encouraging. A means of expression for a lot of people, more people than express themselves through writing operas and writing ballets.'

'Spandau Ballets,' says Mick Talbot.

'Spandau Ballets, yeah,' says Billy Bragg.

By this point, I am bewildered. That is the only excuse I have for my next question.

'Do you think there's a danger in mixing something serious like politics with something trivial like pop music?'

'Well,' Billy Bragg says, 'people have been mixing something as serious as pop music . . . Sorry! Something as serious as politics . . .'

'I think that's the right way round,' says Mick Talbot.

'Yeah,' says Billy Bragg, 'and making serious amounts of money out of it. Just by mixing the two and doing nothing about it except sitting back. This is an attempt to come clean after all these years and maybe throw some of our contemporaries into a different light by showing them to be just, you know, posing.'

Paul Weller joins in. 'But also I don't think it's fair to say . . . what was the word that you used . . . pop music is trivial? I mean, I don't think that's true at all. This tour has proven to me how influential pop music is.'

My friend Alan, from the *Gorgie-Dalry Gazette*, interjects. 'How influential is it, then?'

Paul Weller replies: 'I think the fact that we've drawn all these people in the halls and actually got those people talking, taking the literature away with them, taking the whole thing quite seriously. I think that shows how powerful it is.'

'Is it not worrying that people can be swayed politically by pop music?' I say.

'I don't think they're being swayed,' says Weller.

Tom Robinson of the Tom Robinson Band interjects. 'Are you suggesting that if somebody got up on the stage and said, "Suppose everybody goes out of the hall and jumps under a taxi" they'd all do it because they'd be so easily swayed?'

'No,' I reply, a little testily now. 'I'm suggesting there's a complex web of needs and desires in pop music and people are influenced by fashion.'

'We're not exactly appealing at the fashionable end, are we?' says Billy Bragg. 'All the parties represented here, in our lyrics we all show a slant towards more socially-aware lyrics. So people who buy our records are probably a bit different to people who buy at the more trivial end of the market.'

The chat goes on like this for some time, with the pop stars arguing that they are using the influence that they don't possess to persuade people to engage with 'the issues'. Some of the pop stars hope to change the Labour Party, others seem more focused on changing the electorate. The Communards make a decent argument for gay rights.

Someone asks Paul Weller why he's sitting beneath a Labour Party banner when he previously urged people to vote Conservative.

'I've had this one at every press conference,' Paul Weller replies. 'I still will be voting Tory next time.'

'He's a mole,' says Billy Bragg. 'Central Office sent him down.'

The woman asks again why there aren't more women involved.

'Lorna, would you like to answer that question?' says Billy Bragg.

'I can't answer that,' says Lorna. 'You'd have to ask Neil or Paul.'

42

Shane MacGowan
'I don't give a damn if the bomb goes off right now.'

S hane MacGowan has a question. 'What religion are you?'

'Nothing, really,' I reply.

'Only a fucking Protestant would say that,' says Shane.

It is a sign that my interview with the singer of The Pogues is not going smoothly. There will be other clues.

The Pogues are in Glasgow to record a tune or two for *Halfway to Paradise*, a Channel 4 culture show presented by an actor pretending to be a bingo caller. This character's name is Mr Sinclair and he is, it says here, 'more Sydney Devine than Magenta Devine'. The unsuitable presenter is an effort to shake up the parameters of British broadcasting while also addressing the unsolvable problem of how to present pop culture on TV without looking like an arse.

But none of that that seems to be bothering the band. It is two p.m. in a studio in the shadow of Celtic Park (aka Paradise) in Glasgow's East End and The Pogues are getting in the mood. Shane, it must be said, could be more welcoming. His pallor is mortuary-grey and there are cigarette burns on his forearms. He wears Wayfarer sunglasses, a checked shirt and a badge which reads: 'You piss me off, you fucking cunt.'

Is there a moment when things go wrong? There is. It is the moment when Shane waves a bottle of tequila at me and rasps: 'Would you like a real drink? Would you like something interesting?' I decline because I don't drink and am allergic to interesting things. 'You don't drink?' says Shane, appalled. 'Well, that explains everything. So you're a cynical little bastard 'cause you don't drink. Well, that's a pity. You might as well be a priest.'

It is not, perhaps, the ideal place to start. But it is also the only place, which is a shame, as it overshadows the great artistry of The Pogues and MacGowan's brilliance as a lyricist. On their 1988 album *If I Should Fall From Grace With God* the group presented a startling musical hybrid, a cut-and-shut of Joe Strummer, Ennio Morricone and Kurt Weill speeding into the London Irish punk energy of their earlier, more traditional works.

I try to say this to Shane but he cuts me off. 'It's not different styles to me,' he complains. 'If you go to a Greek restaurant in London, you hear everything. Basically they're the same thing with different haircuts.'

The drink incident, it seems, is not resolved.

'All right,' coughs Shane. 'I'll tell you what I think about drink and I'll also tell you what I think about people who fucking moralise and lecture about fucking drink. They're full of shit, man. Yeah? If people wanna drink, they wanna drink, right? It's better than fucking . . . you know . . . It's better than spending all your time making people bloody miserable, going around . . .'

Shane's flow is interrupted by his bandmate, tin whistle player Spider Stacy, who waves a packet of fags. 'Would you like a cigarette, Shane?' he says. 'Do you have a light, please?'

But the soliloquy continues.

'Who cares who drinks anyway? What's it got to do with anybody except the person involved?'

With this, MacGowan slips into a conversation with the show's director, leaving Spider to face the questions. Still playing the diplomat, Spider suggests that, journalistically, the drinking angle has been overplayed with regard to The Pogues.

'We're adults,' he says. 'We drink. Most adults do. I think that the people who like us don't like us because they see us as loveable drunks. You don't have to be a genius to see that we're normal, intelligent human beings. You want a bit of colour in, obviously. But when it just goes on and on about the one thing all the time it's a bit unimaginative. It's a bit like going for the easiest tag or whatever,' he says, burping.

Booze, of course, is only one element in the formula that makes Pogues live events such festive affairs. Hugely popular in Glasgow, their shows in that city are a good-natured riot of Irish flags and Celtic songs. It's not something they court, Spider claims.

'I'd hate to be bracketed as a sectarian band. Words cannot express the contempt I have for that kind of attitude. But I can see why people do it and there isn't anything wrong with people doing it as long as they're not doing it in a way that's going to make people feel threatened or like they're under attack. There's been times when the audience has been singing the Celtic song, you know – "It's a grand old team to play for" – and I thought, "I wouldn't like to be a Rangers supporter down in the middle of that." But then again, there's probably loads of Rangers supporters down there and because they're not seeking confrontation and not wearing their colours it's OK.'

I suggest that the Pogues crowds tend to be largely male too, hence the football energy. 'There's more truth to that over here,' he says, 'but if you see us in the States or Europe . . . Even here it's much more true of certain towns than others. It's rubbish, really. There are certain times when it seems like that. In Japan it was noticeable that there were more women than men.

'If we appear sectarian, it's to people who are too fucked up to see otherwise. No one could seriously consider us as a Republican band. When we get Irish flags, that's nothing to do with sectarianism. It's because they identify with us because of the sort of music we play and because of the whole attitude. But we're not like The Wolfe Tones. There's no room for manoeuvre at all with The Wolfe Tones – they simply are a Republican band.'

On hearing this Shane decides to re-enter the conversation. Inevitably the talk turns back to ecumenical matters.

'What religion are you, Shane?' I ask.

'Catholic. Lapsed.'

'What has it left you with?'

'Nothing.'

'No guilt?'

'No guilt. I got rid of it recently.' He spits out a laugh like an arrow of phlegm then looks anxious as Spider gets up to leave the room.

Shane opens a beer. 'I fucking hate puritans, man. Particularly self-righteous ones,' he says.

Things falls apart, quickly.

'What are you fucking on about?' Shane demands. 'Why are you on about drinking? Why give me the fucking hassle? Why give me the aggro?'

'It's not self-righteousness,' I protest. 'There's no disapproval on my part.'

'Oh, bloody great,' he says. 'I'll have another one. I didn't ask you for a moral judgement on whether I drink or not.'

'You implied I was making one,' I say.

'You fucking started it,' he replies.

'You brought it up just now when I was talking about something else.'

'You were talking about sectarianism and you just told me you're not interested in religion.'

And so it goes on, with Shane eventually relenting and confessing – or perhaps just suggesting – that he believes in 'something derived from' what is normally meant by God. It transpires he's a Taoist, though he and the now-returned Spider pause to disagree over the small print of Eastern metaphysical dichotomies. Tao, explains Shane, is 'like the life force, like yin and yang. It's just balance. A never ending . . . whatever. We're all part of it.'

'Does Tao make moral judgements?' I ask.

'Course not,' Shane says.

'Do you believe in right and wrong?'

'Yeah.'

'What is wrong?'

'What's unnatural.'

'Isn't that a matter of opinion? Some people would say homosexuality is unnatural.'

'It's not.'

Sensing the impending breakdown of diplomatic relations, Spider intervenes again. 'You can just study nature and it's very easy to see what is unnatural. Murder is unnatural but killing isn't. No animal will wantonly kill another but an animal will kill to eat or will kill in the course of defending territory. Human beings are far more complex than that, so what to an animal is defending territory covers a whole range of things for human beings.'

'But human beings,' continues Shane, 'have gone beyond natural killing a long time back. They don't hunt, which is natural. All animals that kill hunt and they have nothing to help except instinct and skill. But human beings kill the same way as they organise industry. It's disgusting how they kill animals.'

'It all stems down to humanity's fundamental divorce from the world around,' says Spider, slightly self-consciously, as Shane contends that 'machines are unnatural'.

Spider disagrees, saying that though machines themselves are OK, the uses to which they are put are not. 'I'm talking about the actuality of the machines,' Spider says, 'the way they are now. Animals take thousands, millions of years to evolve their skills, but human beings have unnaturally blocked out their skills and instincts and use machines instead.'

The band is called to the stage to play. They display remarkable control, with Shane chewing gum as he sings and swaying on the microphone stand. The song is a lament, so the blurriness in the diction is excusable, appropriate even.

Back in the dressing room Shane's ire is undimmed. 'Books. Drink. Sectarianism. Machines. Ecology. What are you talking to me about ecology for?' he asks.

'You brought it up,' I say, 'and this ecological bent isn't something that comes out in your music.'

'There isn't an ecological bent,' he says. 'This is ecology. Look – there's fucking air out there and it's coming in here.

This is a building. You're a fucking human organism. What ecological bent?'

I try to explain to Shane that I meant no more than to suggest he was concerned about the future of the planet and the way people behaved towards each other.

'Listen,' he says, 'I don't give a damn if the bomb goes off right now. I'm used to that. It doesn't even worry me, I just want to go quick. But when I look at people who are even slightly younger than me who haven't sussed how heavy it is I just think, fucking hell, I don't want these people to have it happen to them. It's not an ecological bent, it's the fucking future of the world. That's what I mean by ecology.'

Again the conversation descends into personal insults.

'You don't seem very comfortable talking about yourself, Shane,' I suggest.

He lurches forward with a Lydon-esque leer. 'It's just boring, totally irrelevant fucking questions and being judged by some prat in the paper.'

'I wasn't judging you.'

'Thank you very much for not judging us, man.'

'Why are you so aggressive?'

'Because you're a cunt. I'm not aggressive.'

'What do you call that, then?'

'You arrogant fucking fucker. Why should you even think of judging us?'

Spider, ever the calming influence, interrupts again. 'Why shouldn't he if he wants to? You've judged him. You've sat there and called him every name under the sun. I think he's got every right to judge us.'

Momentarily chastened, Shane demurs. 'All right. I'm sorry. Judge me.'

Spider laughs. 'Guilty,' he says.

43

Paul McCartney
'I still haven't worked out how
to do it.'

I am sent to ask Paul McCartney a question. It is for an article on love songs. I am supposed to ask Paul McCartney whether there is a secret to writing a good love song. This is because Paul McCartney has written lots of songs, some of them about love. He has also written 'Silly Love Songs', which is a song about whether it is silly to write love songs, in which the answer to the question is, more or less, the sentence: 'I love you.'

Asking Paul McCartney about silly love songs is not as simple as it should be. He is Paul McCartney, a Beatle, and that gets in the way of everything. I am sent to the London Arena, where Paul is giving a press conference. He is fifty years old, which is relatively senior in rock 'n' roll terms but would count as middle school now.

I am not a Beatlemaniac. I have grown up with an attitude of ignorant disdain. I am a punk rocker. It is 1993 but I subscribe to The Clash's formula from their song '1977' in which Elvis, The Beatles and the Stones are despatched. Apart from the Elvis bit. I love Elvis. I quite like bits of The Beatles too. It is unsettling.

The Paul McCartney press conference is not like any other press conference I have attended. It is not Red Wedge. It is not the launch of the Edinburgh Fringe. It is not like the time Robert Maxwell helicoptered into Meadowbank Stadium, and hopped towards the waiting press with one leg in plaster to announce that he was going to save the Commonwealth Games before leaving it millions of pounds in debt. It is not like that at all.

A Paul McCartney press conference is like a convention of European men in leather blousons. It is a like a nursery school show-and-tell in which the children have been instructed to impress a visiting dignitary. Before it begins the European blouson correspondents hover around the empty desk where Paul McCartney is due to sit, placing their microphones at the optimum angle, perhaps hoping to leave a lingering trace of their cologne in the air that will surround the former Beatle.

'Sorry, guys,' says Paul's PR, Bernard Doherty, surveying the men fiddling with their tiny recorders. 'Can we go away from the table now, please? It's like a field day down the Tottenham Court Road.'

The blousons disperse. Paul McCartney enters. The press conference settles into a pattern. Each journalist must ask Paul McCartney whether he has plans to play in their town. Scottish broadcasting legend Billy Sloan is up first. Will Paul visit Glasgow? 'I feel a sympathy with people from Glasgow,' says Paul McCartney. Will he go to Greece, asks a Greek woman, 'And do we see a revival of The Beatles?'

'It's only a little revival,' Paul McCartney says.

Poland? Paul McCartney can't confirm. He has no idea.

The questions drift. Paul McCartney expresses support for Friends of the Earth.

'Do you use the f-word in everyday conversation?' ask a woman in a yellow coat, trying to rekindle an obscure controversy about swearing. Not really, says Paul. 'Instead of saying they're mucking it up for everyone, I used the f-word.' He may have also used the f-word in a song. 'In certain cases, I think it's OK to use.'

There is a question about human rights abuses in Spain.

Mike Donovan of the *Evening Argus* in Brighton asks: 'How much of an albatross is The Beatles? And why do you live in Sussex?'

'The Beatles as an albatross? No, I don't really feel that,' Paul McCartney says. 'As time goes by, I've rediscovered the songs. And instead of the anger and the pain we all felt when we were breaking up, I just like the songs now. They're a pleasure to do. And I don't live in Sussex. He lied.'

It is my turn. I pull up the sleeves on my regulation blouson and raise my hand.

'You are thought of as a writer of great love songs,' I say, rather too loudly. 'Do you think that's fair and is there a secret to writing a good love song?'

'I think it's a compliment if I am thought of as writing great love songs,' says Paul McCartney, ''cause I like a good love song. I also have written some other stuff that isn't like that. I mean, I've written songs like "Helter Skelter", "I'm Down" – pretty hard-edged – but I think people forget that about me. The ones they remember are songs like "Yesterday", "Long And Winding Road", and that. As to whether there's any secret about it, I don't really know. I still haven't worked out how to do it. That's part of the attraction. It's like magic.

Every time I come to do it, I sit down and think, "Oh, will it happen again?" If it does, I'm just very grateful.'

Bernard Doherty points to 'Mike in the leather jacket'.

'Paul,' says Mike in the leather jacket, 'I'm rather surprised not to see the wife here tonight.' The moment, if it ever existed, is gone.

44

Tony Wilson
'The fools in Shakespeare are the only ones that have read the play.'

I meet Tony Wilson in a bland hotel in Glasgow. His lights are not on full beam. He has a cold and seems bored. The film 24 *Hour Party People* is about to come out. It is a fictionalised version of the incredible story of Tony Wilson and his record label, Factory, in which Wilson is played as a cartoon of pretentiousness by Steve Coogan. The real Tony suggests that the fictional film Tony is 'a wanker and a twat' but also 'slightly heroic in some instances'.

Tony Wilson, the real one, is promoting the book of the film. The book is a novelisation of the fiction, which means, as Wilson explains on page five, that the best bits are not true. It's all a bit post-truth before post-truth is a thing. But that's OK. Tony is fond of the oft-misquoted line from *The Man Who Shot Liberty Valance*, the bit where the newspaper-man says to James Stewart: 'This is the West, sir. When the legend becomes fact, print the legend.'

The best bits in the Factory story are Joy Division, New Order, the Happy Mondays, the Haçienda, all that, and the fact that it took a maverick regional news presenter with no business sense to coax them into legend. The point about Factory, if it ever needed anything as flatly functional as a point, is that it didn't bother with London. It decided not to be regional and to make great things happen in Manchester. Because why not?

This, more or less, is the kind of rationale we used at *Cut* magazine, with less success. I could tell Tony that I once appeared fleetingly on his television show, *The Other Side of Midnight*, in a sequence based on John Grierson's 1936 documentary *Night Mail*. I reversed the *Cut* van onto a Manchester railway platform as if to receive a delivery of fresh Scottish magazines, to the soundtrack of W.H. Auden's 'Night Mail'. I could also mention that after this tricky manoeuvre I visited the Haçienda while sober and did not dance because the Haçienda did not seem like the kind of place where sober dancing took place.

I do not tell Tony Wilson these things. Instead Tony tells me the thing he tells business seminars when he gives lectures for £2,500 a night. He tells me a story about Sid Vicious. When Sid Vicious was asked whether he cared for the opinion of the man in the street, he reportedly replied: 'Fuck the man on the street. I've met the man on the street. The man on the street is a cunt.' Did Sid really say that? He surely did, but it also sounds like the kind of thing he might have said if Tony Wilson was writing his lines. Now it is famous for being the thing that Tony Wilson said about Sid Vicious, which is a different kind of true. This is the West, sir.

Does Tony bristle a bit when I suggest that Steve Coogan's impersonation of Tony Wilson is like a more pretentious version of Coogan's own mocking albatross, the idiot Alan Partridge? He does. Then Tony delivers a labyrinthine explanation of how Alan Partridge is not based on him at all.

The story weaves and bobs. It involves multiple Tony Wilsons.

This is how it goes. The *Cold Feet* actor John Thomson is appearing on Piccadilly Radio impersonating Tony Wilson and pretending to snort cocaine. Thomson's efforts on live radio are interrupted by a phone call from his flatmate Steve Coogan, who is pretending to be the real Tony Wilson and threatening to sue. Thomson, at least in the real Tony's telling of this tale, returns home fearful of the legal jeopardy he is in. The pretence is maintained for a couple of hours by Coogan and their accomplice Caroline Aherne (of *The Mrs Merton Show* and *The Royle Family*).

All of which is a very roundabout way of establishing that Alan Partridge is not based on Tony Wilson. But the tale has a coda. On *The Fast Show* John Thomson creates the jazz club host Louis Balfour (catchphrase: 'Mmm, nice!') and later confesses to Tony that the character is forty per cent him. Tony seems proud of this tribute. 'Even though I hate jazz.'

There is, of course, a real man inside these shenanigans, though Wilson tends to wrap his story, and that of Manchester, in the same wax paper. He is like a politician, selling an idea of himself as a kind of self-mocking philosophy. How did that happen?

Tony Wilson's German grandfather moved to Manchester in 1901. The city has always been welcoming to foreigners, Tony says. The family ran a small chain of jewellery shops and moved from Salford to Marple, hoping to give young Tony a more rural upbringing. But Tony won a scholarship to a Catholic grammar school at the age of eleven and commuted back to Salford.

Talking about these days seems to prompt a thought. 'I'm beginning to remember that I probably began hiding behind a persona at about the age of thirteen,' he says. 'Maybe that's just developed over the years.'

Tony says that his parents had worried that he would fail his eleven-plus exam. 'I was an only child and there wasn't much confidence about my capabilities. It was a very pleasant surprise when I got through to grammar school. A bit of a shock that I got into the A-stream. Then at Easter I came top. They also found out that in the entrance exam, out of 950 people, I came top.'

Tony says something about 'the lower middle-class kid's protective blanket of righteous rightness'. He adds: 'Being very clever was a bit embarrassing. And probably the defence mechanism was to be, slightly, the class joker. Slightly the fool.' Naturally, Tony underlines the point by reaching for a literary analogy. 'The fools in Shakespeare are the only ones that have read the play, that know the play. They know they're not a character in the drama. I liked that. And then I hid behind that, and it developed, I suppose.'

I tell him that he has been compared to Peter Mandelson, the Labour spin doctor whose mastery of narrative – his own, the country's – led to him being nicknamed the Prince of Darkness. 'That's good,' Tony says. 'The architect of New Labour. I have no problem with that. I like Mandelson but why would someone compare me to him?'

I suggest that he shares with Mandelson an interest in spin and a pragmatic belief that getting the story over matters more than truth. Tony replies that his real hero is the Sex Pistols' manager Malcolm McLaren, and that he does care about truth.

'The one thing I hate about Mandelson is the Millennium Dome because the Dome is what you get when you ask the great and the good to come up with a creative idea. It was a disaster and I was delighted when it failed. That's the great problem with New Labour – their reluctance to offend the great and the good. You absolutely must offend the great and the good. Margaret Thatcher understood that. She was, in Peter York's great phrase, a Maoist.'

We seem to be edging back towards Sid Vicious and the thing he may or may not have said. Tony returns to the subject of the man on the street.

'If you are your own customer,' he says, 'you deal with yourself. If you love yourself, as you should, you make the best thing you can.

'You know the Walkman was not devised by a focus group? It was devised by the head of Sony, who said, "Can you make me something so I can hear music while I play tennis?"'

How does this apply to Tony Wilson? He built the Haçienda. It was a terrible idea but a pure one. He calls it 'aimless serendipity'. Along with New Order, the Factory crew created a club like those they had seen in New York because that was their vision. It was not a business. It was a dream.

'By not building it for the man in the street we spent five years haemorrhaging money,' Tony Wilson says happily. 'But strangely, in the end, it worked.'

45

A Cup of Tea with Mr Cutler

I go to interview Ivor Cutler at his house. Mr Cutler is a humorist from Glasgow and a cult figure on the John Peel show. His comic vignettes are as sad as they are funny. They are very funny.

I meet him at his flat in Dartmouth Park, London.

It is a small flat. The living room hosts a harmonium and a large photographic print of Mr Cutler in his younger days, looking like Bernard Bresslaw from the *Carry On* films when, in fact, Mr Cutler is actually Buster Bloodvessel, the courier in the Beatles film *Magical Mystery Tour*. Some people say that Buster Bloodvessel is a bus conductor but that seems like a demotion.

There are some preliminaries.

Mr Cutler disappears to make tea.

From inside the kitchenette I hear his tremulous voice. 'Can you handle soya milk?' he asks.

'Yes,' I say.

'You look as if you could handle anything,' he says. 'Except pleasure.'

46

Nirvana
'How many times do people have to rip off Aerosmith?'

I take over the rock column in *Scotland on Sunday*. I am told to change nothing. Just do what you've been doing.

At the *Scotsman* I had been doing whatever I wanted. I had to deliver 800 typed words about something musical every week. I handed in my copy, made no eye contact, left. I received no feedback at any time. There was no encouragement, no discouragement. Occasionally there would be wrinkles in the system, such as the time the *Scotsman* office contrived to lose my irreplaceable Lester Bangs flexi disc, but on the whole the system worked.

Scotland on Sunday is different. The editor, a secret rock 'n' roller, wants the music coverage to be radical, far out, hip to the trip, down with the kids. Scottish, if possible. Plus, none of that weird shit. Nothing obscure. Occasionally, someone from the news desk will chip in with a helpful suggestion, such as 'Have you thought about interviewing Bob Dylan?'

In 1991 grunge happens. As storms go, it is perfect. The band at the eye of the hurricane, Nirvana, is both obscure and everywhere, all at once. Of course, it wasn't really an overnight thing. The distorted underground rock scene of Seattle had been percolating away for a few years before Kurt Cobain's group signed to Geffen and became the world's most successful losers.

I had seen Nirvana on their first UK date, at the Riverside in Newcastle in 1989. They were sandwiched between The Cateran – an Edinburgh band with the melodic fury and dystopian energy of Hüsker Dü – and the headliners, Tad. Tad had a number of things going for them. Their music was loud and nasty, and in Tad Doyle they had a multi-hyphenated renaissance man. One sympathetic reviewer called him a 'shit-kicking, beer-swilling, muff-diving redneck'. In 1991 that was an impressive CV. But it didn't impress my editor, who demanded an inquiry into why I was interviewing fat nobodies from Seattle. Possibly my timing was off. Tad had just been cast in the Cameron Crowe rom-com *Singles*, which in 1992 was to persuasively represent an entire subculture via the medium of Bridget Fonda's page-girl hairdo. Tad was to play 'a beer-drinking big guy watching television. Basically,' he noted, 'being myself.'

For all that, Tad had ambition. He wanted to front 'the loudest, most obnoxious, most earsore and most eyesore' band in the world, and pretty much delivered on these promises at that Newcastle show. Tad even provided a stand-in drummer for The Cateran, whose own drummer had been unexpectedly detained following a bizarre gardening accident.

But the show was really about Nirvana. They were loud and obnoxious and earsore, and angry and self-destructive and petulant and self-harming and righteous. They weren't eyesore. Their singer, Kurt Cobain, was pretty and charismatic and introspective in an exhibitionist way. He was brilliant but reticent. Musically they were a mix of garage rock, bad punk, old blues hollers and slow-burning neuralgia.

By the winter of 1991 Nirvana's fortunes have put them on the cusp of global fame. The single 'Smells Like Teen Spirit' has caught fire, propelled in the UK by a couple of punky television performances. On *The Word* Cobain introduces the song with the unverifiable boast that his girlfriend Courtney Love is 'the best fuck in the world' and changes the lyrics of the song to include a repeated tribute to 'Roger Taylor'. Later, having entered the charts at number 9, Nirvana appear on the British TV institution *Top of the Pops* and rebel by making no effort to mime convincingly. Kurt delivers the song's vocal as a lugubrious parody of himself and changes the opening line to 'Load up on drugs, kill your friends'.

Nirvana's fame explodes after their tour is booked, which is why the hottest band on the planet finds itself playing the Calton Studios in Edinburgh. As a venue Calton Studios doesn't have much to commend it apart from its size. The auditorium is small, the stage is low, the sound is mud.

I am supposed to meet Kurt prior to the show. It doesn't happen. At first I am led through the dressing room, where the singer is bent over in a chair, with a crowd of people around him. I'm led to a tiny kitchenette, roughly the size of a broom cupboard, but with a kettle and packet of Cup-a-Soup in it. I am warned not to go back into the dressing room.

Eventually Nirvana's bass player, Krist Novoselic (then known as 'Chris'), joins me in the Cup-a-Soup kitchenette. The monotonous thump of a drummer doing a soundcheck provides an ominous backdrop.

Novoselic is in a bright mood, at first. 'Ah, *Top of the Pops*!' he says when I mention their absurd rendition of 'Teen Spirit'. 'I think it means a lot more to English people than it does to us. We were told that everybody watches *Top of the Pops*, that it's a tradition. I've seen all the old Stones and Beatles stuff, everybody's been on *Top of the Pops*. We showed up and it's just, you know, TV. TV's just phoney, they just hype up the kids. There's a couple of, like, hype guys who get the kids all hyped up. It's television, that's all it is. We were lip-synching. We wanted to go on there in the spirit of Keith Moon and just lip-synch and obviously look silly. It was just fun, was what it was.'

But Nirvana were cut halfway through the song.

'Well, yeah, you're only allowed three minutes. Every band. Except James got three minutes and fifteen seconds. But, uh, that's cool. More power to James, I guess.'

We talk for a while about Nirvana's sudden rise. 'Yeah,' says Krist. 'Meteoric.'

I ask him about 'Smells Like Teen Spirit'. It sounds like an anti-anthem, I suggest, to his obvious confusion.

'It has its anthem qualities to it, I know. I don't know if that's good or bad, you can take it either way.'

I mean the words are almost the opposite.

'I don't know what you mean by that. Opposite of a traditional love song?'

No – of a rock anthem. It's like the opposite of 'My Generation'.

'Yeah,' says Krist. 'Well, there's a strong statement in the song. It's about American youth, apathy, you know. "Here we are now, entertain us." Give us Nintendo, give us boring TV shows, give us boring mainstream movies. You know? Entertain us, that's all we want. Puppet shows! It starts when they watch puppet shows and they take it all the way to the grave, watching *Golden Girls*.'

The odd thing, of course, is how Nirvana have managed to succeed when their music should have been anathema to conservative American radio.

'It's all corporate,' says Krist, 'it's all very stagnant. I have a hard time, I can't listen to American radio. I listen to college radio because that's where anything's really happening. It's a business – that's all it is. You know? It's really sick, is all it is. It's just like the whole process in America is, like, people are fed garbage and then they're asked what they want and they say, "We want garbage." It's because that's all they know. It's like a circle. It's like a ping-pong game. It goes back and forth. So maybe, hopefully, wishful thinking, our band . . . a lot of people bought our record, they like it, well, maybe they'll say, "Well, where are these guys from, what's their trip?" And they'll find out that there's this whole underground scene with bands like Sonic Youth and Dinosaur and Mudhoney. I could go on and on. You know the bands I mean. There's a lot of bands out there. They'll check 'em out and they'll see that there's a real, happening, vital music scene.'

What's the difference between Nirvana and the Bon Jovis of this world?

'The Bon Jovis just cater. They just cater to whatever, to get money. They're really into being stars. They're into their lifestyles, there's nothing original about it. They just go, "Let's be in a rock band and make money." So . . . how many times do people have to rip off Aerosmith, you know?'

Unsurprisingly Novoselic says that punk had 'a lot of influence' over Nirvana. 'We grew up in a small town. The heavy metal rock that was happening at that time like Def Leppard, like *Bark At The Moon* by Ozzy Osbourne, and the Scorpions – it was just all crap. I couldn't listen to it any more. I had an identity crisis for a while. I turned back to listening to older music, late sixties early seventies stuff. I had very limited knowledge because I was so very isolated, I was just bummed out. I hate heavy metal, I'd say. Then I started hearing punk rock through Buzz Osborne of the Melvins and I was like, "This is right on, this is really happening." It kinda changed my life. A lot of the bands back in the early eighties, like the Dead Kennedys and MDC, had a strong political message, just totally upfront political – "Reagan! Reagan!", you know – that was kinda cool. The energy was there, there was a lot of diversity in punk. Flipper, Butthole Surfers, I mean those are all very different bands but they had the spirit of rock because it was experimental and they were doing something new. It was something for me, for my identity, because I just couldn't have anything to do with the, like, stoner kids and all the rock kids, 'cause I just thought that they were idiots. I just couldn't hang around with them any more.'

Who are the stoner kids?

'Stoner kids are pot smokers wearing denim coats with their long feathered hair, smoking pot. I just couldn't hang around those kids any more. I thought they were stupid. I found this punk rock thing, I started going to Olympia, Tacoma, meeting other people who were into punk rock who I had a lot in common with, who thought society was a joke. There was a lot of ideas going around, and I thank God for that.

'I still had all my Aerosmith and Black Sabbath and Led Zeppelin records. I thought that was cool, too.'

It's odd, now, to spot the distinction between the underground scene championed by Nirvana and the music Novoselic found so tedious. To a first-generation British punk, Led Zeppelin and Aerosmith would have been laughable.

I ask Krist about sex and drugs and rock 'n' roll.

'Well,' he says, 'if that's the attitude of your band, it's a very worn out cliché. That's like the old guard, all the Hollywood Boulevard bands who ride around on Harley-Davidsons and wear bandanas. Our band, it's been written before, we've been known to tear it up. By no means is that a lifestyle. That's . . . One night we all had a hare up our ass, we were drinking a lot of alcohol and we were just going crazy, you know? And sex – I'm married. Everybody has a girl happening. It's not like every night picking up some girl at the show and, like, getting it on. And the drugs part? Sure we drink, smoke pot, you know, experiment with things, but I don't think it's like an image or an attitude at all. So I think we've covered all three bases, sex, drugs and . . . oh! Rock 'n' roll! We're totally into the rock 'n' roll part.'

What does rock 'n' roll mean?

'Rock 'n' roll is like energy, rock 'n' roll is a release, rock 'n' roll is, like, you're totally focused – you're watching a band and you're focused on the band and you're not thinking about anything else apart from the music, and you can feel it and your body kind of moves and it's an emotional thing, passion, you know? That might be the difference between underground bands and mainstream bands. They're over-produced, made-for-product stuff. Indie bands are more into the art of it. That's why there's so much diversity.'

We are talking about Nirvana's song 'Polly' – a rape escape tale based on a true story – when there is an urgent shout from outside the kitchenette. Krist leaves suddenly, saying 'Hang on a second', and I wait in the tiny room for ages, until it becomes clear that he isn't coming back.

Tentatively I step from the kitchenette into the dressing room, where the mood of anxiety has heightened. Kurt is being tended to by a doctor and there is a palpable feeling of dread in the room. A roadie catches my eye and gestures for me to leave.

Subsequently it transpires that Kurt has been told by an Edinburgh GP to rest his inflamed throat but has elected to ignore medical advice, even though it risks damaging what remains of his voice. There is talk of self-medication, of stomach problems. Kurt's ailment, though serious, seems to exist in the realms of understatement. The show is painful. Of course, Nirvana's music is all about pain, and Kurt has a way of representing that pain that goes far beyond performance. There is coughing, phlegm. He means it. He feels it. He is it. But it isn't fun.

In my review I try to fashion a punchline from the fact that the merchandise stand is selling two Nirvana T-shirts. One comes accessorised with the slogan 'fudge packin crack smokin Satan worshippin motherfuckers'. The other celebrates the band as 'flower sniffin kitty pettin baby kissin corporate rock whores'. The riffs, the contradictions, the self-abuse; they were all baked in.

Nirvana was a persuasive illusion. That was its power. That was its flaw.

47

Kate Moss
'I don't look anorexic or like a drug addict or a paedophile fantasy.'

To celebrate her twenty-first year Kate Moss releases a pictorial biography. *Kate* is a handsome book with a portrait by Corinne Day on the cover showing a grainy close-up of Moss's face. The lips are full, the cheeks are freckled, the right eye stares into the light. Are there imperfections? There is a hint of a spot, maybe a mole, above the mouth but the picture is intimate and blurry, the focus sharpening around the eye and the lips. The back cover is a contact sheet, also by Day, of a younger Moss running through set-ups: a smile, a laugh, a tilt of the head. The most interesting frames are the in-betweens, where the pose is broken and Moss's pout dissolves. The shot that has been marked by the photographer shows the model with her mouth open slightly. What is she saying? The picture can't tell us that. There is a faint smile. In this image Kate Moss looks like a Grange Hill *Mona Lisa*.

Kate Moss is called a supermodel but she is something else.

She is plainly gorgeous, accessibly incredible. The photographers who get the best out of her tend to scratch at taboos. Corinne Day's lingerie shot with Kate Moss in the June 1993 edition of *Vogue* does that, possibly because the images are deliberately unrefined. The pictures look tame now, and perhaps they always were, but in the early skirmishes of the culture wars they manage to worry the people whose job it is to be professionally outraged. The question the offensive shoot tries to answer is: 'What to wear beneath effort-free clothes?' The answer: 'Barely-there underwear, naturally.'

There, barely, are pants, vests, a messy bed, a veiled hint of nipples and an eyeful of gusset, with Moss at the centre of the frames looking dead, bored, thin, amused, as always.

And now I am in a limousine with Kate Moss, driving the short distance from the Virgin Megastore in Oxford Street to the Langham Hilton Hotel. What do I want to get from Kate? The sound of her voice and to hear what it has to say. But also a photograph of me with her as proof of something or other. I shake her hand. It is like holding a kitten's paw.

To be clear, I am not alone with Kate in the car. It is crowded for a limousine but exciting too. Kate's agent is here, calling her Katy. Kate complains about the tinted windows because they mean that people can't see her. If a supermodel drives past but nobody can see her, does she actually drive past at all? It's an interesting thought and we almost think it as the limo makes its juddering transit between Megastore and hotel. The mood in the car is philosophical. Kate has just survived a lunchtime book signing. The Megastore crowd was 'really weird, really bizarre', says Kate. 'I'm surprised people came. I thought I'd be sitting there and people would come up to ask where the nearest Anne Rice book was, and I'd say, "Sorry, I don't work here."'

The queue for signatures included a boy who dropped his corduroys and bent over invitingly. 'Yeah right,' says Kate now, 'like I'm gonna sign his bum.'

In the limo the chat spills out of Kate. She was up at 5.45 a.m. It was OK. She might have something nice to wear for her launch party at the Blue Note club tonight. 'I'm expecting something,' says Kate. 'I don't know what it is.'

I ask Kate about the photographers at the signing. They were noisy and demanding but Kate was unbothered. 'They do that at shows when you do runway. The paparazzi at the shows are the same guys that were there. They're quite funny blokes, some of them. They're all right. It's the people who follow you around and try to get pictures of you on holiday or when you're trying to have a private life that are annoying. Otherwise, it's OK.'

Is it intimidating?

'It's all right for the first thirty seconds and then it gets a bit . . . please stop.'

Kate says that Steve from the *Daily Express* has given her a montage of nice photos. 'And a girl came up and said, "Did you go out with Matthew Bailey?" I was about twelve when I snogged him. And she says, "Well, now I'm going out with him."'

After a few minutes of slow London traffic we are at the hotel, in the lift, in the corridor outside the suite. While someone unlocks the door Kate jumps up and tries to form a human bridge between the corridor walls. She wears a silver suit. She is glam. There is a pair of tiny black trainers outside the door.

She is laughing a lot, wondering what the time is in Los

Angeles. (It is 6.30 a.m., Pacific.) 'I think it might be time for a glass of wine,' says Kate.

The room is homely. You might call it messy. There are packets of Silk Cut and Marlboro Lights everywhere and more than three cigarettes in the ashtray. Empty matchboxes abound. There are little piles of Sweet Dreams pillow chocolates. A book, *The Prophet*, is on the settee; Kate's boyfriend, Johnny Depp, suggested she read it.

Coiling her legs beneath her, Kate tips out the contents of her handbag onto the table in search of a light. There are bundles of paper, a passport, a tube of moisturiser.

'The colour scheme in this hotel,' says Kate. 'I just don't know. It's a bit on the brown and orange side. It's very *Good Morning* television. Anne and Nick would love it.'

Kate asks for a glass of red wine but settles for a vodka and Coke.

The clock on the BBC building is visible outside the window, counting down my thirty minutes. I want to ask about growing up in Croydon, about roots, materialism, about dreams. I want to ask whether Kate sleeps easily. But the energy in the room dissolves that. Kate's friend and collaborator Jess Hallett keeps watch as Kate genuflects in front of the tape recorder.

We talk about creative control. About how the book is, and isn't, about Kate.

'I'm at the whim, not of the photographer, but of the hair and make-up and the stylist, and then it's the photographer's vision. But you do have an input in the way that you feel the clothes, so you bring out an emotion which the camera takes. It's kind of an expression of yourself even though somebody's put all this stuff on you.'

I ask whether she was unhappy with any of the looks.

'Yeah,' she says. 'There were a few shoots where I didn't

want to be so unclothed. But it's really difficult when you're young and you're on a set by yourself and you have the make-up and the stylist and the photographer all telling you "Come on, it's fine, don't be such a prude". Because they're artists they will try anything to get you to do what they want. But now I've learned to say no.'

Did she feel exploited?

'At the time I did, in a way. Some of the pictures. But if I really felt uncomfortable I could have said. Like when I was really young I didn't really want to show myself but I was pushed into it, so I was . . . not exploited . . . because they were friends of mine so I didn't feel they were trying to exploit me, they were just doing it for their art. And they are good pictures. It's not like they're really tacky. It's not Page 3.'

Kate talks about photography, saying she may take it up. 'I don't think I would take fashion pictures. I'd take documentary pictures. I find that much more interesting.'

This is a surprising thing to say when promoting a book of fashion photography. I ask Kate whether she expects these pictures to have an impact beyond the thirty seconds it would take to flick past them in a magazine.

'They obviously have,' she says, 'because they've fuelled the media. They must have had some impact, even if it's a negative one. They seem to think it's a negative one.'

We appear to be talking in code, so I ask whether she is referring to the frequent suggestion that some of her pictures have a child-like quality. Others have gone further, suggesting they border on paedophile fantasy.

'Exactly,' says Kate. 'It obviously has had an impact but the wrong sort of impact. But it can have a good impact too, because young people follow fashion, so I think it can have an impact on the way people dress on the street.'

Does she worry about the negative bit?

'I don't lie awake at night,' she says. 'But it does bother me. It does get to be a drag.'

But if you were paranoid, I say, and you saw some of the people who came to see you today . . .

'I know,' she whispers. Then loudly, she says: 'That's when I start thinking maybe they were right. But the thing is, when I'm doing the pictures I don't think about it because it's not me who's making the picture, it's the photographer. They're the ones that are creating. So in all the pictures that I've done, two or three maybe look like they've said. But I don't look anorexic or like a drug addict or a paedophile fantasy. They'll pick one picture where maybe you could look like that and they'll blow it out of all proportion.'

We talk around the subject for a while and Kate seems wearied. She says she hasn't thought about the meaning of her image. Most of what is written about her is lies, she suggests. 'I just kind of am me,' she says. 'I haven't changed for the media. I don't really know if I should or I shouldn't, so I haven't done anything about it.'

Then she says an interesting phrase. 'The more visible they make me, the more invisible I become.'

By now Kate is prowling around the room, still on the hunt for matches. 'It's from Cocteau,' she says. 'I was reading it and I thought: that's so true. I didn't say it, unfortunately. Too clever for me.'

This mention of Cocteau is disarming. What I don't notice at the time is that Kate is quoting from the introduction to her own book, though there's no mention of Cocteau there. The quote will also become the title of a short film made by the photographer Nick Knight, in which he cuts video of Kate modelling for him into surveillance camera footage, so that the viewer's point of view becomes that of a stalker. Years later Johnny Depp will quote the quote, along with the qualification: 'I think it was Cocteau who wrote it.'

I ask Kate whether she has ever considered quitting. She laughs. 'All the time I think about giving up but I've never tried it yet! Too much waiting around. And I have so much nervous energy that I think if I stopped I'd just be . . . nervous.'

The quest for a match is now becoming urgent. Jess is dispatched to another room in search of a lighter and the mood in the room changes again. As we can't dig into the surface reflections of maybe-Cocteau, I reach for the trivia. I ask about luck, suggesting that she has had her share, both in being 'discovered' in an airport departure lounge and in meeting her then-boyfriend, Johnny Depp.

Kate's face glows at the mention of Johnny. 'I believe in destiny,' she says. 'Fate. Like there's a route that you're meant to take, and however you take it you're going to end to end up in the place where you're meant to be. Don't you believe that? Not at all? Do you think we make our own luck? To some extent I do too but some things happen and they're coincidence. And if anything bad happens, I always blame it on fate.'

We talk about star signs. Kate is a Capricorn, Johnny is a Gemini: 'Two-sided personalities.' She tells me about a documentary she saw on palmistry, which showed that people believed what they wanted to believe.

Jess returns. The talk turns back to fame. It takes away something, Kate says. 'Just being able to do things. People look at you. You're always under observation. So you can't really get pissed and walk out in the street and pass out in the street like a normal person would at twenty-one.'

'Or even fade into the background,' Jess suggests.

'You can't not be noticed and just chill,' Kate says. She pauses, as if realising that this sounds like a complaint. 'I don't really take that much notice of it, though. If I'm out, I try to turn a blind eye to it. But you are on display.'

Have you ever thought about wearing a woolly hat?

'I don't get recognised that often, really. When I don't dress up and I'm not in a situation where people would expect me to be, I don't get recognised.' She laughs. 'People always expect me to be taller and more glamorous than I am.'

It seems like a good time to get practical. I find myself asking whether Kate can recommend a good moisturiser. 'There's a brilliant one, actually,' she says, quite enthusiastic now. 'I just started using it. It's called Embryolisse. You get it over the counter. In Paris. That's the ticket, I think. That's the stuff.'

What about cellulite? Does she have any?

'Well, I'm sure I have.' She grabs her upper thigh. 'If I go like that, I have.' She issues a devilish laugh. 'What did Amber call these? Saddles. My friend Amber Valletta, she's another model, we were on a job the other day and she said, "You've gained weight." I said, "I know, I've never had these before. You know, this bit where when you've got your leg like this . . . like hips." I've never had hips before. And Amber was like, "Yeah, I've got them too; as soon as we turn twenty-one, we start getting these saddles."'

Kate says she doesn't get self-conscious about her body. 'Sometimes I think I'm unattractive. Just like a normal person.' The newspapers, she says, are more aware of her body than she is. She has been called 'The Feed Me Girl' and accused of promoting anorexia. For a week she was accused of gaining weight. 'I was like, "Really? Have I? I still fit my jeans." Not that I ever stopped eating chips anyway.'

We have dealt with all the big questions of state, at least the ones a model might realistically be expected to have a view on – astrology, skincare, paedophilia – and I find myself running dry. I reach for the big one. Does she know the price of a pint of milk?

'I'll guess,' says Kate. 'No. I don't go shopping for milk because I don't have a place so I don't have a fridge. When I get a place then I'll get a fridge.'

❈

Did I get what I wanted? Yes, no, maybe. Not entirely. Back at the Megastore I had instructed the photographer to capture an image of me getting into the limo with Kate, as proof. Of what, I'm not entirely sure. These were the pre-selfie days. Shortly after the original interview was printed in *Scotland on Sunday* I received a montage of two photographs. The limousine is clearly captured, as are the paparazzi. There is a shot of me getting into the car and – spray-mounted onto the darkened windows of the limousine – the smiling face of Kate Moss, looking out at everyone else looking in.

48

Juergen Teller
'I was just so shy, and very much taken aback, and I liked the music very strongly.'

There is no delicate way to say it. When I reach the door of Juergen Teller's West London studio my bowels are in ferment. There is no time for niceties, just a blurted apology. 'I'm sorry,' I whimper. 'Can I use your toilet?'

The photographer ushers me in. 'Up there,' he says, waving at a staircase. It is hard to take in the layout with my gut in revolt but I realise as I climb the stairs that the room is peculiar. You might expect a photographer's studio to resemble a film set. This goes further. The room looks as if it has been partially demolished. The stairs go up to a landing, on which there is a toilet. Not a bathroom. There is no bath, no room. Just a toilet, in the open, without walls. Seeing it triggers my intestines. I need to go. But here, in a room without a wall? Is that how it is with fashion people? They must be used to the functional intimacy of the changing room, but shitting in public?

I am exploding. I reach for my belt. No time for shame. We're all men here. At this point, Juergen Teller glances up. 'No!' he shouts, with obvious alarm, 'not there!' He gestures frantically towards another toilet. This one is more conventionally situated, in a room, with a wall and a door and a lock.

Juergen Teller arrived in London from Munich in 1986, not knowing what kind of photographer he was. His attraction to photojournalism was countered by laziness. 'To travel the world and wait for that decisive moment, and to take that picture of some misfortunate accident . . . I find that sometimes quite questionable.'

Instead, though he was naïve and 'too shy to communicate with the girls or the guys I was photographing', he gravitated towards style magazines such as *i-D* and *The Face*. 'It was mostly musicians, and within these portraits things melted into each other. In a picture of Kurt Cobain, is it a fashion picture or is it photojournalism? Is it a record cover, or a portrait, a time document, or what is it?'

In his 1996 book *Juergen Teller* there are three photographs of Kurt Cobain, though his face barely registers in any of them. The pictures were taken in 1991, just as 'Smells Like Teen Spirit' was propelling Nirvana to a destructive level of fame. 'An American magazine, *Details*, asked me to go to Germany for a week with some band with long hair and holes in their jeans. I didn't have much money, I was not very well. It was November and it gave me a chance to go to Germany, which I was longing to do.

'I was very, very taken by them. They really intimidated me. I met them in Heathrow, we stayed in the same hotel, drove around. They made their rehearsal, they were eating, and then they were doing their interviews and they had their concert. So I've seen the whole thing, four times in different cities. I was just so shy, and very much taken aback, and I liked the music very strongly. I very much liked them, especially Kurt. He was very introvert. He was very shy himself and I felt so intrusive, I was just sitting there having the meals with them, talking to them. I never did a picture. All these other photographers and journalists, Germans, they came in, everybody had like five, ten minutes, and they were bombarding him. Then suddenly I realised that the trip was nearly over. We were there to do a big story and I didn't do any pictures. But I think that picture where he's down like that – I like the picture a lot – it's how I see him, and how I was, and it's totally him.'

The Cobain picture Teller is describing shows the guitarist hunched over his guitar, the fingers on his left hand curled over the strings, the head bowed, the hair hanging down. Another shot shows Kurt in the corner of a dressing room, as a woman – possibly Courtney Love – attends to him in ways that are intimate but indistinct. A third shot has Cobain side-on, holding his guitar in his left hand, his face masked again by his hair. The singer is hiding in plain sight.

Creatively, Teller's progress was intuitive. He says he didn't understand fashion photography but took it up 'because I thought it was an easy way out of saying something'. At first, he says, he was naïve. 'I didn't really have too much of a strong self-opinion about my work.'

As his confidence grew Teller developed an informal style, quite at odds with traditional fashion photography but in tune with others, such as Corinne Day. Both of them pursued an anti-glamour aesthetic that had something in common with the art photography of Nan Goldin but also contained echoes of grunge. The fashion industry absorbed the style but not without prompting a confected tabloid outrage in which Teller found his work being dismissed with the short-hand insult 'heroin chic'.

'I got criticised for glamorising the fuckedupness, the heroin chic,' Teller says, justifying his disdain for the traditional sensibilities of the fashion industry. 'When these women come to me I find some of them very attractive the way they are. I don't mind whether they have a big ear . . . or whether they have dark rings under their eyes. It's all in their personality.

'I never meet anyone in my whole life who looks like a *Vogue* cover. They portray, they glorify a wrong view of women's lives. They push people towards cosmetic surgery and to some perfectionism which doesn't even exist. They push themselves – people get anorexic and aware of everything. It's all money. They put a stupid credit there that says, "Cosmetics by blah blah blah". It's all fucking rubbish. It's all airbrushed. There's no bloody make-up on it. I think that's quite questionable.'

Amongst all this sex and vacancy the Kurt pictures stand out, possibly because the singer is so obviously in retreat. But Teller also gets the best out of Kate Moss, whose great skill seems to be her versatility and her intuitive sense of how to make a picture.

'I just love her in a way,' Teller says. 'She's very full of life and very enthusiastic. She initiates things, she does things, she's not so passive. She also has the possibility, as a model, to completely understand, and some models can't. For some actresses, they only play their one role. She's able to completely understand clothes. She slips into that role without me having to explain a lot to her. We don't have to talk much and we totally understand what we're trying to do. She understands the clothes. The way she sits. She always does things. If it's some elegant thing she becomes gracious, or if it's some slutty sexy thing she's able to slip into that. Or some sweater and she becomes a young teenager. She's incredibly versatile and she really works with you, to get that thing done.

'I think she changed a lot of beauty perceptions in the industry, in the world. She looked really young and quirky and suddenly she became a sophisticated woman. Also, what I like about her, she truly enjoys working. She's not afraid. She doesn't hold back, at least with me. She has a certain element of trust and she just gives it to me.'

Teller says he is aware of the responsibility he has as a photographer. 'A lot of photographers, they got blamed for heroin chic, and quite rightly so in some cases. But if a magazine asked me to photograph John Galliano, Chanel, Dior, Alexander McQueen, and I'm trying to choose a model, I have to get somebody who is absolutely super-skinny. It is the fashion designers who are on the first rung who present their look with these skinny models walking up and down the catwalk. And that piece of clothing doesn't fit anybody else.

'Nobody blames the fashion designers for anything. It's the photographers who get blamed. And I don't think that's right. Most fashion designers, the way they see women is a very abstract one. Most of them are gay, they don't have much to do with tits. They'd rather not have them. And it's some sort of idealised gay man's fantasy.

'Kate opened the doors. There's a group of photographers, including me, who changed the way we see these models and brought back some humanity. People seem to be able to relate to Kate and all the models afterwards. They are not so tall, they are a little bit quirky, they have red hair. Everything seems to be so much more possible. Real beauty. So I can relate to it, instead of Stephanie Seymour looking like some sex doll. You don't see that very often on the street.'

As an example of the strange relationship between wealth and fashion, Teller worked extensively with Seymour, a supermodel whose husband happened to be the industrialist, magazine publisher, film producer, art collector and billionaire Peter Brant. In his 2002 book *More* Teller documented his lengthy collaboration with Seymour, and only a viewer inoculated with inordinate wealth could fail to detect a satire of conspicuous consumption in his treatment of the model's opulent Connecticut home. What was the photographer trying to say? There's a clue in Teller's self-titled monograph, where a snapshot of a blank-faced Seymour is juxtaposed with a study of a frozen dead dog dumped in a Czechoslovakian dustbin.

I ask Teller to show me his favourite photograph of Kate Moss. He retreats into a storeroom, returning with a print taken on the day after the model's twenty-fifth birthday at the Ritz Paris. Kate is lying on the bed in a white robe, looking sleepy and fragile but also intensely relaxed. On the bed beside her are toy animals – a cheetah and a snake. Teller suggests that the photograph reminds him of pictures of the Austrian-born actress Romy Schneider, or Marilyn Monroe. 'The air was full of flowers,' he says, celebrating beauty, hinting of tragedy.

49

The Many Moods of Iggy Pop
'This is not an act of savage nihilism.'

1 Telephone Box
It is 2013. Iggy Pop is on the telephone. Iggy is promoting a new record by Iggy and the Stooges. It is not his best record but there are great things on it. It follows the pattern of many late-period Iggy Pop records, mixing vulnerable introspection with unvarnished animal urges. Both approaches have their adherents. Possibly, one is the product of the other. But the impression remains that Iggy's instincts veer towards emotional reflection while commercial pressures insist on the hymns of praise to gargantuan bosoms.

Bra-size commentaries aside, the news has just emerged of a film project that proposes to tell the story of Iggy and David Bowie's much-fabled time in Berlin, a period in the mid-1970s that prompted their best records.

'That sounds like some corny shit,' Iggy says of the film idea, before delivering a nostalgic reverie about his time in that 'twentieth-century island'. It was as if time slowed down, he says. 'You could be an artist. You could experience real humanity. You could walk down the street without being rushed.'

There were strange characters everywhere in 1970s Berlin: grumpy draft-dodging German students, Viennese chefs, Macedonians, Serbians, Russians. In this Cold War idyll a man could step out for a boiled egg in the morning and it would be cooked on a proper iron furnace, and the tables would be made of wood, not 17-ply Formica, and there were *eckkino*, small cinemas on every corner, 200-seaters, where you could watch three or four old black-and-white films for fifty cents US.

'It was just a nice time,' Iggy concludes. 'If you pretend it's New York, it was as if the Russians got Wall Street and everything up to Times Square, and then the US, Britain and France divided Central Park, Queens and the Upper East Side.

'A silly example of the atmosphere would be that once I got very stoned and drunk and I went to use a telephone box at three in the morning. I happened to be one of fourteen victims that night of somebody who went around and locked people in phone booths all over Berlin. I was terrified because the only way I could get out was to call the police. Somebody had to call the police for a key. And, you know, I was holding [drugs]. But there was nobody really in charge at that time, and nobody cared, so they just helped me up and took me home. They didn't search me, they didn't question me, they didn't hassle me for being drunk.

'It was wonderful! It was a very laissez-faire and relaxed place with room for the intellect. There was something very cosy about it and at the same time you never had to worry about a parking space.'

❋

2 Toilet Break

I am watching an Iggy Pop performance. Memory lies but it must be around 1980. Most of the details of the show have dissolved. I don't know the venue. I have lost the ticket. I am aware that the Iggy Pop I am watching is a few years past his peak but it is still a thrill to be in the presence of a legend. Iggy has destroyed rock 'n' roll, invented heavy metal and been crowned the godfather of punk. He is old. Maybe around thirty-three years old.

I remember two things about this show. First, Iggy sings 'One For My Baby' and muses aloud about the brilliance of Frank Sinatra. This is not a very punk-rock thing to do, unless in saying punk rock we employ the classical definition: defying expectations, thumbing your nose, staying alive by refusing to conform to the rules of engagement and just generally doing what you want in the way that you want. In which case Iggy Pop singing Sinatra is very punk.

Second, Iggy needs a shit. Perhaps this is the sort of thing you might expect from the godfather of punk but it's a startling moment. What happens is this. Iggy discusses his defecatory needs with the audience and threatens, for a while, to do the deed right there, on the stage. Perhaps he does this every night. Maybe it is a routine. But it seems urgent. Eventually Iggy leaves the stage for a while, has a comfort break, and resumes the show as if nothing has happened.

3 The Guy Who Put Dostoevsky in 'Louie Louie'

I am in a hotel in London with Iggy. Coffee will be served in china cups, with shortbread. Iggy is promoting *American Caesar*, one of his better late-period albums. Iggy is in spectacular form, quiet and gracious, talking at length about how he has been putting his affairs in order, taking control of his back catalogue, extracting royalties from bootleggers, writing prose, acting, penning an advice column for teenage girls. He is, he says, at the end of a ten-year plan to become a viable artist and not a marginal one.

That's business. Then there is art.

Iggy is talking about his recent visit to Europe, notably Madrid. He went to the Prado art gallery. 'The fucking Velázquez!' he says. 'Just really, really big for me.'

Velázquez, says Iggy, 'paints people's character in much more depth than the other Spanish or Flemish painters. And he has a sense of politics. There's a very worldly sense on those paintings that I really appreciate.

'Then I got to the bullfights. I'd been to the bullfights before but this time we got seats on the edge, right there where he's kicking dirt and you hear him smarting and you see the whole thing going down.'

Iggy talks for a while about Edward Gibbon's *The Decline and Fall of The Roman Empire*. He read the version abridged by Dero Saunders ('butchery!') and blended this with his half-memories of old gladiator movies – 'some of these funny movies where they always hire Peter Ustinov to play Nero' – to create his American Caesar. And now he has an unabridged set of the funky Gibbons. 'I've been reading it and loving it. The set I've got has some really nice etchings.'

This does not sound like the usual small talk of a wild man of rock 'n' roll, though Iggy has always been able to mix the two elements: the ennui and the double-Ds.

He talks about reading as if it is an act of mental refuelling in which the reader is collaborating with the text. 'Basically you're making the words, and as you pour them into yourself . . .

'You know,' Iggy says, spooling back to one of his signature songs, '"Search And Destroy" . . . that was a column heading in a *Time* magazine article about how we were going to win the war in Vietnam. That's all it was, a column heading. I saw it in the bold print. SEARCH AND DESTROY . . . ooh, that's good. Search and destroy, indeed. I always used to read *Time* just as a spy would. A spy trying to see what they're thinking, all the people that believe this shit.'

Reading, Iggy reiterates, has always been vital. 'But I don't have a balanced knowledge about anything. I'm just a crack-pot!' He laughs. 'A little knowledge is a dangerous thing!'

I suggest that he is the first person to incorporate Dostoevsky into the lyrics of the garage-rock anthem 'Louie Louie'.

'This is right,' Iggy says. 'This is really good! It takes a guy like that to put Dostoevsky into "Louie Louie". Somebody who really knew all about Dostoevsky wouldn't do that. I read *The Idiot* 'cause it's the shortest book! I tried to plough through a little bit of *The Gambler*. That was years ago. I have more patience to read, so I might be able to do better now.'

There is a word people use to describe the outlook of Iggy Pop, particularly his early work with The Stooges. Those records didn't sound like the hippie orthodoxy of the time, they were in opposition to all that, and to everything else. Over the years Iggy will fashion an explanation of his musical choices but perhaps the most apposite image is his suggestion that he absorbed the Motown clang of the Detroit car assembly lines.

When people talk about Iggy's worldview, the word they use is nihilism.

Iggy is not keen on being labelled. 'Whatever they call me, it's pretty much bullshit,' he says.

'Of course, I had my beliefs early on. I had my feelings and beliefs but they were too dearly held for me to come out. I was young and idealistic. The things I really felt, I wasn't gonna come out and trumpet to create wealth for myself. I felt the wealth should be created on the basis of a penetrating vision in music: I would try to take as hard a look as I could at everything. That's what I thought I could offer as an artist.'

'But the value system you had,' I say, 'or the way you expressed it in the late 1960s, was the opposite of what everyone else was doing.'

'I wouldn't paraphrase my own work,' says Iggy, 'but I had a song that said, "It's 1969 okay/All across the USA/Another year for me and you/Another year/With nothing to do." I did mention me and you.

'One thing that gets distorted is the intent with which I said these things. Because I never ever yelled or screamed on those records. If I screamed, it was between words. I never yelled a word at ya, I never screamed a word. I almost spoke the words. You could always hear what was being said and . . .'

We are interrupted by the rattle of bone china. The coffee arrives.

'I don't know if I would call it composure,' Iggy continues. 'I had the confidence in the weight of what I was saying to calmly state it, so you could hear it. I always did that. Even if you listen to "Search and Destroy", I practically whisper the song. A lot of people came after me thinking perhaps that they were doing it like me and it was all' – he elicits an animal howl which makes the china cups rattle – 'it was like rabbits on aggressive drugs or something. That was never what I was into. The points were made but there was always a reasonableness about it. "No Fun" says "no fun" but it also says "no fun to be alone". Even in "No Fun" I call my mom on the telephone in the bridge. This is not an act of savage nihilism.'

Iggy says the first person to call him a nihilist was the exuberant critic Lester Bangs. 'Lester had a big heart,' he says. 'And Lester breathed forth, "He is a nihilist!" And everybody who was assigned to cover me for twenty-five bucks and free tickets and didn't want to do the work went, "Oh, Lester said he's a nihilist – right! He's the nihilist rocker!" Then they add, "The nihilist rocker who rolled in glass." "The nihilist rocker who rolled in glass who ate the shit." It becomes like a litany. It becomes like a mass, and as time goes on they just keep hanging little things on your altar, haha, until you've got these great garlands of garlic and you're trudging around with all this crap on, you know?'

Iggy takes a sip of coffee. He winces. 'It's kinda funny in a way. But I never thought of it as nihilism. The nearest to that would be – I have a song called "Death Trip". Hahahaha. That's one of my positive numbers. I really liked that one on *Raw Power* because it upset everyone. The manager was so upset. "Death Trip!" Oh my God! It just looked great in print, "Death Trip!"'

'Some milk for your coffee, Iggy?'

'Yeah. At the time it was really heavy to name a song "Death Trip". Now there's death metal and snuff metal, and rap is all "I'm gonna shoot you in the dick and then I'm gonna eat it. I'm gonna fuck your mom." But then, nobody said it. Death trip! I was just singing what I really thought. I just thought I was doomed.' He laughs. 'But the reason I thought I was doomed was, I was getting no support for the kind of music I wanted to make. I knew that and I made a conscious decision: I'm going to make it anyway. I had offers to give me a great deal of support, from management

226

and people around me, if I would do a different sort of music. If I would misuse my charisma to make a sort of emasculated music. I just wasn't ready to get my dick cut off.'

Iggy says he was being urged 'to make something suitable for radio'. This suggestion will become a recurring theme in his career.

'I had this other thing in my head,' he says, 'and I knew it could sound very exciting and I wanted to make that. So I made it. I'm glad I made it, and like anybody who's out there trying something for the first time I made funny mistakes doing it and stumbled a lot. A lot of it was hilariously overblown, like "I have to be naked to sing the vocals." So I had to do all the vocals naked for that album, *Raw Power*. And I burped by accident before the cut 'Raw Power', which is how the song starts out. You hear it on the record. "That's it! That's great! That's right!" That's genius. It's silly too. Maybe that's where the nihilism was creeping in. Even on *Fun House*, the second album, I realised I was going to get no support. And I thought, "Well, that's OK. I need to do this anyway." I knew' – he slips into a nagging managerial voice – '"but tomorrow you're going to wake up and you're not going to have a record company or a job or anything else, and what with all your other problems, your drug habits, your real problems, you're gonna be really fucked". So it was kinda like that. I'm glad I stuck the way I stuck.'

'You made the records you wanted to make,' I say.

'Yeah,' says Iggy. 'Uh huh. That's the main thing. When I hear the records I get excited, I'm happy.'

At this point we are interrupted by a waitress. 'Is there a Stefan Handjob here?' she asks.

I look at Iggy.

Iggy looks at me.

227

'What is your view of Christianity?' I say, because someone needs to say something.

Iggy confesses he is not a big Christianity fan.

'Turn the other cheek?' he says. 'Hahaha. I've not been baptised. My father was agnostic and didn't want me to be raised within the Church, so when I was about seven or eight I heard about this God deal and I thought: "Oh my God, I'm not gonna go to heaven and I'm gonna die." I used to think about it at night a lot. I never think about it any more. I realise now, the closest thing to God is my own death. I'm at a time of my life now where I can see it coming. And you kinda start to see a continuum. Well, I got born, OK. That's started. And I'm gonna die and that's gonna end. There is a finite quality. For some reason that works as a comfort in my life. It makes me not quite so uptight as I would normally be, like if I was going to have ten shit-fits a day instead of only one or two. The rest of the time I'm more able to laugh. The other thing is it allows me to enjoy little stuff.' He looks around the hotel room. 'Like a really good croissant. Yeah! A really good cup of coffee. Little things that are really big, that's nice. A good newspaper!'

4 Pomona: The Local Kicks
On holiday by mistake in Southern California, I come across an Iggy Pop concert at the Glass House, a small venue on a strip called the Arts Colony. The venue is a bit like a Scout hut. Concert-goers are searched for weapons on the way in. No gun, no entry.

Iggy's veins are bulging, He sometimes looks as if he is going to shed a skin and re-emerge as a younger version of himself. He is not self-destructive. The concert is a model of control. It is a tug of war between adulation and revulsion.

It is a modern dance. Iggy is half Nureyev, half Beowulf. He rips through 'Raw Power'. He poses with the microphone stand looped through his arms, like a crucifixion. The band are blow-dried drongos who drive with both cowboy boots jammed on the accelerator. The one song Iggy introduces is the one where he actually sounds as if he means it. This is 'Look Away'. There's a line in this song about how becoming straight means becoming narrow. It is a small-town love song, a drug cartoon. It is about keeping your feelings in check. It is like a Johnny Cash confessional in heavy disguise. 'This is how I cope,' Iggy sings. 'Now,' he says wearily at the end, 'back to the same old shit.'

Maybe it's a routine night, and Iggy's roots are showing, but it's great. When Iggy plays 'The Passenger', perhaps for the millionth time, the awkward boys crowd around the microphone and the pretty girls dance. What else is there to do?

5 Chateau Marmont: Clichéd Psychoanalytical Shit
Iggy looks calm, maybe a little nervous. He wears black jeans with Chelsea boots, a black vest and a leather jacket. He is tanned. His hair is freshly platinum. 'I'm the victim of a domineering hairdresser,' he says. 'It happened stage by stage.'

I am at the famous Chateau Marmont in Los Angeles to meet Iggy for the debut issue of *Blah Blah Blah*, a British version of *Ray Gun* which will share its parent publication's penchant for impenetrable design and raw copy. The lads' mag *Loaded* is also in the room and its unathletic gonzo reporter has plans to share an exercise workout with Iggy, for the purposes of comedy. This does not happen. I am supposed to referee a chat between Iggy and Beck. This doesn't happen either. A man called Edmund, from a cable music channel in Dortmund, is also here. Edmund is expressing his surprise – and perhaps regret – that Iggy is not writhing around in his own faeces with a live electrical cable sparking between his shattered teeth. (He doesn't put it exactly like that.) I ask Iggy's manager, Art, whether the singer still has the capacity for wildness. Yes, he confirms. Just the other night Iggy had picked up a chair and smashed it against his dressing-room wall. 'People were a little surprised,' Art says quietly, 'but he was just getting in the mood.'

Iggy can't quite see it yet but his reputation is about to be significantly enhanced with the release of the film *Trainspotting*. Director Danny Boyle will repurpose the dark energy of 'Lust For Life' for the opening sequence in which Renton and Spud chank through the streets of Edinburgh.

'Have you heard of this film, *Trainspotting*?' I ask.

'N-yeah,' Iggy replies. 'They sent me a script. I remember it was kind of wacky and I think they asked me to do a little bit on it and I wasn't ready that day, put it that way. I think they're using some of the music.'

Iggy tells me the story of writing 'Lust For Life'. Like all the best rock 'n' roll anecdotes, it involves ukuleles and sausages.

'I was living in Germany in a fourth-floor walk-up,' says Iggy. 'A cold-water flat with no central heating. It was in the same apartment house that David Bowie lived in, behind his place. It was the first place of my own that I'd had, where I paid the rent, in my life. I had just turned thirty and had my first real tour, the Idiot tour. I was torn between everything I had lost – my meandering band life – and everything that was about to face me, which was the responsibility of being a solo performer. The two were really fighting inside me. I still liked drugs,' he chuckles, 'and things like that.'

The story of the song's composition is well known. Bowie borrows the Morse code riff from the American Forces Network, picks it out on a ukulele, fiddles around, Iggy tapes it and retires to his own flat to work it up. Bowie suggests the title. 'I went from that concept. As a device to get into the lyric I used a lot of the Burroughs imagery from, I think it was *Soft Machine*, where he talks about everybody searching for love and what a con that is, and Johnny Yen, the Venusian green boy who sells you love while he takes your energy. It's about me trying to go straight a little bit and also basically about getting fucked over because I have enthusiasm. The subtext of the song is that the assholes always seem to come out on top with the goods. That's pretty much what I was feeling.

'I slept in a cot and I had a small Chinese rug which I'd managed to scam a couple of hundred bucks for. I was so happy like that. I did that album on German beer and sausages. I particularly liked bratwurst, some knockwurst, German beer and Coke. Berlin for me was like a dark playground. To me it was Jamaica, a wonderful island, and I just loved it very much. Of course, while I loved it I was screwing myself up. I was a neurotic wreck but I thought the song was good.'

The other thing that made the *Lust For Life* album good, Iggy says, was his haircut. 'Bowie had said, "You're getting too pretty, boy, you're not so interesting any more. I dare you to cut your hair." I had been on the road, scoring lots of chicks and playing rock star, and he thought I was getting too big for my britches.

'I cut it to a quarter-inch. I gotta tell you, I've got a funny-shaped head. I looked so miserable with that quarter-inch haircut and all of a sudden I couldn't get any chicks.'

He laughs. 'And also my eyes were just starting to fail so I wore glass spectacles too. I was like the ugly duckling and that made the album more intense because I was more miserable.'

Iggy digs misery, it seems. But his was not total. 'I was not working at the Burger King.' He likes a bit of pain, the kind of thing you feel 'when you're out and alive and reaching for some kind of joy, and you'll probably get a night of it, then you're going to get whacked with a big right fist of pain to your head and you go down'. That kind of pain. 'These are things that enable you. These are song enablers.' Evenness, Iggy concludes, 'gets miserable'.

We talk about pain. We knock it around for a while, kick its tyres, while Iggy resists all invitations to explore the roots of his own discomfiture. Then he says: 'Of course, the pain comes from all that fucking clichéd psychoanalytical shit. Your childhood and all that stuff. Sure. I don't have a problem with that. I can deal with it. You're never gonna lose it entirely. We are who we are in this world. I am what I am. I'm not interested in changing what I am. I'm going to be what I am until I fucking croak. And on the way I'll do my work and I'll place it right up there and people can see what the fuck it's worth, motherfucker.' He is laughing as he says this, but still.

The album we are here to discuss, *Naughty Little Doggie*, is not Iggy's best but there are great things on it. The album includes the song 'To Belong', which sounds like Nirvana. The first verse is about a bird with a broken wing. I ask whether it is about Kurt Cobain.

'No,' says Iggy. 'It's about me. The key line is "To belong here I'm giving up my soul". That's basically what I've been experiencing since I started building my career back around the mid-seventies. Particularly the last ten years. I've been engaged in trying to make an art of compromise, and there has been compromise. To become part of the society there's a constant battle and many times I feel like my soul's getting snatched. So rather than say I'm not giving up my soul and trying to play the hero, I just said what I felt. With me, the best lyrics come out of my mouth before they are considered. I find many of those to be more true. Like a critic, I look at what came out of my mouth and say, "What the hell did I mean by that?" and I then go "Oh my God!" and see how I feel. It's a form of therapy, I suppose.'

The rage Iggy admits to most readily seems to be business related. He expresses undiluted contempt for the music business people he has to butter up and also bemoans the unrelenting pressure to live up to the extremes of his own legend. 'But also, the more they cast it up the bigger it gets,' he says. 'It doesn't hurt, in a way.'

'But the torment,' I say, 'the rolling in broken glass, that was real.'

'It's still real,' Iggy says. 'There's still a lot of that going on with me. I've just managed to build a stable home for it.' He allows himself a laugh. 'But it's still going on. There's still plenty of mess going on, it's just not as evident on the surface.'

'Do you understand what it's about now?'

'No, I still don't quite know where it comes from. It still happens, is what I'm saying. I just keep it quieter. That's all. But it still happens.

'I still get cut. Literally. Just not as badly, generally, and not as often. There's a lot of anger in me, basically.'

The famous glass-rolling incident occurred at Max's Kansas City in New York, when The Stooges were promoting the release of *Raw Power*. A table overturned while Iggy was clambering through the audience. Glasses fell, Iggy bled. He kept singing. He kept bleeding.

'Were you trying to kill yourself that night?' I ask.

'Not really,' he says. 'I was very stoned that night. Hahaha. I'm not sure what I was trying to do. What precipitated it, more than any other single thing, was that the gig was wrong. I was put in a room to play assaultive rock 'n' roll with an audience of a hundred and fifty New York journalists and scene-makers sat in folding chairs. They were sat in little folding chairs in rows, facing the fucking Stooges. Playing that kind of music. Playing something at the speed of "I Got A Right" to people sitting in folding chairs staring at me, trying very hard to be New Yorkers. In other words, you were throwing it out and nothing was being given back except a little bit of spite. Resistance. That set-up precipitated a lot that happened that night. Also, I was very stoned. Hahaha.'

'He didn't know what he was doing, Your Honour,' I say.

'That's right! And anyway, society was to blame. Haha. But it's a fair cop! I did it.'

Iggy suggests that by the time of the Max's show the drugs weren't working. Famously, in the Stooges period, Iggy used to make potent drug cocktails. His performances existed, he says, in the 'grey area' between being in and out of control.

'When I used to make the cocktails I never had a problem with that,' he says. 'Work is work and I know how to do my work. When I was sitting down to make a cocktail for work it would be fine. I could do my work and deal with the consequences later. When it got to be a problem was by the time of that Max's gig things had spiralled out of control and I would just show up in whatever state I was in. Then the drugs were not being used properly.'

'They were starting to use you?'

'Exactly, and it wasn't a cocktail it was just, "Oh, this afternoon I've been on this." I was very unhappy. I was not getting any support from the world for the sort of music that I thought was the best way to go. I heard it first. Nobody else heard it.'

'Now it sounds timely and timeless.'

'Yeah. It was against nature and, even more sinful, it was against the industry and they're bigger than I am.'

'Were you conscious of how out-on-a-limb it was?'

'Yes. Of course. I'm intelligent. I have the soul of a child but the wiles of a sophisticate. I know where I am, you know?'

I suggest to Iggy that the attraction of rock 'n' roll, for performers and audience, is that it represents a suspension of normal rules of engagement. The reason people get screwed up is that they can't cope with it.

'Sure,' says Iggy. 'That's absolutely right. I've gone through that and continue to wrestle with that. But I think it's important to go out there, whatever your situation is. When there are possibilities open to you, you pretty much have to explore them because of what you'll make up in your head if you don't. Your fantasy will be worse than the reality. That nightmare is really bad. I think every man or woman, you've got to go out there and experience what you can. You don't have a choice. Having said that, if you go one step too far you're gonna be a dead doggie. Ha!'

'You went quite far.'

'I've gone far. I have many wounds. And I have whole entire parts that are dead.'

'What doesn't work any more?'

'All kinds of bits. It's just normal. It's my life.'

Iggy wraps up the conversation about the damage he has

done to his bodywork, and the intensity of his performance, by comparing himself to a vintage sports car.

'You can take a really nice MG convertible and you can go out and smash it into a lorry and you can pee on it: it's still going to be a nice MG convertible. The bones are the bones. And that's that. Sure, it would be nicer if it was fully restored . . . or would it? Sometimes you see these guys with their restored cars and their little caps on and you think, "You dick." You know what I mean? The essence of how somebody does something, that's the way they do it. Personally I feel it's nice to have a complete line of choices! In other words: would you like the model that can only stand up for twenty minutes and is on vodka and methedrine? Well, you can have that one. Or would you like the new improved "I can do two hours and tell you what the song was about" version? You have a choice there. I don't see any reason to disown either one. Ultimately the essence isn't that different.

'Personally I'm interested in the whole thing. I can see both sides. I sit on a fence.'

Of course, I say to Iggy, the performances still include things that would make regular mortals feel self-conscious. The trousers come down within minutes.

'Did you see the gig here in LA?' asks Iggy. 'No trousers down. Trousers up all the way, mate! Trousers are up in New York too.'

Iggy says that he still gets lost in the performance, to the extent that there is an exchange between performer and audience. Both are reacting to each other. 'I get affected by who's around. I am present in the hall. I am not just some guy coming through, where the format is everything. This is not a Pink Floyd concert. This is not, "Yes, and then we're going to fly the pig."'

Time is almost up. Across the lobby the man from *Loaded* is in his metaphorical leotard, doing his warm-up stretches.

'The large and ponderous conclusion,' I begin.

'Which you may have drawn before this interview started,' says Iggy.

'Presumably when you were a teenager you were sensitive and to some degree withdrawn . . .'

'OK, and I wanted to make sensitive music and I found out what they want?'

'That's not what I'm saying.'

'OK, what are you saying?'

'When you're lost in the performance do you feel like you belong?'

'Oh, like I'm more part of the gang, you mean?'

'Or do you still hate the gang?'

'Very good question,' says Iggy Pop. 'I don't have an answer.'

50

Tilda Swinton
'I need dungarees. Help me.'

The first time I meet Tilda Swinton there is a diplomatic incident involving dungarees. It is my fault. It is her fault. It is John Gordon Sinclair's fault. It is nobody's fault but mine. How does it happen?

John Byrne is making a TV drama for BBC Scotland. It is a sequel to *Tutti Frutti*. What was *Tutti Frutti*? For viewers in Scotland, *Tutti Frutti* was *Lanark* for television. All the things that people ascribe to Alasdair Gray's mad, confusing, fabulous novel applied to *Tutti Frutti*, plus it was fun. *Lanark* isn't fun. *Lanark* is Scottish alienation and shy sadness refracted through science fiction and poetic realism in an ambitious echo of James Joyce. *Lanark* is brilliant. It was brilliant. It will be brilliant. It is weird in all tenses except the strictly nostalgic. But, however you boil it, the book has a hint of yellowing Y-fronts about it.

What does *Tutti Frutti* have to do with that? Nothing and everything. John Byrne is not Alasdair Gray, though both of them are art school painter/writers. With John Byrne the language is musical. It is about words. It is about tunes. It is about the liberating gestures of post-war America reflected through working-class Scottish experience. It is about middle age. It is about men being fuds and women being smart. It is about having a voice and hearing your voice bouncing back and suddenly making sense.

What does this matter? Because John Byrne is following his rock 'n' roll midlife crisis series with a country 'n' western drama called *Your Cheatin' Heart* and BBC Scotland has given the first set visit to an English Publication. This is clearly an outrage, and after a stern expression of editorial pique I am dispatched to the outskirts of Aberdeen.

I have never done a set visit before. The truth about set visits is that they are useless. In PR terms they are a way of steering the coverage towards colour rather than criticism. The programme or film is not finished, so criticism is premature. Instead you can see the actors, see the settings and have a chat. As journalism goes, the set visit is promo only.

What I do is sit on a bus and wait. I am waiting for John Gordon Sinclair. I wait. I am bored. I don't protest. The odd thing is, I am at the front of the bus and John Gordon Sinclair is at the back. I wait. For what, I do not know.

As I am waiting Tilda Swinton strides past the bus. She sees me. I am a fresh flea in the jar. 'What are you doing?' she asks. 'I am waiting,' I say. 'Come with me,' she says.

What can I do? Tilda Swinton is persuasive. Tilda Swinton is confident. Tilda Swinton is better than waiting on a bus. 'I need dungarees,' she says. 'Help me get some.'

We go from the outskirts of Aberdeen to the centre. It is nostalgic for me. I haven't been back to the Granite City since university and we do a lot of talking and reminiscing about our different lives, me and Tilda. Tilda is fantastically posh, which I have heard about, and Scottish, about which

I have no clue. The Swintons do amazing stuff: inventing tanks and television, that sort of thing. The Swinton family motto is *J'Espere, Je Pense*, which is 'I Hope, I Think' in French. I think. I hope.

I know that now. What I know then is that Tilda is a free spirit from the experimental end of the artistic spectrum and that buying dungarees with her and talking about Derek Jarman and Princess Diana is better than sitting at the front of the bus, waiting.

We arrive at Burton's on Union Street. Or is it Top Man? It isn't Top Shop. We are in the men's bit, me and Tilda Swinton, shopping for dungarees. I have never done this before. I have never shopped for dungarees. Never felt the urge. I have gone dungaree shopping by mistake. I can't quote what Tilda says because the Dungaree Incident has been declared off the record but I may paraphrase. Roughly speaking Tilda says: I want the finest dungarees known to humanity and I want them now.

Amazingly Burton's, or possibly Top Man, obliges. They mostly have suits in putrescent shades of maroon but they also have dungarees. They serve the lady. She buys the dungarees and we return to the outskirts of Aberdeen, where I have inconvenienced everyone by not waiting for John Gordon Sinclair. It is awkward. But not a complete waste of time. From my long chat with Tilda I remember one thought, which I paraphrase later in my story. Tilda says that she is disappointed with the crew who are working on *Your Cheatin' Heart*. She says that some of them give the impression that they would rather be working on a golf documentary. I write this in my entirely sympathetic promo-only feature and it annoys everybody. Perhaps that was the point.

Now it is years later. On this day Tilda is promoting *The Deep End*, the film that will be considered her breakout role, a mere fifteen years after her actual breakout debut in Jarman's *Caravaggio*. In film parlance breaking out involves playing the game. Playing the game means attending the junket.

There is something odd about the situation. The interview is taking place in the Scotsman Hotel in Edinburgh. The hotel occupies the building that used to be the offices of the *Scotsman* newspaper. There are many rooms in the Scotsman but, of all the rooms on all the floors, the junket is taking place in the cubby hole that used to house the *Scotsman WeekEnd*. (Before that it was the home of the *Weekly Scotsman* and it had a map of Scotland on the wall. Above the map of Scotland were the words: The World.) I am sitting in the exact corner of the narrow vennel where I used to labour, looking out of the windows to the grim space beneath the North Bridge arcade, where bewildered pigeons nest in giant extractor fans and a phantom drummer exorcises his inner Cozy Powell. It's like I'm playing myself in a Japanese novelist's dream.

'It's like we're acting something out,' I say to Tilda.

'Aren't we?' Tilda replies.

We fall into our roles and Tilda offers serious answers to quite routine questions. She says something that I can never forget, even if I can't tell whether it's true or not. What she says is: 'All art is about loneliness.' It's a thought that can't be unthunk and she delivers it pretty much out of the blue. This is not what usually happens in junkets. 'A junket?' says Tilda. 'Is that what this is?'

Usually, in junkets, personal details are kept to a minimum by the lack of time and the fact that the interviews are stacked like commuter jets over a fogbound regional airport during a hoax terror alert. Junkets are all about the nausea and the desperate urge to disembark. But Tilda has said that all of her work is autobiographical, so nothing is off-limits. There is a but: everything is rendered in abstract terms. In this instance Tilda says her interest in the film was cinematic. She wanted to explore acting in close-up.

'It's the thing about being unwatched that is the real challenge. That's what makes film stars. That's the game of it. A film star is someone who is projected upon but any artist in any medium, or any human working in any field whose work is responded to and liked by other people, provides company for those people. You go and love a painting, you've found a friend. That artist is a new friend.'

It's possible that I once understood this statement. The last bit is clear. I know about artists being friends. With me, mostly, it's songwriters. The first bit, who knows? Tilda goes on, talking about 'the theme tune of her work'. It is, she says, 'a general question about whether it is possible to live an integrated life. How is it possible to make friends with all your virtual selves? How is it possible to resist lopping off bits of yourself and bear the pain of them growing back and then having to lop them off again? Part of that inquiry has been a gender inquiry. And now I am, fairly obviously, turning into a woman, it's interesting to look at the strains that come with being a mother.'

Here, perhaps, we have arrived at the junction where Tilda's professional and private lives overlap. She is a mother. I have met her children. She is talking about motherhood. 'I feel freer now,' she says. 'That's partly because the children look at you and they see a human being. Every time you look at them, you see that in their eyes you *are*, and that your

242

task is simply to model a human being to them. That's how I see being a parent. That's my job. And so, for me, that brings with it an extraordinary freedom because I know what they need me to do, which is to live my life. That's all they need me to do.

'But also you see the way in which they see you and the way in which they just love you. You are so acceptable to them in every way. You end up loving yourself a lot more, even liking yourself, which seems to me a lot harder.

'I think liking people is a very undervalued thing,' she says, 'and is much harder very often than love, or what's talked about as love. And just to have the company of children is such a relief. I don't feel alienated in the way I used to. Maybe it's because I have the company of people whom I love and who seem to like me.'

On the subject of alienation we talk for a while about boarding school. Famously, among other top schools, Tilda went to West Heath Girls' School with Diana Spencer (later to become Princess Diana, Queen of Hearts). Tilda tells me that on leaving school she – Tilda, not Di – was furious to discover that punk had been going on in the outside world: the school rules allowed no music. 'Beyond anything else that's such a cruel thing,' she says. 'Who cared about boys? It was the music. The music.

'But actually there are so many things that I happened to get out of that whole experience. Getting to grips with loneliness is not a bad thing. And – I'm going to sound like an advertisement for boarding school, which is a joke – faith. And that all bad things come to an end. And also the possibility of comradeship in the trenches. That's wonderful.'

I mention the dungarees. 'I remember that!' she says,

slapping her hands together. 'Very, very big ones. I wish I'd kept them. They'd be quite radical now.

'Maybe,' she says suddenly, 'what I am is seriously, energetically opposed to being shanghaied by anyone else. That is where my energy goes. It's my life, I'm not giving it up to anybody.'

51

Mo Mowlam: Diplomacy

I go to interview Mo Mowlam, the Labour politician whose informal 'tea and diplomacy' helped broker peace in Northern Ireland.

I go with a photographer.

I knock on Mo's door in Hackney.

The door opens.

'He's the photographer and you're the journalist,' Mo Mowlam says.

'How do you know that?' I reply.

'Because he looks open and friendly, and you're tight-arsed.'

52

Rod Stewart
'I wanted to show my dad I could do something really well.'

Few things are more worthy of repressed shame than buying a record because it has Britt Ekland simulating an orgasm on it. That was 'Tonight's The Night (Gonna Be Alright)', a tune on which Rod Stewart teased some of his boastfulness and all of his soul into a *Lolita* fantasy about a lusty man harvesting the virginity of a young girl. Was it a real orgasm? This seems unlikely, given the record's peerless attention to sound design. Britt's orgasm was musical, a melodic feat previously attempted by Jane Birkin on 'Je T'Aime . . . Moi Non Plus', though the role of the woman in Rod's song is more passive than it is in the Serge Gainsbourg tune. Perhaps if Rod had sung in French, his predatory lyrics about drawing the blinds and disconnecting the telephone would have seemed more poetic and the metaphysical sub-tleties of the lyrics could have been more fully appreciated.

Critical consensus now suggests that *A Night On The Town* – the album which hosted 'Tonight's The Night' – is a career highlight for Rod. This is obviously contentious, unless the yardstick is commercial. Artistically Rod's highlights are the four albums he made between 1969 and 1972. On those records he establishes himself as a singer with a rare ability to inhabit songs, a stylist whose music rambles carelessly through folk, soul and blues in a way that seems natural and unaffected. Rod's success was built on these rough, soulful recordings but mass acclaim also meant he was never able to recapture their ramshackle charm. It's also possible that he never tried.

Fame turned Rod into something else. It turned him into the kind of singer who could insert an image of himself into a vandalised version of Renoir's *Bal du Moulin de la Galette* on the cover of *A Night On The Town*. 'How poncey!' Rod will tell me later. 'I don't know how I got away with it.'

This image might have been just about excusable at the start of 1976. By the end of that year, with punk rock setting a match to rock 'n' roll decadence in all its manifestations, the image of the singer as a sun-dappled rake in a straw boater left a bad impression. *A Night On The Town* was one of the albums I disposed of in the great punk putsch.

Rod survived this slight, flitting in and out of fashion, remaining never less than massively successful. But his fame is rooted in a less ironic age. He comes from the time when being a pop star was like being a footballer – a childish aspiration, a dream that was no more plausible than winning the pools. Being Rod Stewart was like being George Best. Which may be why I spent so much time trying to get him to explain where it all went wrong.

My interview with Rod was a bit uncertain from the start. All I knew was that Rod was flying in for the Scottish Cup final between Rangers and Aberdeen at Celtic Park and I'd hear more later. I started the week imagining I would have several days to write my story – honing, whittling, draining it of spontaneity – given that the interview was likely to take place on a Saturday, and *Spectrum*, the features section, was completed by Friday night. No. Rod was a special case. He couldn't wait. For the first and perhaps the only time, the front page of the features section was to be held, the presses stopped. My interview was to be treated like a match report.

Obviously I complained. There wasn't time. It wasn't possible. I would have an hour to write 2,000 words. These complaints had the effect of making the editor more enthusiastic.

Waiting for Rod to finalise his plans, I did some research. The only way I could possibly write the interview live on the day was if I cheated and wrote most of it in advance.

Long John Baldry was on tour and due in Edinburgh the same weekend. Famously Baldry discovered Rod Stewart and when I rang him he was happy to tell the tale again.

In 1964 Baldry had a residency on Eel Pie Island, on the Thames at Twickenham, west of London. 'I lived in Hampstead,' Baldry said, 'so I would catch the train from Twickenham to Richmond and then get the North London line, which took me directly into Hampstead. I was on the railway station waiting for the Richmond connection. It was a very cold, foggy January the 7th, 1964 night, and I heard the sounds of 'Smokestack Lightning' coming from the other end of the platform on a blues harmonica. That had a very famous riff – duh duh, duh-duh du-du du-du – and I thought, "Well, that sounds pretty good, that sounds pretty authentic", so I went down the platform, saw a pile of coats with a nose coming out of the end of them, and I said, "Why don't you come down and play some harmonica with us on Tuesday at the Eel Pie Island club?" He said yes and came down and it was a lot of fun and he stayed for ever.'

Rod joined Baldry in the Hoochie Coochie Men and his subsequent group, the Steampacket, playing the blues mostly. 'Rod was a very shy individual,' Baldry recalled. 'He used to hide behind amplifiers on the stage. He was terrified of the audience. Of course, it's completely the other story now.'

I asked Baldry whether Rod drank heavily before performances. He hesitated before answering. 'I tend to think, knowing Rod as I do, that he wasn't such a heavy drinker unless somebody else was buying.' A chuckle. 'If it was on his own dime, he didn't drink so much. And of course he never smoked. From his wages, which I paid him back in those days, he was canny enough to save enough to buy a house. His only extravagance back then was clothes.'

Baldry said that the Rod of the mid-1960s looked very similar to the Rod of today. The hair was 'more or less the same except a trifle longer and instead of being cut into the spooky fashion it was backcombed with copious application of hairspray to hold it all in place'. The use of tartan as an accessory can also be traced back to a tour date in Aberdeen. 'I had no right to be wearing tartan because I have no Scottish roots at all but we both bought Stewart tartan trews for our trip up to Scotland.'

Baldry noted that Rod did not seem ambitious. 'Who was, back then? We were all doing it for the fun of it and the fact that we occasionally got paid was a great bonus. The fun of it and a few beers during the evening – it was a very enviable lifestyle. Rod is a similar person to myself. We both share that eternal gypsy spirit.'

❄

On the day of the cup final everything is a rush. When I arrive at One Devonshire Gardens – Glasgow's swankiest hotel – I am shown to a lounge. Rod's lunch is over-running and the sounds of merriment can be heard leaking from the restaurant. The photographer, Drew, is also waiting. At Rod's insistence he has entered the hotel not by the door but through the windows of the dining room.

After an age, Rod arrives. He is tanned and well-watered. He wears a light pinstripe jacket and a dappled tie, loose at the neck, with light flannels and white shoes. His hair is expertly tousled and streaked and his face looks as if it is starting to dissolve. He is accompanied by a man he calls Doc, who seems to be performing a protective role. 'My second father,' says Rod. 'Or as close as you can get to it.' What I don't know at the time, because the introductions are brisk, is that Doc is Dr Bob 'Painless' Paterson, who gained his nickname while working as the Ayr United doctor under the club's charismatic manager Ally 'Tartan Army' MacLeod. Today, instead of giving painkilling injections to crocked knees, he is the responsible adult administering the magic sponge to the interview process.

As time is short I try to win Rod over by mentioning his extended family in North Berwick.

'They're all bloody dead now, aren't they?' Rod replies cheerfully.

'Dennis,' says Doc, reminding Rod of the owner of the town's Nether Abbey, a drinking establishment favoured by rugby enthusiasts and lobster fanciers in the Royal Burgh's west end.

'Dennis is still there, yeah,' Rod agrees, a little woozily. 'Cousin long twice engaged. Cousin, yeah.'

'I'm going to have a big brandy,' says Doc.

'Me too,' says Rod. 'I'll be excited by that.'

I mention that I have been speaking to Long John Baldry.

'No!' shouts Rod. 'Bless 'im.' Rod confirms the story of how Baldry discovered him on a railway platform and agrees that he was 'far from' ambitious in those early years. 'I wanted an excuse not to have to do a regular job,' Rod says. 'It was either playing football or singing. So I tried my hand at football. Well, that's all history. You know all about that.'

The truth of Rod's football career depends on which version the singer decides to tell. In his 2012 autobiography he downplays his previous claims of being an apprentice at Brentford FC. 'I no more signed with Brentford than Gordon Ramsay played for Rangers,' he writes. Which is to say, he didn't. But that doesn't mean his love of the beautiful game is any less intense.

'The attraction of football – I'm very drunk, you'll have to excuse me – is I grew up among a family of footballers. My big brother. My two big brothers. They played football. Dad was a great footballer. He was a Scot in the family and he put among us that Scottish football was the greatest in the world. We grew up with pictures of Eric Caldow and Bobby Evans, all those players. So he was a big influence on us. And it's survived. He died three years ago.'

Rod is a purist of the old school. He likes to see clean football, with wingers. Is coming home a way of keeping in touch with things?

'I wouldn't say coming back to Glasgow. It's coming back to Great Britain. I like to keep in touch with football in Britain. And the reason we're up here today – the team I play for in Los Angeles, called the Exiles, have sworn by Scottish football. Hopefully you're going to see a great game today. I fucking hope it's going to be a good game.'

Rod's devotion to playing football has not dimmed, despite injuries. His advancing years are pushing him further back on the field, from attack to defence. There is talk that his skills have been diminished by arthritis. 'No, no,' Rod says. 'I had a cartilage problem. You operate on it, Doc. These are two of the guys who play on the team. Nathan over there and this guy here – he used to play for the Greek national team. They just qualified for the World Cup. First team to qualify. SO HERE'S TO GREECE QUALIFYING FOR THE WORLD CUP!'

We talk for a while about Rod's recent records. There are two. Both seem designed to prompt a re-evaluation of his talent. Rod is oddly dismissive of the *MTV Unplugged* album ('a collector's piece, really'), preferring to talk about *Rod Stewart, Lead Vocalist*, a grab bag that adds a few new recordings produced by Trevor Horn to archive cuts from the Jeff Beck Group and the Faces. The five new tracks are cover versions. 'This is the best vocals I've delivered in a long time,' Rod says.

I suggest to Rod that his talent has long been overshadowed by his image.

'Oh, absolutely,' he says. 'I indulged it as well. I absolutely enjoyed it. I believed everything I read about myself in those days, in the period between, say, 1978, '79/'80 to '81, I believed everything. And I agree with every critic, especially the guy from *Rolling Stone* that said I betrayed my talent and copped out. He's absolutely right.'

Does it worry you?

'Nothing worries me. Nothing worries me. Nothing worries me at all.'

We talk a little more about music. Rod suggests that he still feels that he has 'the masterpiece album' in him. His voice, he says, is 'fucking great, I tell you. I'm so proud of it. You listen to the *MTV Unplugged* album. The voice is so rich and big – it's as good as it's ever gonna get now, I think. I even shock myself sometimes.'

He is marginally less ebullient on the question of song-writing, admitting that his ego had taken 'a bit of a bashing' when his last three hits came from cover versions. 'I thought, "Fuck, I can't write songs any more." 'Course you can write songs – if it's in you, it's in you. You just need to rest from it, take a little step back, look at what's happening in your life and hopefully write about it. Would you like a drink now? You're really fucking boring. You know that, don't you?'

'I try,' I say, 'but cheers.'

'Nah, I suppose you're not going to the game. I wish I was going to an England–Scotland match. I really miss those games. I miss 'em. The atmosphere.'

It's just about notable that Rod has reverted to football talk as an escape from introspection but it's also true that the mood in the room mitigates against thoughtful reflection. We talk more about music and Rod says he is 'still moved' by Sam Cooke, Muddy Waters and Otis Redding. He just about concedes that singing 'Da Ya Think I'm Sexy' can be tiresome, before adding that the song was not auto-biographical. 'It was in the third person. I was the voyeur, if you want, looking at these other two people. So it wasn't about me. It was supposed to be called "Da Ya Think They're Sexy" but my manager at the time decided to call it "Da Ya Think I'm Sexy".' And 'Hot Legs'? 'There was nothing wrong with that. It was a rock 'n' roll song and it was a rock 'n' roll video. I still love singing that song.'

I suggest to Rod that many of his early songs are about people dreaming and there is also an element of autobiography.

'I've worked between those two spheres, really,' Rod replies. 'The autobiographical and the running away.'

I ask whether the boy that Long John Baldry saw on the station platform could have foreseen where he would end up.

'Not in a million years,' Rod says. 'I must admit when I first started singing the first thing that was on my mind was not to become wealthy. It's the typical rock 'n' roll story, really. I wasn't great at school, I was only good at playing football and singing. Those were the two things and I wanted to show everybody else I could do something really well. I wanted to show my dad I could do something really well 'cause he had big, high hopes for me as a footballer, as he did for all three of his sons. I was the one who came closest to being a professional. When that all fell through he never wavered, he said if you're not going to do football I'm right behind you with the business. In other words, if you're happy with what you're doing, I'm happy. Which I admired him for, bless him, I wish he was here today. And he gave me so much support. The family gave me so much support. These two brothers of mine, they used to lend me twenty quid, thirty quid, brilliant. That's why I do this for them now – fly 'em all round the world to watch football matches – it's my way of paying 'em back. Would you like a drink now?'

Rod pours another brandy. I suggest to him that his existence is almost royal. 'Yeah, it is,' he says, regally. 'It's wonderful, believe you me. I never want it to go back the other way. I quite enjoy being famous and I enjoy being wealthy. If you're a public figure, you've got to enjoy being in public. If you don't then fuck off! Leave it to somebody else. There's plenty of people trying to be famous. I enjoy every minute of it.'

We talk for a moment about Rod's father, Bob. Though Rod was born in Highgate, North London, his dad gave him his strong sense of Scottishness.

'Doc,' asks Rod, 'how old was Dad when he moved down to England? Sixteen, seventeen?'

'Yeah,' says Doc, 'he spent a spell in the merchant navy, didn't he?'

'Yeah,' says Rod, 'how old was he when he moved to London?'

'I would say early twenties,' says Doc. 'No more.'

'Early twenties.'

'He was born in Leith,' says Doc. 'During the war he was up in Monkton, Ayrshire.'

'You never fail to find out more things about your dad,' says Rod. 'I never knew that.'

'Funnily enough,' says one of Rod's brothers – whether it's Don or Bob is hard to say – 'Gordon Strachan, who I know quite well, and Rod knows quite well, his grand-mother went to the same school probably at the same time as my dad.'

'If they'd have shagged each other, we'd have a footballer,' says Rod, delicately.

'As Rod said,' says Rod's brother, 'with a little bit of eh . . . he could have been his uncle's auntie's sort of . . .'

'How's your father?' says Rod.

Time is wearing on. Kick-off is in forty-five minutes on the other side of Glasgow. The photo is still to be taken. 'We've just gotta go and put our make-up on,' says Rod. Rod, his brothers and most of the LA Exiles football team disappear into the powder room. Muffled echoes of bawdy songs can be heard. Moments later the door bursts open and Rod leads the gathering in a conga line through the lounge and into a hallway. Rod has a laundry basket on his head. 'Just one with the basket for me,' Rod says to Drew.

'Quick, Rod, honestly, we're gonna miss the kick-off,' someone says.

'We never see the kick-off and we never see the end,' says Rod.

'Has anyone seen my face?' says Rod's brother Don as the laundry basket is placed over his head.

'What do they do at the kick-off?' says the other brother, Bob. 'Do they throw the ball up in the air?'

'Actually there's a coin involved,' says a third voice.

Rod, his brothers and the laundry basket are now posing for a portrait.

'That's good with the background,' says someone encouragingly. 'Sultry look, sultry look.'

'Take your trousers down,' says someone else.

A riotous chorus of the traditional Scottish song 'A Gordon For Me' breaks out. 'Gordon for me, Gordon for me, if you're nae a Gordon then you're nae use to me.' The photo shoot is over ninety seconds after it begins.

We clamber onto the bus. I am seated up the back near Rod. A radio is turned on for a pre-match report.

Drew takes a picture.

'No more pictures,' says Rod.

The tickets are divvied out along with the passes for the Jock Stein Suite.

'What's the next question?' Rod shouts.

What about the rumours that you've settled down, I say.

'What does it look like?' Rod says. 'I'm a Jekyll and Hyde. I enjoy a couple of days out with the boys and I enjoy being a family man.'

I have to shout to be heard now. 'Do you live primarily in LA?' I ask.

'Yes.'

'What's it like?'

'What would you think?'

'I would imagine you don't live in South Central.'

'No, I try to avoid that area as much as I can.'

Who are your neighbours?

'No one. I've just built a new house. I don't know who my neighbours are.'

'What's it like?'

'What's this got to do with music?' Rod says.

I suggest to Rod that he might try and recapture some of the magic of his early records by reuniting with the musicians. He looks baffled and says that he can't because most of them are dead. We go round in circles for a while, with Rod also ruling out a reunion of the Faces. 'The only reason we'd get the Faces together would be to raise money for Ronnie Lane. I don't think the world needs a Faces reunion. I think there's enough good bands around.' He rules out playing in smaller venues because he would disappoint so many of his fans. I realise that I am now getting into George Best territory, asking Rod why he doesn't do the things he did when he was much less successful.

Another song erupts on the bus. It is Irving Berlin's 'When I Leave The World Behind', which tells the story of a millionaire who is 'burdened down with care'. The singing is riotous now. 'TA-TA-TA-TA-TA-TA-TA-TA-TA!' Rod shouts, impersonating a snare drum.

The song collapses into drunken cheering.

'I like how we broke into that, impwomptu,' says Rod.

'Impromptu,' says someone.

'Impwomtu,' says Rod as the chorus now switches to 'Me And My Shadow', with vocalised jazz drumming. The bus is now on its way through the East End of Glasgow. Someone is whistling 'here we go, here we go'.

'There's the Barras,' says someone as we approach the famous market.

'Trendy Fashions,' Rod exclaims, noticing a modestly boastful clothes shop. 'Togs! Price War Fashions!'

'Dress yourself here, sneeze and you're naked,' says someone.

'Oh, there's the Barrowland,' says Doc. 'Christ! Barrowland! I used to dance there to Billy MacGregor. Do you remember Billy MacGregor?' MacGregor and his band, The Gay Birds, were the resident entertainers at the famous ballroom. 'No, you're too young. Fucking magic.'

'That looks like our type of place, Doc,' says Rod, gazing at an intimidating-looking bar.

'This is some area, this,' says Doc. 'The Chrystal Bells down there too. You know the Chrystal Bells? The only place I saw a razor flashed properly.'

'Operation Blade,' says Rod, referring to a knife safety campaign. 'You hear about that a lot.'

One of Rod's brothers is enquiring about the possibility of a stop on the way to the stadium.

'Stop what?' says Doc.

'Well, there's the public hoose,' says Rod's brother, gesturing to a pub surrounded by Rangers fans. 'Next round's down to Doc Paterson.'

'I'll pay for it,' says Doc. 'I'll pay for it all. Open the window and make an order.'

'Do you think I could do that?' asks Rod. 'Just pull up on the wrong side of the road and I'll buy all the boys a drink.'

By now the mess is threatening to get messier. Doc asks whether I come from Glasgow. No, I say, Edinburgh. 'That's a bit fucking awkward,' he says. 'Leith?' says one of Rod's brothers hopefully. I mention North Berwick. 'You mean Dennis Stewart and the Nether Abbey and all that shit? I know them so well,' says Doc.

'And the Iona Hotel,' says Rod.

'The Iona,' says Doc. 'And the Golf. The Castle at Dirleton. The Open Arms. And The Ship Inn. I know The Ship Inn. Nice place. I went to North Berwick twenty years in succession for my holidays.'

Rod starts to sing an old music hall verse about a girl 'that married dear old dad'. 'She was a pearl, and the only girl, with eyes so blue, one who loved nobody else but you,' he croons. A chorus of Gershwin's 'Swanee' with Rod on lead vocals follows. 'My mammy's waiting, praying for me,' Rod sings as the rest of the bus attempts a complicated harmony part. 'Strolling' by Flanagan and Allen follows, and Rod concentrates on the line about how he doesn't envy the rich with their automobiles.

'Rod,' says Doc. 'How many times have we fucking heard this?'

'Ratatatattatata,' says Rod, now moving back into vocal percussion. 'Shall we get out?'

We are almost at the stadium and the bus has slowed to walking pace. An air of reminiscence has settled on the bus.

'Three goals up at half-time and we're off,' says Rod.

The doors open and the noise of the crowd rushes in as the LA Exiles, Doc and Rod spill, almost literally, onto the street.

'There's Rod Stewart,' a passing fan shouts to his mate. 'He'll get you a spare ticket.'

＊

Years later I interview Rod again, this time at a rehearsal studio in North London. It is a less ebullient affair, though it finds Rod's reputation more in keeping with the times. The new man has been replaced by the lad, and rock 'n' roll and terrace culture are aligned once again. Rod professes his admiration for Oasis. 'I like the guy in Oasis,' he says. 'He's all mouth and trousers. I like that spunky, rebellious approach.' Rod also reveals that at the age of fifty he has installed a full-sized football pitch – 'bigger than Ibrox' – at his Essex home and is hoping that Frank Lampard Sr, then the assistant manager of West Ham, will join him for training sessions.

I mention to Rod that he reminds me a bit of George Best. 'Yeah,' he replies. 'He's probably shagged some of the same women, if we were to compare notes.'

53

Dolly Parton
'It seems like you're in another world, but it's very close.'

In the middle of the war on terror, routine questioning from border officials is a thorny affair. There is no room for flippancy. But what happens when the truth sounds like cheek?

'What is the purpose of your visit?' the border man asks at Atlanta airport.

'I'm coming to meet Dolly Parton.'

'Oh,' he replies, his features visibly stiffening. 'And where are you going to do that?'

'Dollywood.'

'Dollywood,' he says. 'Of course.'

I do meet Dolly Parton. I join a long queue of people having their photograph taken next to Dolly on the Dollywood stage at the Celebrity Theater, and though I miss the gaffer tape mark on the floor I manage to look half-sentient in the picture while Dolly resembles a bisque doll of herself refashioned by Jeff Koons, all porcelain radiance and sculpted charm.

In real life this princess in tailored rags is a brilliant impersonation of an exaggeration of herself.

It is extraordinary, literally so, because Dolly, the flesh and blood person, has applied such care and attention to her image that she now inhabits a kitsch cartoon, if not a *Westworld* simulation, of Dolly Parton, and she does it so successfully that this is not a criticism. Dolly has a joke about this which she can be relied upon to deliver: 'It takes a lot of money to look this cheap.'

Before meeting Dolly, I meet Dollywood. As country 'n' western theme parks go, it's a tasteful affair, not least because the Dolly theme has been applied to an existing park which had already worked its way through a couple of nostalgic iterations.

It opened in 1961 as Rebel Railroad, offering a steam train, a general store, a blacksmith's and a saloon – a capsule of nostalgia at the gateway to the Great Smoky Mountains. In 1970 it became Goldrush Junction, a retreat into the nostalgia of the American frontier, which was further confirmed in 1977 when the park twinned with Silver Dollar City in Branson, Missouri. Dolly bought into the business in 1986, bringing investment and opportunities for marketing and rebranding. So while Dollywood hosts a gospel music museum, it also offers the usual thrills and spills of a fairground resort: river rafts, abandoned mines, a gorge, mountain trails and canoes. There are horse-drawn wagons and funnel cake. There is a five and dime, a be-bop shop, a doughnut factory, duelling banjos and racks of Betty Belle dresses. There is a mock graveyard with rough-hewn monuments to fictional individuals such as Big Louis Free ('His axe fell himself instead of the tree') and Dr Samuel Brown ('Tread this ground with gravity, Dentist Brown is filling his last cavity'), plus memorial markers for country singers such as Conway Twitty and Tammy Wynette, whose spangled lives had at least one boot in non-fiction.

As a memorial to an idealised America, Dollywood is almost Cuban, with ice cream-coloured Cadillacs and endangered crafts ('Live sheep demo. Ask the shepherd.') In Craftman's Valley I meet Lee Warren, a carver, who is happy to talk me through a varied career which included drumming in Shamrocks, a 'James Brown-sounding' soul-rock group, and being a movie stuntman. 'I helped train the guy that doubled Dennis Weaver on an old TV series called *Gentle Ben*,' he tells me. 'Clint Howard, Ron Howard's brother, was the star.' Sensing the way things were moving, Lee switched from being shot at in the wild west show to chiselling wooden Indians.

In the centre of the park is a reproduction of the Tennessee mountain home previously eulogised in Dolly's 1972 hit song. Parton was raised in good-natured poverty on Locust Ridge, not far from Dollywood, where her sharecropper father tended a tobacco patch to provide for his large family. The cabin is life-size but tiny, crammed with beds and patchwork quilts, and lacks the romance evoked by Parton's song. In this context it serves as a homely reminder of an escape, or at least a graduation, from childhood penury. My guide, Ruth Miller, points to the soap by the sink in the replica of the kitchen. 'Do you have lye soap? That's made from when you would kill your hog in the fall. It's made from the pig fat. It's supposed to be good for if you've got poison ivy or athlete's foot.'

Dolly doesn't live in Dollywood but she does make a phantasmagorical visitation a couple of times a year, gliding through the crowds in a horse-drawn carriage, performing a show for the fans at the Celebrity Theater. It's almost royal.

The mock streets of the park are cordoned with incident tape and a regal Dolly wafts on by, waving a gay hello. It's outside the theatre that I meet her, though the girlish trill of her voice arrives first. She sounds amused, as always. Dolly is always on and an on-Dolly is a full-beam presence. Dolly is at once tiny and larger than life, dressed today in a denim jacket with rhinestones and a mini-mini skirt. Her wig is very blonde. Her legs are amazing. Her legs are bare. She uses them like pinking shears, cutting the small talk into pretty ribbons.

Dolly's time is short, so I share her with my friend Patrick, who is after musical and cinematic facts. I am trying to capture Dolly essence, which is like catching moonbeams in a Mason jar.

There are some facts in this fairy tale. Dolly has polished them so often that they now seem like plot devices.

The parable of Dolly Parton has two poles. There is the start and there is the destination. In between there is fate and talent and hard work.

Dolly Parton was born in 1946 and raised in Locust Ridge, ten or so miles from Dollywood.

'Country miles!' she says, scissoring her legs for emphasis. 'Ten to fifteen country miles! That's like sayin' "wider than the mountains". It seems like you're in another world but it's very close.'

The fourth of twelve children, she grew up 'poor, very poor' in the mountains of East Tennessee. Her first memory – though she admits there may be an element of post-rationalisation – is being bounced on the knee of her 'Aunt' Marth, who owned the land on which her father farmed tobacco.

'She lived in this old shack since long before I was born, and I must not have been more than two. I remember climbing up on her steps and walking into her house and smelling this odd smell. She used to burn some stuff because of her asthma and she had a rocking chair and a spinning wheel. And she would sit me on her knee and she would sing "Tiptoe tiptoe, little Dolly Parton/Tiptoe tiptoe, ain't she fine?/Tiptoe tiptoe, little Dolly Parton/She's got a red dress just like mine". I remember saying, "Sing it again, sing it again." I remember her before I do my mom and daddy or anything. It's the strangest thing.' In other tellings of this tale Dolly notes that Aunt Marth's spinning wheel seemed as big as a Ferris wheel, and it was magical, almost as if it was spinning dreams out of thin air.

Parton's magical realist childhood is explored on her early records. Though they offer a first draft of Dolly's industrial persona, the sweet purity of those songs is a revelation. There is mawkishness but the apparent simplicity of the songs contributes to their emotional power, and on the album *Just Because I'm A Woman* the title track wears the resilient smile of feminism country 'n' western-style.

Parton wrote her first song, 'Little Tiny Tassel Top', at the age of five. It was a hymn of praise to the doll her mother made her from a corn shuck. She realised 'when I was a little, bitty child' that music was something she could be good at and it stopped her getting 'lost in the shuffle' among her siblings.

'I realised very early on that people were noticing me because I learnt to play, I could sing and I wrote these songs. People would say, "Oh my Lord, did you hear that song that little thing wrote?" I saw I was getting a lot of attention, so it made me want to sing better, it made me want to write more.'

Stylistically Dolly absorbed a mix of mountain influences, but bluegrass and southern gospel were dominant. 'My mother's people were all very musical. My grandfather played piano and fiddle and guitar, and my aunt was like a Pentecostal preacher, she would sing and really pray, so I really believe that my great world influences came from my own family. I don't know who all they were influenced by – maybe the Carter Family, Kitty Wells and Hank Williams – but they were influenced more by those people than I was. It worked out anyway!'

Dolly has a joke that if she wasn't a singer, she would have been a missionary or a prostitute, and if she'd been a prostitute she would have done it in the missionary position. Really, she thinks she might have been a beautician. 'I just like putting make-up on. It's not that I think I can't be real without it. It's just that I never know who's gonna come by. I have to be at my best. When I get up in the morning I put on my make-up and fix my hair 'cause I think my sisters may come by. I don't want to open the door and scare the hell out of somebody. So I just get my make-up on and get ready. I don't know what the day's gonna bring.

'My look came from a very sensitive place,' she says, 'as a country girl's idea of glamour. I wasn't a natural beauty and you have your complexes and all your insecurities, so you try to make the most of everything. I always try to make positives out of any negatives and try to put things to where I'm comfortable with myself, where my personality can show but where I have a support system with it. And although my look may make some people uncomfortable, it makes me comfortable. If I'm comfortable with who I am and how I present myself then it allows my creativity and my personality to shine.'

I ask Dolly whether she has always been shy and retiring. She collapses with mirth, placing a cool hand on my arm. 'Actually, to be honest with you, when I was little I was always kind of hyper. I had a lot of energy but I was kind of bashful with strangers. I know that sounds funny, saying that I was ever shy or bashful, but there are times even now where I'll find myself feeling very shy.'

She considers the matter again. 'I don't know – that sounds stupid. I'm very comfortable in my area, where I know I can present myself, but there are times where I revert back to that little shy girl.'

Age crops up frequently in Parton's conversation. The death of her parents was a significant landmark. Dolly bought 'the ol home place' and her parents' farm. 'As you get older, you tend to want to migrate back to home. I find myself spending so much more time here now than I did in years past.

'I kind of fix up all our family places. I buy up all the stuff from where any of our family lived and I share it with the rest of my family. It's real special to me.'

There were also signs, after the terrorist attacks of September 11, 2001, of a more pronounced spiritual side in Parton's writing. 'Go To Hell', on the patriotic album *For God And Country*, found her confronting Satan: 'Take your weapons of mass destruction, terror and sleaze/Go to Hell with your corruption, just get away from me.'

'That was my cry for help,' she says. 'But I've always been very spiritual. Not religious. Even now I don't say I'm religious. The kind of religion I grew up in, the Pentecostal holy rollers, that was exciting because it was the music of prayer and I learned a lot from that. I guess you always get more religious-minded as you mellow. But I don't really think about it a lot. If I died today, I'd be just as happy to go to Heaven or Hell as I would if I'd spent the rest of my life reading the Bible or praying, because I think God judges us with a tender heart . . . and if not, I should burn in Hell!'

54

Willie Nelson
'I think I could sell a vacuum cleaner if I had to.'

Willie Nelson's bus is parked on the pavement outside the stage door of the Usher Hall in Edinburgh. Nelson has just finished a concert with his band, rushing through his hits and rephrasing the lyrics so that the lines zipped past impatiently. At times Nelson's singing seemed to be at odds with the music, not only in its irregular timing but also its stylistic qualities. Nelson's band was playing country, albeit a brand of country that was having a flirtatious conversation with the blues. The voice was singing jazz.

A queue of fans with dog-eared albums awaits Nelson's autograph at the stage door. Before that can happen, I have an appointment to meet him on his tour bus. Unfortunately there has been a double booking. Kristina from the Finnish Broadcasting Company is here too. She has a cumbersome tape recorder. She struggles with the machine's bulk as I follow her onto the bus. First there is a stairway and then a black velvet slipway. Everything is black. The band, the

Nelson family, are on a sofa behind the driver's seat. We creep towards the rear of the bus, Kristina and me, easing through a heavy curtain. With each step the air grows sweeter, smokier, fishier. Finally, as we squeeze pasts the bunks, Nelson's ancient face appears in the gloom. The singer is in an advanced state of relaxation. He is drinking black coffee from a tin mug. A fish supper is laid out in front of him.

Everything is a bit awkward. There are several layers of diplomacy at work. Willie wants to get stuck into his chips. Kristina and the Finnish Broadcasting Company want to record station idents to promote his upcoming shows. I want to waffle on about the ancient lore of Nashville.

Kristina and I agree to take turns. Willie is wired up to the war correspondent tape machine. Kristina has ways of making him talk, though not necessarily in an interesting way. 'How do you choose songs that end up to be in your concerts?' Kristina asks. Willie replies in a voice so quiet that the levels on the tape recorder barely flicker.

'We just play songs that we really like,' he whispers. 'All these songs are songs that we enjoy doing.'

Undeterred, Kristina continues. 'But you have so many songs that I would imagine it must be difficult to decide which ones to do.'

Is this a question? Even with the uncertain cadences of a Finnish accent, it sounds like a statement. Willie contemplates a chip. It is a fine chip, almost fresh from the fryer at the Kingfisher of Bread Street, an establishment that serves the patrons of Edinburgh's famous 'pubic triangle' – a tight confluence of roads where the city's go-go bars are located. Decades later the Kingfisher will close down after receiving a TripAdvisor review comparing its onion rings to Shrek's foreskin but Willie cannot know this. To him it is just a chip, or possibly a French fry. Chewing now, he gives a functional answer to Kristina's observation. There is a basic show, he says. There are certain songs that the audience expects, so they will be played. But the sequence changes every night to keep it interesting.

'That's good for us,' Willie says. 'It keeps us alert. If you try to do it the same way every night it really gets boring.'

Kristina drills into the boredom. 'But does it ever get boring to do the same songs that you might have been performing for years, because I am a producer for radio too and sometime I think: "Haven't people already got fed up with this song, we have played it so many times?" Don't you ever get tired of doing the same songs that people expect?'

'Fortunately I don't,' says Willie, looking distinctly underwhelmed. 'I enjoy doing "Funny How Time Slips Away", "Crazy", "Night Life", "On The Road Again". The songs that we do on the show are songs that we really enjoy. Occasionally I'll get tired of one and we'll drop it out of the show. "The Red Headed Stranger" is one that I recorded and that has a whole lot of verses. Occasionally I'll get a request for it, so I'll do it, but I sort of stay away from it because it has so many verses.'

'You looked as if you enjoyed the blues numbers,' I say and Willie's face brightens a little.

'Yeah, oh yeah,' he says, taking a swig of coffee. 'I'd like to do a straight blues album sometime with some of my blues brothers. B.B. King. And there's lot of great blues guitar players around. George Benson. He would be good, wouldn't he?' (Three years later, Willie and B.B. King's duet on the Nelson song 'Night Life' is released. The song swirls around the phrase 'the night life ain't no good life, but it's my life'. The duet is a beauty, not just in the way the voices complement each other but in the way the song's easy rhythm expands to allow contrasting guitar solos from each man. Nelson's guitar playing is as much a signature style as King's. He leaves gaps and echoes where King paints his licks in curlicued gold leaf.)

'When you have a new record out do you still get excited?' Kristina continues. 'Or are you so used to it that you don't really?'

Willie answers with appropriate patience that some records are more exciting than others but his latest is a whole lot of fun. 'I'm excited about this one because it looks like a lot of promotion is getting behind it,' he says. 'It's going to be out there. If someone wants to buy it, they can.'

By now I'm worried. Kristina's idea of a joint interview is less collaborative than was previously advertised. I start thinking about one of Willie's most famous songs, 'On The Road Again'. With a rhythm like a runaway train, it celebrates his love of touring; the sense of restlessness, of being in permanent motion, of visiting new places and hanging out like a band of gypsies.

'So,' Kristina says, 'uh, do you need to take care of your voice in any way, being on the road?'

'Occasionally, not often,' Willie whispers, 'I'll get laryngitis. It hasn't happened in a long time and usually when it happens I've done a whole lot of shows in a row. But I started out working clubs in Texas where we'd play from eight p.m. till midnight and on Sundays we'd go from ten till two, Sunday afternoon matinees and then come back again Sunday nights. So I was used to playing long shows and singing a lot.'

There are police sirens outside the bus. Does Willie stiffen a little? The air is still clogged. I ask about his voice. There is a common perception that Nelson was uncertain about his singing when he started out. He was, and remains, an extraordinary vocalist, intimate and soulful, yet conversational.

'The truth of the matter,' says Willie, 'is that I had felt I didn't really sing that bad but when I got to Nashville they didn't consider my voice that commercial. They didn't know what label to put on me. I wasn't exactly country as they knew country to be. I wasn't exactly anything, so I wound up falling through the cracks. But I didn't give up. I stayed with it, and Faron Young was an old friend of mine and he recorded 'Hello Walls' right back in the sixties. He used to tell me, "Willie, why don't you stay in Nashville and write songs and let me go on the road? You write 'em, I'll sing 'em." Maybe I should have but I'm glad I didn't.'

'We are glad too,' says Kristina brightly. 'You said you kept going. What gave you that motivation? In your first years you were struggling like so many people are when they are beginning. Did you believe that one day you are going to make it and why?'

'The people,' says Willie. 'Every night I was singing and the people in this club was liking what they was hearing. I knew I wasn't a terrible singer. I knew I wasn't Frank Sinatra but I felt I could hold my own. So I had a lot of confidence when I went to Nashville. Just because I didn't make it in the beginning as a singer, it didn't really dampen my enthusiasm. I was still coming back to Texas and working the clubs and drawing crowds there, so my ego was getting built up enough that it didn't matter if it got deflated a bit in Nashville.'

'So you say that one of your personal characteristic traits is that you would contribute to being where you are today,' Kristina continues. 'What might be the others? What has it demanded?'

'I really enjoy what I do,' says Willie, looking increasingly baffled. 'My philosophy is to have a good time and enjoy yourself and do what you really want to do. I've been able to do that . . . I don't really understand your question that well.'

Kristina explains. 'Because I meant that I like what you said, you were confident to go on in the bikini . . .'

Willie's eyebrows twitch. The smoke clears. She hasn't said 'bikini'. She has said 'beginning'.

'. . . so is it one of the characteristics of your personality that has helped you, that has contributed to where you are today?'

'Well, I've been able to make a few dollars singing,' says Willie. 'Not a lot of money in the beginning. You work for the door. If it seats fifty people and you charge a dollar, you make fifty dollars. But that was a nice fifty. It was a pretty good day's wages. I always knew that I could do this as long as I wanted to. I could play clubs for the rest of my life because I have a lot of friends who have never made it and are doing well. Drawing crowds and taking care of their families. I had that much security in my mind. So if I hadn't made it in Nashville I would still be somewhere doing it.'

He talks about Nashville and how there is a new generation of younger performers and younger audiences. 'The odds against makin' it are probably worse than they were when I was there and they weren't that great then.'

There is a sense that Willie's attention is beginning to drift. Kristina asks how it feels to be a living legend.

'I just lived a long time,' Willie says. 'There'd be a lot more legends if they would just live a little longer. I've been very fortunate, if you believe in luck, and I do. "Fortunately, we're not in control" is our motto.'

I ask Willie he thinks about Garth Brooks – at this point the most popular entertainer in the world – mentioning that Nelson's friend, the singer and comic novelist Kinky Friedman, has dubbed Garth 'the anti-Hank'.

Willie issues a long, throaty laugh. The laughter echoes back from the front of the bus.

'Oh, he's crazy, he's funny,' Willie says, meaning Kinky. 'What I like about Garth Brooks is that he draws a lot of people and he doesn't tour that much, so these people have to go and see somebody once he gets them stirred up. We see them at our places.'

By now it is obvious that the double interview isn't working. The cowboys of Lothian Road are growing restive. Willie has grown distracted by percussive banging on the window. The Kingfisher chips have congealed. Kristina is staring anxiously at the recording levels on the tape machine.

I decide to rush my questions. I have my notes about Nelson's first marriage, to Martha, their arguments, their divorce (in 1962), his spells as a salesman hawking bibles and vacuum cleaners. The seven years he spent as a DJ in Texas, Oregon and California before he started performing. I swallow them and ask: was taking to the road a route out of the straight life?

'Well,' says Willie, 'if I hadn't been able to make a living out of music I had some things that I could fall back on. Still do. I think I could sell a vacuum cleaner if I had to.'

Nelson's first record was a self-released single in 1957, a brisk seventy-eight seconds of boom-chicka-boom called 'No Place For Me' with the Leon Payne song 'Lumberjack' on the flip side. He advertised it on his Oregon radio show, *The Western Express*, and threw in a signed 10 x 8 photo. Over the years the contrast between the short-haired, sharp-suited singer who toiled in Nashville and the weed-loving sage with the pigtails has tended to overshadow the consistency of his writing, some of which was made famous by other singers. Patsy Cline's immortal hit 'Crazy', for instance, is one of the building blocks of the mythology of Nashville and country music. What was the inspiration for the song? 'Aw, who knows?' Willie says. 'I don't.' The story of how Cline came to record 'Crazy' has been embroidered and contested over the years but it revolves around a meeting between Nelson and Cline's husband in Tootsie's Orchid Lounge.

'When I came to Nashville, Tootsie's was one of the first places I went to,' Willie says. 'I had "Night Life" [a hit for Ray Price, which along with 'Family Bible' financed his trip to Music City] and they put it on the jukebox for me. At Tootsie's I ran into Charlie Dick, Patsy Cline's husband. He liked "Night Life" and heard "Crazy" and said Patsy should do that. So he got that one recorded for me. But I had 'em before I went to Nashville.'

Nelson's career is defined by his decision to move back to Texas and his ability to attract a less conservative audience. Creatively his breakthrough was the 1975 album *Red Headed Stranger* but his collaboration with Waylon Jennings, Jessi Colter and Tompall Glaser on the album *Wanted! The Outlaws* crystallised his image as a rebel. The outlaw tag 'was originally started as a label to sell records', Nelson says, 'and there wasn't much more to it than that'.

The drumming on the window resumes. Willie pulls back the curtain and peers out. 'I'm not really getting annoyed by it,' he says. 'If it's sold some records I think that's fine.'

So you never considered yourself a rebel?

'To me that's what the word "outlaw" meant. It was somebody who really didn't want to do it the way that this guy said it should be done. I'm talking about music. So in that respect I'd be proud to be called an outlaw.'

In 1990 the Internal Revenue Service took a jaundiced view of Nelson's rebellious stance and recovered $16m in back taxes. The singer released *The IRS Tapes: Who'll Buy My Memories?* to pay off his debts. 'He certainly takes his cut,' Nelson says of the taxman. 'He's the biggest outlaw.'

Anxious, perhaps, to end the conversation, Willie reveals that he is about to record a video in London for his playful duet with Frank Sinatra on the song 'A Foggy Day (In London Town)'. The two men didn't meet. Frank was live with his band somewhere while Willie was in Austin, Texas. 'Would you like to hear it?' he says, fiddling in vain with the bus's music system. He stands up suddenly and heads into the toilet cubicle. As he goes, Willie forgets that he is wired up to Kristina's tape recorder and she leaps up to rescue the machine.

Our time has slipped away. Willie records a trail for his upcoming show in Turku and descends from the bus with a Magic Marker in his hand.

55

Shirley Manson
'I felt like I was from Mars.'

Shirley Manson stands in the middle of an *Edward Scissor-hands* street in Ventura, California. She wears a Day-Glo vinyl mini-skirt, a sleeveless top and shoes that could have been designed by a perverted ankle doctor. She cradles an old radio to her ear, though the only noise puncturing the stillness is the eerie whistling of wind chimes. For a moment she becomes self-conscious. 'My hair is a big bush!' she shouts. Then, prompted by a request for a smile from Valerie, the photographer, she starts laughing. She doesn't stop laughing. Shirley says that sometimes, when she is out driving with a girlfriend, they challenge each other to laugh. At first it comes in self-conscious bursts. Then the laughter becomes so infectious that it won't stop. Some people do it as a kind of therapy, Shirley says.

The sun is hot, so we walk the three hundred yards to the San Buenaventura State Beach, where Shirley stands in front of the volleyball nets and the *Baywatch* tower. She looks like a punk's dream of Twiggy, her fair skin in danger of incineration after an hour in the ultra-violet. The incongruity of the setting prompts a thought. Shirley confesses that she is a fan of Pamela Anderson. 'I know this will come out wrong,' she says, 'but I saw her interviewed and she was very smart.'

Yes, Manson agrees, the *Baywatch* star knows she is a cartoon character but she is happy to play along. 'She's everything I thought a woman should be when I was young,' says Shirley. 'The only thing that I don't like is that she's had plastic surgery.'

You don't have to be in Manson's company very long to realise that she has done a lot of thinking about the pressures that conspire against a woman in the public eye. After a decade of preparation, much of it on the fringes of success with Goodbye Mr. Mackenzie, a Bowie-influenced group from Bathgate, near Edinburgh, she is experiencing the first flushes of real fame as the singer of Garbage, an electro pop group assembled by Nirvana producer Butch Vig.

I first saw Shirley at a post-punk event in Edinburgh. She was modelling in a fashion show at the Missing Link, a creative arts hub in the shadow of the St James Centre, run by John McVay of Visitors. I performed a song called 'President Nixon's Funeral' with a pop-up pop group called Bingo Lovers. 'President Nixon's Funeral' was a ferocious rumination on the rehabilitation of a corrupt president. I forget the lyrics. Shirley was in a fashion show for the Edinburgh clothes shop, the Ivy League. She looked amazing. She was almost topless, with concentric circles painted on her breasts. I also bared my chest, to reveal a slogan on my torso. I have no memory of what that slogan was.

I reviewed Goodbye Mr. Mackenzie for the *NME* and in the absence of musical insight resorted to physical insults. I am confident that Shirley won't remember this.

'You called me a pirouetting bog brush,' she says.

'I did,' I reply. 'It was a compliment.'

I try to ingratiate myself by mentioning the fashion show.

'I've never been freaked out by my body,' Shirley says. 'I remember I did a fashion show in a see-through wedding dress. It was plastic. My boyfriend at the time stormed out and wouldn't speak to me for days because I had revealed my body in public. That's ridiculous. It's a real male, British attitude: "Only I should look at my woman's body." Oh fuck off, give it a rest.' She laughs.

But it was still a startling thing to see, I suggest, at least in Edinburgh.

'I know,' Shirley says. 'I had no fear. It's only as I've gotten older that I've developed fear.'

'Would you do it now?'

'No, I wouldn't do it now. Not unless someone paid me millions of pounds. Then I might consider it.'

'You could command a higher fee now.'

'Hee hee hee hee hee hee. Yeah. Oh God.'

'Did you think you might be a model?'

'Oh no, I always knew I was chancing it. I was too small and too strange-looking and too funnily shaped. I think a lot of people wanted me to do it because I had a certain look that they liked. People at the art school, students, liked me. I didn't look like your perfect model.'

In the distorting mirror of pop celebrity, not looking conventional and not beating yourself up about it is the thing that will define Shirley Manson's fame. She will speak up for misshapes of all kinds while exploring her own neuroses.

Did she really feel ugly?

'I still feel horrendous. I can't even explain it. My mother is very upset every time she reads this in interviews. You

279

become very aware of yourself. I see all the faults before I see the good points. And that's been my saving grace. People can fall in love with their media-created images and then they try and live up to it and become immersed in it.'

Was she ever anorexic?

'No, never. I have my mother's genes as regards my body. I've never been anorexic. I've always eaten like a pig. During adolescence I battled with my body. I hated it. I loathed it with a vengeance. And I hated when I started getting an arse and hips. I hated my body.'

Shirley says that even now some people expect her to be more beautiful in real life. 'I've battled with ugliness all my born days, so it's not too freaky for me to have people disappointed in my physicality.'

When I meet the band at the Doubletree Hotel in Ventura, California, they have been touring for almost six months. It has been 'a long slow grind', Shirley says, but the work is beginning to pay off. The distortions of celebrity are being experienced for the first time. The night before, after performing at the KROQ Weenie Roast, the group had driven to McDonald's. Shirley stayed in the van. While she waited a group of youths started peering through the windows. One shouted: 'Yo! Is the chick from Garbage in there?' Shirley squatted in the back of the van, hiding beneath her hoodie, muttering 'tell them to go away' until the moment passed. 'Mostly, the people that come up to us are really cool,' she says, reflecting on the strangeness of being recognised.

'We go out to meet the fans after the shows,' says Shirley, 'and they're high as kites. Often it's been their first rock concert ever. It sounds like a boring cliché but it really is a big thrill, a big honour, because you know they'll never forget that until they die. Or you meet teenagers. Young kids come up and they chat with us and they're just beginning to bloom. It's so lovely to see them fighting with the onslaught of adulthood and hormones.'

I suggest to Shirley that many of the concerns on Garbage's first album are adolescent. They are about wondering whether there are other ways of seeing things.

'I don't know if they're adolescent concerns,' Shirley says. 'I think they're basic concerns. The record is mostly about overcoming negative circumstances. I think everybody can relate to that. A lot of adults are battling with that.'

Famously Shirley was invited to audition for Garbage when the band saw a video of her singing with Angelfish, a reconfigured version of Goodbye Mr. Mackenzie. Butch was attracted, at first, by her voice. 'A lot of singers have this kind of screech,' he says. 'In order to convey intensity, they scream. Or they have this pretty little girl voice. Shirley had this low, understated quality that was more intense and more subversive than anything we'd heard. Kind of a Patti Smith thing. A little bit of Chrissie Hynde in her voice. But it was her voice. We didn't know there would be this sensibility that went with the kind of music we liked: kind of the darkness that melded the music to the lyrics.'

For Shirley, Siouxsie and the Banshees were an inspiration. She saw them at Clouds discotheque in Edinburgh and at the Playhouse. 'Lyrically, Siouxsie always made me feel empowered. I felt that she was in control of her situation. Although a lot of the songs were angry, I always got the feeling that she was the one that came out tops. That really inspired me at an age when I really felt totally ill at ease. I felt so ugly and unhappy. For no reason. I had a great life. But I think a lot of people feel like that, particularly when hormones are oozing through their body.'

The next day, in search of fresh hormones, we proceed to Malibu, where Garbage are to appear on MTV's *Beach House*. It is ten a.m. The band were up till three the night before. The joke in the van is that they will be met at the gate and told: 'Here's your Speedos, here's your guitar.' This proves to be an understatement. An over-stimulated representative from Garbage's record company leans his head into the van and without forewarning shouts: 'Your record is blowing up like a motherfucker!'

'Is that good?' mutters bass player Dan Shulman in response.

MTV Beach House is filmed inside a converted ranger station. The stage overlooks the ocean. Garbage have a dressing room that comes fully stocked with Cheerios. Giant chairs and sofas are arranged round a pool. There is a basketball court, a fake cactus and a statue of a spaceman. Shirley, her hair and skirt bright orange, her Scottish skin swathed in sun-block, is the least-tanned person on the set, though Californian ska-punks No Doubt are also backstage and singer Gwen Stefani is similarly bleached.

Garbage endure a bleary soundcheck. 'Lo-fi,' Shirley says, to no one in particular. 'It's hard to get psyched up to play so early,' Butch says, slapping his legs into life as the kids are shepherded around the pool. 'God,' he adds, 'I haven't worn a bathing suit in about five years. I take one on the road with me but there's never time, or the pool looks too lo-fi, or you don't feel like exposing your white body.'

There is blast from a megaphone. An MTV youth-wrangler is explaining to the partygoers that for technical reasons 'all white T-shirts must be removed'. He adds: 'And girls, if you have bathing suits on underneath we'd prefer those also.'

When the 'Big *MTV Beach House* welcome' has died down, the bikini girls drag themselves from the pool and start dancing. A woman runs round the perimeter shouting 'Guys! Can you dance?' and another group of beauties is led in. 'We want you to act crazy, OK?' they are told. Garbage bash out a grungy version of their hit 'Stupid Girl'. There are cheers and whoops. The crowd goes crazy on cue. There is a heckle. 'I don't understand American,' Shirley replies.

Afterwards Shirley says: 'I've never seen boys and girls stripped like that. I come from Scotland. It doesn't happen. I felt like I was from Mars.'

'It's the first time we've played a beach,' guitarist Duke Erikson tells an MTV interviewer, with almost imperceptible irony. 'It's the first time we've played a swimming pool.'

'A lot of the songs seems to be about not being happy, not fitting in, being imperfect, pissed off,' I say to Butch.

'And here we are in this perfectly surreal California paradise with girls in bikinis and studs in their G-strings. Yeah, it's ironic. This red-headed Scot under the blazing sun. It's ludicrous. All I have is black jeans and black T-shirts. That's my entire wardrobe. And to sit out here when you're baking under the sky is . . . funny.

'People like darkness in music,' Butch continues, 'and they like weight to it, depth to it. I'd much rather listen to dark, sad, slow stuff that bums me out than – what was the song? That one song that I absolutely hated on the radio . . . Oh, "Don't Worry, Be Happy". I can't remember who did it but every time I heard it I wanted to kick the dial out of the radio. Why, I don't know.'

At this point, the choreographed cheering resumes. It is time for No Doubt, or perhaps Everclear, to have their turn in the sun.

'People have a thing about this record being dark,' says Shirley. 'I don't think it is. On every single song we went to

283

great lengths to ensure that the words resolve themselves positively, ambiguously. If you wanted it to be positive, it was there.' She says she writes about triumph, not failure. 'Not losing it is positive.'

Shirley talks for a while about fame, and self-esteem, and the way the process always seems to be 'seducing your resolve'. She cites a line she saw in *Vanity Fair* about society parties. 'It said, "Parties are never thrown for you, they're thrown against you."'

'People have always looked at artists to journey for them,' Shirley says, 'or to speak for them because they're unable to deal with it themselves. But mental illness is still looked on as glamorous. A great story I'll always remember. Me and my pals always used to go and see *Betty Blue*. That was the movie to see. My girlfriend went to see it with her boyfriend and at the end he was going: "That was brilliant, she was gorgeous." The girlfriend was a bit angry, saying: "What do you mean?" He said: "She just epitomises the most perfect woman for me. She's just so impetuous and crazy." And my girlfriend took a pint glass, poured it over his head and said, "How's that for impetuous?"'

56

Encore

In the lost summer of the pandemic I went on holiday to North Berwick to stay in my childhood home for the last time. It was poignant. Time was upset. I didn't want to leave. I couldn't get out quickly enough. The bricks and mortar were the same and the remaining detritus of my teenage years was in boxes on the floor. It was pure nostalgia, if nostalgia means oscillating between fragments of memory.

There was no going back but there I was, communing with ghosts. I was old enough and tired enough to appreciate the extreme beauty of the place I was so desperate to leave. I loved it. I love it. I love it because it is my past and because it has changed, not always for the worst. It used to be the whole world. Now it is just the centre of my universe.

The town is more than twice the size it used to be. The fringes are creeping outwards. The fields are filling up. The houses are bigger, vast Bantustans of executive ambition and negative architecture. The magical spaces where I used to walk and play are disappearing. The grand houses of Glenorchy Road now have smaller houses in their gardens. The old abbey on Old Abbey Road is surrounded. Trainers Brae, then a hilly track between the old doocot and Grange Road, lined with electric fences for the livestock, is a hamlet of detachment.

I can't be snobby about this. The two houses my family lived in were new-builds. We were the newcomers.

My house is up from the railway station, next to the Field. The Field is long gone. My old walk to school has been diverted. It now follows the new road. There is no ducking through the woods. On a dreamless night in your parents' old bedroom it is possible to hear the hooting of owls in the trees. In daylight a more pedestrian reality takes hold. The trees have been cut back to provide distant sea views for the big houses in the grounds of the bigger houses. The drives are full of frustrated SUVs. The new houses squat precariously, stretching the boundaries, endangering the town's fragile ecology. It's nobody's fault. There's nothing to be done. Something is lost.

Following the road through the Field, there is an open patch of land with goalposts. The grass is striped, mowed by tractor. Someone has planted wildflowers. A sign warns that they should not be cut. The caravan site at Gilsland has crossed the road and is now full of stationary caravans that are almost houses. The ancient farm machinery still decorates the verge where the shop used to be. The peacocks are gone.

I walk out of town and keep on walking. It is the route we should have taken for the high school cross-country run, if we had followed the rules and not cut across the fields. It is misty for summer, hot and cold by turn. The summit of the Law is swathed in cloud. There is no traffic. There are faster ways to leave town, more direct routes to somewhere else. But on this aimless day normal life is furloughed.

Even so, there is a strange air of exposure. On the beaches there are signs urging visitors to 'leave nothing but your footprints'. Outside the town, walking away feels like an act of subversion. Going nowhere slowly invites suspicion. Sometimes the cars slow down out of concern. More often they speed up, just in case.

How to describe the empty solace of that walk? In the mist the cultivated beauty of the farmland is all that is visible, and the narrowness of the road. There are passing places. Were they always there? They seem like a recent thing, if recent means any time within the last forty years. The hedgerows are loud with birds. At the first corner there is a farm with a red corrugated barn and a smaller shed with green garage doors. In the distance, the sound of the Edinburgh train.

I follow the road to the left. A Tesco bag wrestles with a tree. A white Range Rover speeds past, forcing me into a ditch. I trudge along the verge, following the road to Kingston. Kingston was a destination on childhood cycle rides. It is not a place to stop. It is mostly isolation and a postbox.

I trace my way towards the back of the Law, facing the traffic: faster cars, angrier cars. The sign on the gate post of Bonnington Farm is crowned with a metal silhouette of a bull, tail aloft, chasing a man. In the verge I stumble over a decomposed deer, eye sockets empty, mouth open, hide peeled away to reveal a smile of ribs.

As the road curves back into town there is another new-build estate. At the edge of the development there is a recently constructed ruin of a house with a large sphere in front of it. The fake house has small figures inside its stepped windows. The concrete sphere is decorated with wheat-sheaf patterns, a developer's idea of conceptual art. From just behind the school playing fields the Bass Rock looms over the houses of Lochbridge Road as it surfaces from behind the mist. The scale seems wrong. From here, the island is huge.

I walk past the school. The gates of Law Primary are locked up for lockdown. A rainbow of woollen pom-poms is tied to the fence. The ground by the gate is decorated with painted pebbles and shells; rainbows, hearts, smileys and messages of gratitude to the NHS. 'Bee Happy' says one stone decorated with a smiling insect. 'Miss you P1B,' says another, 'love Mia.'

The primary school has doubled in size in recent years. It's a school I never went to. I was in the last primary seven at the old school. We made a mosaic to be displayed in the new foyer, symbolising continuity. The old school had rats. You could smell them in the assembly hall. The building was reborn as the town's community centre. My mum did patchwork classes there until the stairs got too much. The Commercials used it as a practice room.

When it was being built there was much excitement about how Law Primary was going to be open plan. All the classrooms were to be linked, with no doors between them. Did that work? It seemed radical at the time. The only time I ventured inside the building was to attend an election meeting held by the former prime minister Sir Alec Douglas-Home. I went with my brother and we sat cross-armed in the front row, radiating contempt. At the end the old politician disarmed our youthful fury by thanking us for coming and saying how encouraged he was to see young people at a hustings.

I take one last circuit of the town. I walk east, through the scheme, past the telephone box where we used to ring Dial-a-Disc, hoping to hear the first strains of 'Tiger Feet' before the pips intervened. The architecture is austere. There are occasional cottages marooned among harled streets that mimic their shape.

On the road towards my old house at Lady Jane Gardens there is a small wood, criss-crossed now with paths for accessibility. The old Store on Dundas Road where I used to collect morning rolls and Co-op stamps has become a Loco, the windows decorated with outsized images of pizza, red wine and baguettes. The Store never sold these things. Wine was limited to weddings or a petrol-station glass from a bottle of Mateus Rosé. Pizza was a pie served folded in half and deep-fried at the chippie. Baguettes were a rumour. This was a time when sliced bread was the best thing since sliced bread and the main choices were sliced pan or that west-coast aberration, the plain loaf.

I pause at the back gate of my old house. Behind me is the hedge I sheltered in at the age of seven, having run away from home for twenty minutes before deciding to return because, actually, life was great and I wanted to be seven for ever. Looking up at my bedroom I catch the eye of a woman inside the house and hurry past. That is the window I used to open to serenade the neighbours with a blast of Gary Glitter.

What was going on with the Leader of the Gang? Let's not go there again.

I hurry on, down Brodie Avenue, past Tubby's house and onto the recreation ground. There are all-weather football pitches now. The rugby club has grown. I sat in the doorway of the rugby club once, reading Heinrich Böll's *The Train Was on Time*. That was my idea of fun, not rugby.

The recreation ground is different. A skate park intrudes on the site of the old football pitch. The goalposts and pavilion are gone. Over the road the Ben Sayers' golf club factory has given way to sheltered housing.

I duck into the Glen, a small burn running through trees to the Glen Golf Club. We used to catch sticklebacks in jam jars in the Glen. It seems tiny now, though the space has been augmented by information boards celebrating the birdlife and the history of the Glen. Thrush, blue tit, great tit, wood-pigeon, chiffchaff, chaffinch, dunnock, blackbird, robin, wren. There are ruined mill buildings scattered around the water. The sign in the Glen quotes a sentence from Robert Louis Stevenson's 'The Lantern-Bearers', an essay that details the boyhood pleasures of summering in North Berwick; not so much golf as marbles and knucklebones and haunting recollections of tortured fisher-wives hag-riding his memory, deadly squalls and fear, exultation, the coil of equinoctial tempests, scouring flaws of rain, tragic fate. From this ferment, a pretty sentence is plucked. 'You might secrete yourself in the Lady's Walk,' Stevenson writes, 'a certain sunless dingle of elders, all mossed over by the damp as green as grass, and dotted here and there by the stream-side with roofless walls, the cold homes of anchorites.'

I walk back along the beach, past the hill where the witches were burned, past the rocks where Brigitte Bardot melted the sand, past the boating pond, past Anchor Green and the memorial to art student Catherine Watson, who drowned in 1889, rescuing a boy from a stormy sea. 'The child was saved,' the red granite monument reads, 'the brave girl was taken.' I keep walking, following the beach to the west golf course where I sit on my dad's memorial bench before making my way back to the house.

This is it, then. My car is full of old photographs and school magazines. I have the Turner seascape I inherited from my gran's house in Montrose. I have the glass model of the Pink Panther I got in Ibiza on my first foreign holiday. I have my dad's Edinburgh Crystal decanter, which he never drank from, so the whisky just evaporated over years. I have a live tape of The Commercials which will be fantastic or unplayable. I will find out when I have access to some obsolete technology. I have everything packed into the metal trunk my dad used when he went to sea, which is heavy, and has frayed ropes around the handles.

It is time to turn the key. I go into the living room for the final time and ask my phone to play '5.15' by The Who. It is the first song that was played in the house and I want to play it again, for the ghosts.

Acknowledgements

Thanks to the late Beatrice Colin for commissioning the essay which led to this book. Versions of some of the chapters appeared in *Cut* magazine, *Scotland on Sunday*, *The Scotsman*, *Blah Blah Blah*, *The Independent*, *North Edinburgh News*, *Gaudie* and *Algebra*. Thanks to all my editors, notably Nigel Billen, Allan Campbell, Brian Groom, Rebecca Hardy, Alan Jackson, Andrew Jaspan, Iain Martin, Craig McLean and Alan Ruddock. Mostly, thanks to my mum, who had to put up with the music, and to Charlotte, who still does.